European Society

William Outhwaite

polity

First published in 2008 by Polity Press

Polity Press
65 Bridge Street
Cambridge CB2 1UR, UK

Polity Press
350 Main Street
Malden, MA 02148, USA

ISBN-13: 978-07456-1331-4
ISBN-13: 978-07456-1332-1 (pb)

A catalogue record for this book is available from the British Library.

Typeset in 11 on 13 pt Berling
by SNP Best-set Typesetter Ltd., Hong Kong
Printed and bound in Great Britain by MPG Books Ltd, Bodmin, Cornwall

For further information on Polity, visit our website: www.polity.co.uk

CONTENTS

List of Maps, Figures and Tables   vi
Acknowledgements   vii

1   European Culture and Society   1

2   Europe: East, West, North, South   23

3   The European Economy   44

4   The European Polity   72

5   Social Divisions and Social Identities   99

6   Conclusion: Europe in its Place   133

    Notes   142
    Bibliography   158
    Index   193

Maps, Figures and Tables

MAPS

1.1   The European region of Unep   4
2.1   Regional per capita GDP in Purchasing
      Power Standards   40
5.1   The migration divide in the 1960s   118
6.1   European cities and capitals of culture   139

FIGURES

3.1   Amable's five models of capitalism   51
5.1   Sociology after postmodernism   109

TABLES

5.1   The Sinus-Milieus® new model 2005 for
      Germany   114
5.2   Explaining variance in levels of European
      identification   122–3

ACKNOWLEDGEMENTS

I should like to thank Hettie Peters, Daniel Steuer and participants at seminars at SOAS, Kent and Sussex for their comments on a much earlier version of what appears here as chapter one, and György Széll, who subsequently published it in an edited volume (Széll, 2001). My discussion of postcommunist Europe is substantially shaped by my work with Larry Ray on our joint book *Social Theory and Postcommunism* (Outhwaite and Ray, 2005). Jacqueline O'Reilly and Sabina Avdagic generously shared their knowledge of contemporary European political economy and commented helpfully on my autodidactic efforts to catch up with this rapidly growing field. A work of synthesis such as this inevitably incurs huge debts to the Europeanist community as a whole, as reflected in the footnotes and bibliography.

1 EUROPEAN CULTURE AND SOCIETY

1 Introduction

Why yet another book on Europe? Well, systematic attempts to discuss European society as a whole are actually rarer than one might think. There are of course innumerable histories of Europe, the best of which attempt to avoid national or regional biases in their treatment of the continent.[1] There are what one might call long-essay books, such as those by Romano Prodi (2000) and Zygmunt Bauman (2004). There are excellent detailed studies of the European Union as a whole (Rumford, 2002) or, more often, specific aspects of its workings. Finally, there are books, often multi-authored, which discuss Europe piecemeal according to disciplinary or national divisions.

The genre to which this book aims to contribute is marked out by a (so far) smallish range of key contributions: Therborn (1995); Crouch (1999); and Münch (1993); more recently, Beck and Grande (2004); Delanty and Rumford (2005); and Delanty (2006b). It is one informed by the social theory of the last few decades – in particular, the revival of historical sociology and, more broadly, theories of modernity and, secondly, the growth of postcolonial theory and its application to European history. These two theoretical revolutions coincided, of course, with the anti-communist protest movements of the 1980s, the anti-communist revolutions of 1989 and the postcommunist 'transition' which followed. It is, in short, a contribution to what is sometimes called the new direction in European Studies (Rumford, 2007; see also Calhoun, 2003).

The main argument in this book is that it makes sense to treat Europe as a whole, rather than the sum of its component states and regions. This does not mean that there is some sort of essence to Europe, emerging historically and realizing itself through successive centuries. Rather, Europe should be seen as a region of the world, with an open frontier to Asia (of which it forms a peninsula) and close links of various kinds to the other continents of Africa, America and Australasia. The European region came to be perceived, and to act, as in some respects a single, if complex, entity. In particular, it functioned as a crucible in which social forms of production and organization, often imported from more 'advanced' civilizations elsewhere in the world, were developed and subsequently re-exported. The technologies of textile production and warfare are examples of this, but so are democratic politics, individualism and other aspects of what is generally known as modernity. This contentious yet fundamental link between Europe and modernity means that to study Europe historically one cannot treat it as just one world region among others, even if a global frame of reference is the most appropriate one to use (Bhambra, 2007). It is only in the recent past, as the economic and political forms of modernity have spread, if unevenly, across the globe, that we can ask what, if anything, is distinctive about *European* modernity, modernity *in Europe*.

The following chapters attempt to do this. This chapter examines the geographical and historical background to European culture and society, setting the scene for the more detailed discussions which follow. Chapter 2 looks in more detail at Europe's internal geographical differentiation and its location as a whole between East and West, North and South. The third chapter is concerned with the two economic formations found in contemporary Europe, capitalism and, for much of the past century, state socialism. Whereas the socialist economies followed more or less closely a standard Soviet pattern, European capitalism is differentiated between the extremes of Anglo-Saxon liberalism and the more statist or otherwise institutionally embedded economies of continental Europe. Chapter 4 looks, in a complementary way, at Europe's characteristic forms of state: the liberal (and eventually democratic) state and the totalitarian or authoritarian dictatorship. The second type is found in fascist Europe in the mid-twentieth century, surviving longest in Spain and Portugal and with a brief resurgence in Greece under the Colonels' regime, and in the Soviet-style Marxist-Leninist state. Liberal democratic forms of rule are again differentiated according to, crudely, the greater or lesser role of the state apparatus. Here we find a third type of polity emerging, in the form of the European Union: one with affinities to the historical empires in Europe and elsewhere but fundamentally different in its democratic structure and what has come to be called 'soft power'. Chapter 5 examines the divisions and commonalities of European society and societies, according to class, ethnicity and gender and the ways in which these operate in different parts of the continent. The concluding chapter attempts to situate Europe as a region of a globalized world. This is a world substantially shaped by Europeans in the long century of European hegemony running from the late eighteenth century to the mid-twentieth, but it has become a world in which Europe, rather like classical Greece, now has to take a more modest place.

2   What is Europe?

The question 'what is Europe?' can be given a very short geographical answer and a very long historical one. The geography need not detain us long. What we call Europe is a Western peninsula of Eurasia, mostly surrounded by sea (and some islands, including the one I happen to live on) and with a land frontier conventionally located at the Ural

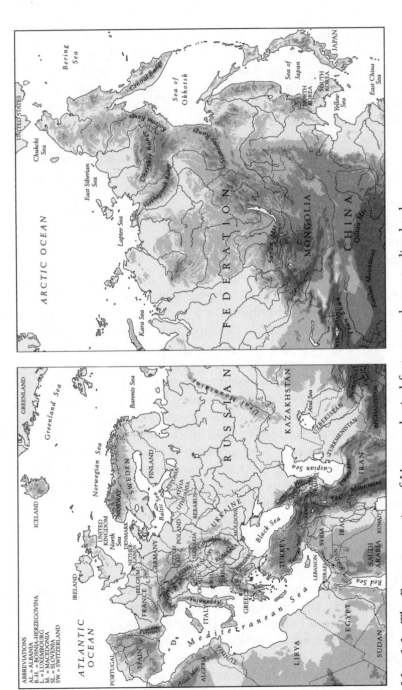

Map 1.1 The European region of Unep – physical features and surrounding lands
© UNEP/GRID-Europe

mountains and somewhere between the Black and Caspian Seas. At the borders of Europe, both Turkey and Russia have small 'European' parts and much larger parts outside Europe, but both are often included as a whole.

The historical answer is necessarily much longer and more complex, since 'Europe' is a historically developing and 'imagined' entity. It is clearly anachronistic to talk about 'Britain' or 'France' in the Stone Age, and by the same token also to talk about 'Europe'. At some point, then, the people of Europe, or what we now call Europeans, come to define themselves and/or be defined by others as Europe(an). And this definition can of course be questioned (Delanty, 1995). If we think of the defining structures and events of what we now call Europe, we need to reflect on which of them, singly or in combination, are distinctive of Europe. Ancient Greek polyarchy as a form of intra- and interstate organization clearly deserves a mention, as do the Macedonian and, much more importantly, Roman Empires. The latter of course intersects with a third crucial element, the somewhat unexpected rise of Christianity in the Roman Empire and subsequently as a defining element of Europe as a whole, just as Islam became a defining element of the 'Middle East'.

Yet, just as it is artificial to separate out English history from the rest of European history before the fifteenth century, it is similarly anachronistic to think of Europe as a distinct entity before that time. Charlemagne's empire of the early ninth century may have covered the territory of the original European Communities and lent his name to a building and a prize, but it had nothing to do with Europe as such (Fried, 2003). The Crusades of the thirteenth century are resented, with some justification, as inaugurating Europe's continuing interference in the Middle East, but they are more appropriately seen, like the rest of the history of that half-millennium (and arguably the following one too), in a broader Eurasian context. A recent popular book (Aust and Schmidt-Klingenberg, 2003: 89) contains a map of the trading network of the Hanseatic League around 1400 labelled 'The EU of the middle ages', but the irony is of course intentional.

In what Europeans call the fifteenth and sixteenth centuries, however, something distinctively European begins to emerge, marked by the conjuncture, roughly speaking, of the Renaissance, the Reformation and the beginnings of the voyages (anticipated much earlier of course by the Vikings) of discovery and conquest. These were not, to say the least, unique or endogenous 'European' developments, but they do initiate a distinctive path. This line of development runs in three directions:

(i)   from the Renaissance to the scientific revolution and the Enlightenment;
(ii) from the Reformation to the religious wars and the 'European' state model consecrated in 1648 after perhaps the first genuinely European war;[2] and
(iii) from Columbian adventures to the European colonial and semi-colonial empires of the eighteenth, nineteenth and twentieth centuries.

In the last of these, the 'discoveries' were reflected in the culture shock of Europeans confronted by alterity, otherness, and perceiving themselves in its mirror.[3] A different form of alterity closer to home was provided by the Turkish victory at Mohács, Hungary, in 1526.

We might, then, roughly mark out three interlocking spheres of transformation marked by the crude labels of Renaissance/Enlightenment, Reformation/state formation and world-system/imperialism. The first directs our attention to ideas, which of course are also, as Marx put it in 1844, 'a material force when they seize the masses'. The second refers us to the European national-state model, seen both in its domestic aspect and as part of a system of such states, and the third to Europe's economic and political domination of much of the rest of the world in the second half of the last millennium. The interrelations between the first and second spheres have been fairly well discussed, though there is little agreement over the relative power of ideas or more material political or economic processes. The relations between the first two and the third, however, have received much less attention and are finally getting it under such rubrics as postcolonial theory and critiques of Eurocentrism. Did Europeans colonize America and Australasia, almost all of Africa and much of Asia because they had a sense of intellectual or cultural superiority and believed that the particular Middle Eastern religion which they had adopted as their own was the Truth, to be disseminated as widely as possible, or because of economic and/or military-strategic interests and capacities arising out of their particular state forms? Both elements undoubtedly played a part.

Let us trace these processes rapidly down to the present. It is difficult to escape from the haze of self-congratulation in which intellectual developments in Europe over the past half-millennium have tended to be discussed. In the late twentieth century there was a long overdue corrective movement, marked by a number of works which showed the dependence of Greek thought on regions to the East and South (Bernal, 1987), of the Renaissance on past and contemporary Islamic scholarship (Jardine, 1996), of Chinese anticipations of much of what has been attributed to the 'scientific revolution' of the seventeenth century (Needham, 1969) and of movements outside Europe and its settler colonies paralleling the European religious Reformation and Enlightenment. For all that, there did develop in Europe a powerful set of syntheses of practical and speculative thought, inspiring transformations in science and technology on the one hand and forms of political rule on the other.

One quite plausible attempt to explain the dynamism of a region which had previously been rather backward stresses the combination of a common ideological and political framework (Christendom and, for much of the region, Roman Law) with the political diversity of relatively small emergent states (Mann, 1986, 1993, 1998; see also Jönsson, Tägil and Törnqvist, 2000: 20). The creative tension between religious and secular power and the multiplicity of competing jurisdictions may have encouraged the development of individualistic ways of thinking and liberal political thought. The etymology of the word 'liberties' and its equivalents points to this: initially meaning privileges or exemptions, it comes to have a more universalistic sense in which, as the nineteenth-century Russian anarchist Mikhail Bakunin put it, I can be free only if all others are free. In the rather diffuse development of European conceptions of individualism and of human and political rights and freedoms, the French Revolution clearly deserves a central place as the defining feature of the European political imaginary (Furet, 1981; Best, 1988). This is no less true of the conservatives who rejected it (Mannheim, 1927), or of the socialists and communists for whom it was just a prelude to a full social democratic and anti-capitalist revolution.

Concurrently, the American Revolution inaugurated another form of republican constitutional government and, perhaps more importantly, the first major postcolonial state, what the American political sociologist Martin Lipset (1964) called 'the first new nation'. For progressive Europeans, this was one more victory over the old aristocratic order, and the French aristocrat Alexis de Tocqueville found in the US in the 1820s what he expected to be the democratic and egalitarian future of France and Europe. Geopolitically, the American Revolution marked the beginning of the provincialization of Europe, the relativization of its power in between the United States and Russia, which Tocqueville also foresaw less than forty years after the French and American Revolutions (and an even shorter time since Napoleon's short-lived European empire) and when Europe's imperial power was still on the rise.

Imperialism was of course a European transformation both of Europe itself and of much of the rest of the world, running alongside the extension, within Europe itself, of capitalist production and industrialization. From now on, though no one was yet thinking in these terms (except perhaps in relation to the contrast between the old and the new worlds), there were multiple modernities and a post-European future. What Fernand Braudel and Immanuel Wallerstein called the capitalist world economy or world-system largely pre-dated systematic imperial conquests, though not of course the Middle Eastern 'Crusades'. Debates still rage over whether imperialism should be seen primarily as what Lenin (1916) called the highest stage of capitalism or more as a matter of geopolitical competition, with economic interests secondary. (The neo-imperialist adventurism of the US in the early twenty-first century provokes of course similar disagreements.) Imperialism and colonialism also transformed the European societies themselves. On the whole they got substantially richer, whatever happened to the wealth that was accumulated; the poorer and more peripheral states of Europe such as Spain and Portugal acquired or preserved a great power status. Germany started two world wars in large part out of resentment at its lack of a 'proper' overseas empire and the attempt to catch up (in the First World War) or to colonize the East of Europe and Russia instead (in the Second World War).[4] Domestically, many states (not just the fascist ones) re-imported military and policing tactics tested in the colonies. Finally, the former colonial powers tended to attract (and often to recruit) immigrants from 'their' territories in the 'thirty glorious years' of capitalism from the late forties to the mid-seventies. As a result of these flows both from outside Europe and from its poorer peripheries, Europe became more substantially multicultural, though not without a good deal of resistance and denial on the part of the 'natives'. (The fiction was maintained, for example, that the German Federal Republic was 'not a country of immigration'.)

Back home, Europe experienced three further transformations, all in one or another way associated with notions of citizenship. First, there was the slow extension of political democracy, finally reaching adult women in most parts of Europe by the middle of the twentieth century. Second, the nationalism which was already implicit in the political structures of much of Europe became more forceful across the continent as a whole, in part as a reaction to Napoleon; this development, culminating in the post-First World War settlement, consolidated the (Western) European nation-state model. This model, with its prioritization of nation-state citizenship as a defining identity, swept the world wherever the European states had not established colonies or, as in South America, were expelled from them. In the second wave of decolonization in the mid-twentieth century, it was considered automatic that the colonial territories, already carved up into what Europeans considered state-sized chunks, would be set up as European-style national states. Half-hearted supranational economic arrangements, in East Africa and elsewhere, rapidly succumbed to political contingencies. Third, there was the dual response to the 'social question' in the form of welfare states (Donzelot, [1977] 1980, 1984) and social democracy. The former is the beginning of the 'European social model' and social conceptions of citizenship based on social rather than just political rights (Marshall, 1950). The latter, social democracy, is the source of what can be called the European political model, the left–right division between the ostensible opponents and the all too real defenders of capitalism. This opposition structured much of European politics and tendentially the politics of much of the rest of the world until at least the end of the twentieth century. As early as 1906, Werner Sombart (1976) was taking this as the norm and asking 'Why is there no socialism in the United States?' Despite the vogue of 'third way' politics in the UK, Germany, and much of the rest of Europe, it is far from certain that European politics is moving 'beyond left and right' (Giddens, 2004).

In Russia, of course, after the Bolshevik Revolution, there remained only the left. The thoroughly European ideology of Marxism took hold in Russia, China and elsewhere outside Europe, with the Russian export version of Marxism (Stalinist Marxism-Leninism) re-imported into much of Europe in the aftermath of the Second World War. Russia's land empire had of course been a classic case of European 'internal colonialism', the securing of control over peripheries. The Soviet Union also presided over the last quasi-imperial structure in Europe, with the so-called 'Brezhnev doctrine' of the limited sovereignty of Warsaw Pact states. The Soviet empire differed from the 'normal' imperial relation in that here it was the hegemonic power which supplied its more developed client states with cheap energy and raw materials in exchange for relatively advanced consumer goods.

If, then, these processes of transformation have left us with something called Europe, whose geographical parameters and defining historical events are reasonably clear, we might naturally go on to ask whether there is something like a single European culture and society, or, more probably, several forms of culture or society *within* Europe. We would have to take this second alternative if we were thinking, say, of Africa, with its now crucial divisions between the North and the South of the Sahara.[5] The same goes for Asia, with even more massive differences between what Europeans tend to call the Middle East, and North Americans the Near East, and the huge areas of central Asia, the Indian subcontinent and East and South-East Asia.[6] Europe, however, is small enough for the question of a single culture, like a single market, to be a realistic one, and the fact that it has an emergent form of state covering almost all of the West and a very substantial part of the East gives some support to the first answer. If there is something like an emergent European state and legal regime, however patchy at present, then one might perhaps expect to find something like a society and culture to go along with it.

Historically, of course, this last way of framing the question is a peculiar one. What is now called the European Union is only half a century old. If there is something like a European culture or a European society they can hardly have come into existence so rapidly, or have been conjured up by such a half-hearted entity as the EU, which has not even sought, like the eighteenth- and nineteenth-century European national states, to impose a common language and culture. For all this, I think one can claim that there is something like a European culture and form of society which operates as a kind of background to the operations of the national states within Europe, as these became first more nationalistic, in the sixteenth to nineteenth centuries, and then more oriented towards supranational integration in the second half of the twentieth.

Without, then, making the strong claim that the term 'European culture' refers to a unitary phenomenon, I do believe that one can ask meaningful questions about the

degree to which cultures, understood in the broadest sense
as including material elements such as systems of production as well as those more often assigned to the domain of
'culture', are unified or diversified. If I board a train at St
Pancras Station in London, things are very different depend-
ing on whether I travel to Sheffield or to Lille, even if the
journey time is about the same. Both cities, however, also
have features in common which would distinguish them
from comparable cities in, say, India.

An emphasis on diversity, fragmentation, the inadmissibil-
ity of unifying concepts and so forth is now firmly associated
with the intellectual current known as postmodernism. As
I have argued elsewhere, however, an awareness of social
and cultural diversity and of the uncertainty of all assertions
in the human sciences has been a feature of most if not all
social theory (Outhwaite, 1995). In sociology, in particular,
the exploration of subcultures went along with and fuelled
a critique of the functionalist conception of shared cultural
value-systems. What Margaret Archer (1988) has aptly called
the myth of cultural integration has long been recognized as
such. Archer takes her account of the myth from Etzioni's
denunciation of '"one of the most deep-seated fallacies in
social science . . . the . . . assumption of a high degree of con-
sistency in the interpretations produced by societal units"'
(Etzioni, 1968; cit. Archer, 1988: 2); she traces its effects
through anthropology, functionalist sociology and the sociology of culture. Nor is there anything particularly new in
the rejection of general concepts, categories and theories:
here the most fashionable postmodern critique converges in
practice with an empiricism which would allow one to talk
only of individual cultural items. Both, I suggest, impose an
unnecessary straitjacket on theorizing in the name of liberation from dogma. But we have ways of dealing with and
correcting incautious theorizing without ruling out theorizing as such.

As we saw earlier, the question 'what is Europe?' can be
conveniently broken down into two separate but related
questions: 'where is Europe?' and 'what is European?' The

first question can be resolved to most people's satisfaction without much dispute, though borderline issues arise, as noted earlier, in relation to Russia and Turkey (both of course associated with major empires). The second question is much more difficult to resolve. These complexities are perhaps greatest with respect to culture, again conceived in a broad sense to include ways of life as well as more specifically cultural artefacts. European culture, if there is such a thing, is a culture of import and export, in constantly shifting proportions and configurations.

Europe, as I suggested in the introduction to this chapter, can be usefully seen as a crucible in which social and cultural forms, whether indigenous or imported, are warmed up and (re-)exported to other regions of the globe, where they develop in ways which often eclipse their European variants. This can be shown in relation to capitalism, individualism, the nation-state and so on. The nation-state, for example, rightly seen as somewhat passé in Western Europe, remains the dominant political form on the world stage; the European Union itself, even if it achieves full political union, will arguably only be one (very large) state among others. Communism or Marxism-Leninism is another striking example: unsuccessful in the more advanced parts of Europe at the end of the First World War, it gained a foothold on the edge of Europe, in Russia, whence it was imposed on much of the rest of Europe in the aftermath of the Second World War and the substantial Soviet contribution to the defeat of Nazism. Now largely repudiated in Europe, communism remains a significant political force in India and elsewhere.

The question 'what is European culture?' is, of course, a minefield of dubious assumptions which have given rise gradually to ongoing controversies. In recent work, as we have seen, this question has most often been given either a historical answer, emphasizing the non-European origins of European culture in opposition to long-standing myths of Europe's unique creativity, or a contemporary answer, focusing mainly on the globalization and Americanization of popular culture. In what follows, I shall try to bridge this gap in the way recommended by Homi Bhabha (1990: 142) in his account of 'nation':

> Historians transfixed on the event and origins of the nation never ask, and political theorists possessed of the 'modern' totalities of the nation . . . never pose, the essential question of the representation of the nation as a temporal process.

Bhabha's focus here is on the nation-state and on processes of representation; I am concerned more with the re-presentation of these cultural forms from one moment and region of European and world geo-history to another. In particular, again, the question I am aiming to address is what is distinctive about European culture in the early twenty-first century – what if anything distinguishes it from other globally available cultural forms of advanced modernity.

A quick answer to the contemporary form of the question, 'what is European culture?', would be to say, borrowing Henry Kissinger's comment on Eurocommunism, that it is just culture in Europe. This will clearly not do. Nor however can one simply point to a set of cultural elements which have the equivalent of a food additive's 'e' number printed on them. Whatever moment one picks on the temporal trajectory of European history, culture in Europe has always involved a complex mixture of elements of local and external origin, the latter more or less fully assimilated. Rather than asking of any of these cultural configurations, whether the Renaissance or a day's programming on a European TV channel, 'how European is it?', one should try to situate these phenomena in the trajectories of European culture as a whole, in which processes of importation, assimilation, re-export and reassimilation of the exported content interweave with one another.

This is one of the principal vectors of European culture, expressed in cross-cutting processes of nationalization on the one hand, notably in the construction (or sometimes reconstruction) of national languages and literatures, and cosmopolitan internationalization on the other. A good example of the interplay of these processes can be seen in relation to language and the internal democratization of European high culture. A cosmopolitan clerical elite stratum, communicating across the continent in Latin, gives way to a more independent cultured elite, also writing initially in Latin, then increasingly in vernacular languages. Among these, French acquires a special place as the medium of elite cross-cultural communication or lingua franca, losing this place to English in the course of the twentieth century. One or both of these languages is now routinely available to school students throughout Europe as part of universalistic educational programmes, and they may well then use these in international business and intellectual and cultural life. Further down the social scale, there is a more functional cosmopolitanism among travelling people and those in frontier regions, where what has been called the 'dialect continuum' (between, say, the eastern Netherlands and the extreme north-west of Germany) often makes cross-border communication easier for 'dialect' speakers than for speakers of the distinct formal versions of the respective national languages. (The broader issue of the relation between national and sub-national societies and cultures, notably in relation to European integration, requires of course fuller attention than I can give it in this chapter; see chapter 5, below.)

There are also long-term trajectories from one geographical area to another, as discussed in chapter 2. These include the diffusion of culture in early modern Europe from South and East to North and West, followed by a predominantly West–East movement of material culture and technologies of all kinds which continues to the present. We tend to think it is elite culture which is essentially cosmopolitan and international, but commercial opportunities and pressures mean that mass culture is also increasingly internationalized, albeit often in ways which conceal its national origins (dubbed television programmes, etc.).

I shall be very brief in discussing the debates around the beginnings of European culture. It is important, however, to address them because of the way in which they have been central both to Eurocentric mythologies and to critiques of them. It is salutary for Europeans like myself to learn how many of the cultural items which we take to be peculiar to Europe, and even to European modernity, were imported from further East or South, or independently developed there. It is even more salutary to learn about the ways in which these achievements were belittled or ignored, in order to make the 'European miracle' stand out more brightly and to make European colonialism seem both necessary and benign (cf. Bernal, 1987, 1991; Amin, 1988; Blaut, 1993).

These and other critiques of Eurocentrism are well taken, and there remains much more to be done in this area. For someone like myself, who is primarily concerned with Europe (with the justification that even a sociologist has to draw limits *somewhere*), the lesson is I think that in studying Europe one must constantly keep an eye on the rest of the world. As Kipling might have said, 'What should they know of Europe, who only Europe know?' Against this comparative background, however, one can, as Dieter Senghaas (1982) put it in a classic book, 'learn from Europe' – learn, that is, both from the peculiarities of the European experience and from what certain European states and regions had in common with non-European ones on the eve of modernization.

World history has of course come to the aid of such perspectives, as Europe as a region of the world is increasingly sidelined militarily, politically, economically and to a considerable extent also culturally. The old Eurocentrism now looks not only pernicious, but parochial. And world history is also a world court with Europe in the dock – the image of Europe no longer so much vanguard as vandal, rampaging around the world in a manner which one might describe (in Eurocentric terms) as Hitlerian. Here, as well, the dust has still to settle. And inevitably judgements about Europe tend to get mixed up with judgements about modernity, industrialism and so forth – inevitably because of their original conjunction. The postmodern version of this critique makes things too simple in throwing out the babies of modernity, rationalism and so forth along with the admittedly often polluted European or American bathwater which was all they had to bathe in.

Having skated on thin ice over a number of minefields in the preceding section, let me try to clarify the relation between Europe and modernity today. Some writers draw a distinction between culture and civilization, in which the latter has a primarily material reference. So, for example, my Japanese or Chinese DVD player is part of a global industrial capitalist technical civilization, while the discs I play on it happen to be largely European or export-European (mostly North American). It would be stretching things to call the equipment residually European because of some story about the history of radio and television featuring Marconi, Baird and so on. In the case of the content, things seem more complicated. How about a tape of a US TV broadcast of the Tokyo Symphony Orchestra playing Brahms? Is a film about North American adolescents in some sense residually European because the Western Canadian towns and farms featured in it are outgrowths of a European settler culture, or because the sexual mores described in the film are more like those of Western Europe than of, say, parts of South or East Asia?

What in any case should we understand by modernity? The concept has dominated social theorizing in the 1980s, replacing the previously fashionable terms 'industrialism' or 'industrial society' in the 1950s and 1960s and 'capitalism' in the 1970s. The underlying rationale of the shift to 'modernity' was, I think, to move attention away from what in Marxist language would be called the forces of production or the social relations of production towards more cultural and political dimensions of modern societies. This is where the fun begins. If one takes advanced modernity to include not just industrialism and capitalism, urbanism, mass education and so forth, but also certain traditional Euro-American conceptions of citizenship and the public sphere, with roots in the French and American Revolutions, these are not always part of the export package. I once heard a Japanese sociologist argue that Japan had not had a public sphere in the usual understanding of the term because its political culture had been so dominated by the cult of the Emperor, and similar debates arise in relation to, for example, Russia. There has also been a good deal of debate about whether the state socialism developed in the USSR and imposed on large parts of the rest of Europe should be understood as a variant of modernity, just as it was in previous decades as a variant of industrial society (Aron, 1958), or as in some sense insufficiently, incompletely or unstably modern, in its socio-political structures no less than in its automobile industry. On this view, for example, the 1989 revolutions could be seen as a process of catching-up or rectification (Habermas, 1990; cf. Arnason, 1993).

I share Habermas's view that modernity should be seen, among other things, as an unfinished and indeed open-ended project. Most importantly, the element of self-reflection which I would argue is built into the discourse of modernity implies that all our practices and ways of life are in principle open to questioning and attempts to justify them. They become in Habermas's sense post-conventional. Habermas, has, for example, defended a conception of 'constitutional patriotism' based not on membership of a particular ethnic or national community or Volk but on a rational and defensible identification with a decent constitutional state, which may of course happen to be the one whose citizenship one holds and/or the one in which one lives.[7]

It is interesting to ask what happens even to prejudice and to xenophobia under these conditions. A newspaper report that students participating in international exchange programmes often returned home more, rather than less, hostile to foreigners was neatly illustrated by a cartoon in which one (male) student says to another: 'I hate foreigners because they've turned me into a xenophobe.' In conditions of advanced modernity, I suggest, misunderstanding and prejudice have become reflexive, in the sense that an awareness of the possibility that they may occur, and of ways in which their occurrence might be understood, forms part of the context underlying them – just as, in Anthony Giddens's words, 'Anyone who contemplates marriage today . . . knows a great deal about "what is going on" in the social arena of marriage and divorce' (Giddens, 1991: 14). And so even the fundamentalist defence of tradition or the xenophobic resistance to alien influence becomes one option among others – thus changing their character.

What can be said in the end about the residual distinctiveness of Europe as a cultural region of the modern world? A familiar theme, invoked even in an advertising series by Shell some years ago, is diversity, notably the diversity of languages. Compared to the largely anglophone societies of North America or the area sharing Chinese pictograms, or even large regions such as India or the former USSR with an established lingua franca, Europe looks rather a mess. One may wonder how far such a perception rests on overlooking linguistic diversity elsewhere in the world, but Michael Mann (1986, 1993) may well be right to emphasize the combination of competition between smallish units and the unifying umbrella of Christendom. It is at least true that in the European case a pattern of linguistic variation largely coexisting with the boundaries of developed modern states creates powerful entrenched structures and interests which, in turn, act as obstacles to cultural and political integration. (It is obvious, at least to this particular English speaker, that the official language of the European Union ought to be English, just as it is obvious that its principal institutions should all be centralized in Brussels, but no one quite dares to say so.)

The contours of Europe's main divisions are shifting in dramatic ways. It is not just that the old political East–West division has now been replaced by an economic one. The cultural North–South divide within Europe, marked for example by the line between potatoes and pasta, remains important, but is changing in many ways, with the modernization of (parts of the) Southern European societies. It is now for example Italy, with its poor public provision for childcare, rather than the Protestant Northern welfare states, which apparently puts work before children (Therborn, 1995, 2004).

Europe's position as a major cultural producer is of course one of the effects of its previous world hegemony, partly preserved in that of its world languages: English, French, Spanish, Portuguese and to some extent even Dutch. It has also stood up in many ways to the challenge of North American imports. This applies not just to cultural commodities such as films, but also to material aspects of life such as the car-based civilization; despite everything, most European cities remain less car-based and suburbanized than US ones. For a time these might have seemed like cultural lags. Now, however, it appears that in many ways parts of the US are returning to more 'European' modes of life, including railways and urban mass transit systems, delicatessen food (even cheese) and niche markets for cult movies in some of the cities. Colin Crouch (1999: 395) has suggested classical art, music and association football as three areas of substantial intra-European interaction; all three also however involve more or less worldwide activity, with the exception that the US remains relatively free of soccer. And if there is, as Crouch (1993) also argued, a European model or set of models of industrial relations, this may well appeal to other regions of the world too. (In the European context, the UK governments of Thatcher and Major, and to a lesser extent Blair, were out on a limb in wanting to abandon some of the benefits of the European system and adopt largely misunderstood Asian models instead.) Europe also appears 'modern' in relation to the US and many other regions of the world in the extent of its secularization. Whatever the difficulties of measurement in this domain, it is clear that religious belief in Europe has mostly ceased to have the kind of importance for social life as a whole which it has retained elsewhere, even in officially secular states like the US or India.[8]

The big question, I think, and it is one where expertise in relation to non-European societies is more relevant than mine in relation to Europe, is, to put it simplistically, what fits together with what: in other words what effects different cultural items or forms have on one another and with what degrees of compatibility, assimilation or rejection. Here again the 1989 revolutions in Europe offer an interesting example of what may have been a cultural or civilizational collapse as much as a more narrowly political or economic one. The communist regimes were ageing not just in the senility of their political elites, their technology or the state of their housing stock but in their whole ways of life. We are familiar with arguments about the corrosive effect of material progress on traditional ways of life, but it could be argued that rock music and youth culture, for example, also had an important effect in undermining the credibility of the post-Stalinist regimes.

Similar challenges probably confront other regions of the world. There are of course significant fundamentalist counter-movements, calling forth in their turn responses such as that by Samuel Huntington which manage to be at once hysterical and cynical. But fundamentalist movements, whether outside or inside Europe, are unlikely in the long term to be able to resist pressures from the Euro-American cultural area, or from East Asian producers moving from control of the hardware markets into the sponsorship of content. So far, it seems to me, Japanese influences on European culture in the late twentieth and early twenty-first centuries have not been particularly striking, despite important exceptions in management styles and some areas of design. More generally, the privatism of European ways of life has probably reduced the impact of other cultural influences, despite significant migration from outside Europe in the middle decades of the twentieth century. Multiculturalism is an important ideal, but perhaps not yet much of a reality.

On the issue of compatibilities and incompatibilities, Max Weber borrowed from Goethe what remains perhaps the most useful concept for addressing these issues: the chemical concept of elective affinity (*Wahlverwandtschaft*). But if this provides a useful way of thinking about such relations, it does not give us much of an idea about what fits with what. What is clear is that human societies are much more ingenious in their bricolage than we can predict (see, for example, Gilroy, 1993). The current attention to conceptions of hybridity is helpful here, though even this term risks implying a certain reification of the initial entities between which hybridizing occurs. But even if something like European or North American modernity does continue to spread over the more fortunate areas of the rest of the world, its inflections and modifications will continue to surprise us.

As we have seen, it is extremely difficult to separate the question of Europe from that of modernity as a form of life which happened to develop in Europe and was adopted, voluntarily or involuntarily, in much of the rest of the world. The following chapters explore this issue in more detail, focusing first on Europe's geographical divisions, then on the European forms of economy and state, and returning to the issue of social divisions of class, ethnicity and gender as they play out across Europe. The concluding chapter aims to situate Europe as a region of global modernity.

2 EUROPE: EAST, WEST, NORTH, SOUTH

I referred briefly in the previous chapter to the diffusion of culture in early modern Europe from South and East to North and West. In Italy, the term 'Italian Renaissance' would sound pleonastic, and the notion that there was also a 'Northern' Renaissance in Poland, the Netherlands, France or the British Isles tends to be met with scepticism. Italy was of course a privileged site not just because of the classical Roman heritage, but also because it was a channel and focus for the processes of migration of people, artefacts and ideas across the Mediterranean region as a whole. This configuration in the early modern period was followed by a predominantly West–East movement of material culture and technologies of all kinds, epitomized by Peter the Great's 'stage' in the Greenwich dockyards in London and his imitation of Venice in St Petersburg. As with the so-called European miracle, it is hard here to detach reality from myth.

Europe itself is between East and West in an obvious geographical sense: between the Asian continent, of which it forms a peninsula, and the Europeanized societies of the Americas.[1] Until recently, it was of course geopolitically partitioned between East and West, as the front line of, respectively, the Warsaw Pact and NATO. Berlin, itself partitioned, was both a Western metropolis and an Eastern capital, with American GIs, off duty but in uniform, strolling through the latter and the occasional Soviet sentry in the former. The residues of the East/West partition of Europe are still with us, not least in Berlin itself, though they have again been overlaid, as they always used to be, by other geographical and social divisions. It now makes sense once again, as it did for a year or two after the Second World War, to think of a political Europe which in principle includes the whole subcontinent, although East and West experienced radically different trajectories over the second half of the twentieth century.

Europe's Eastern border will remain an issue for the foreseeable future. At the time of writing, the question of Turkey's membership of the EU is still not finally resolved. Even if we take that proleptically as achieved, along with the accession of the Western Balkan states of former Yugoslavia and Albania and perhaps of Ukraine and Belarus, there remains the open question of Russia and the rest of the Commonwealth of Independent States. Many of the latter states, if they are not unequivocally European, would certainly pass the 'Turkish test' as substantially secularized and Westernized Muslim societies. Whereas the Western end of Europe is clearly marked by the Atlantic Ocean, its Eastern edge is not just imprecise, but fundamentally indeterminate, in the sense that any attempt to fix it conceptually or politically generates paradoxes which undermine the attempt. As Liotta (2005: 69) puts it, 'In the broadest sense, the "new" map of Greater Europe includes Turkey, Ukraine, the Russian Federation, and perhaps even Christian Armenia and Georgia and Muslim Azerbaijan.' (See also Lavenex, 2004; Rumford, 2006.)

Europe is also between East and West in a more internal sense, with substantial populations in many parts of Europe identified with Asia in one way or another and/or with 'Eastern' religions such as Islam, Hinduism and Buddhism. This is of course true of North America or Australasia as well, but in Europe it is a much more prominent feature, with several prospective member-states of the EU predominantly Muslim by religion. Even excluding central

Asia from consideration, we have Turkey, Bosnia-Herze-govina and Albania as prospective member-states with sub-stantially Muslim populations.

To register these facts is to confront a Europe which is not so much between as *beyond* East and West (Delanty, 2006b; Wang Hui, 2005a, 2005b), just as much as hyper-modern Dubai, Singapore or Hong Kong. At the same time, however, the internal East–West divide remains an impor-tant structuring feature, not just of Europe as a whole but of many European states and even many European cities, whose smart Western suburbs are upwind of the central and Eastern quarters. The East–West 'wall in the head'[2] is not confined to Berlin, nor more substantial walls to Jerusalem. Most fundamentally, the East–West divide has been shaped by ideologies of European (and, within Europe, Western) superiority which continue to influence such concrete issues as the EU enlargement negotiations of the twentieth and early twenty-first centuries.[3]

To think about Europe, then, at least the Europe of the last half-millennium, is to think, however sceptically and critically, about modernity, and this inflects the notion of the West. Since around halfway to two-thirds through the last millennium, Europe has come to see itself and portray itself to the rest of the world as 'Western' in an evaluative sense, and its neighbours and its own Eastern or Southern regions, and parts of its populations, as less Western or less than Western. This is an approach appropriately described and rightly condemned as Eurocentric in relation to the rest of the world, and Western-centric or Occident-centric within Europe.[4] It is of course integrally linked to imperialism and to the processes, within Europe itself and its component states, of 'internal colonialism' (Hechter, 1975).[5]

One way of framing this is in terms of the notion of a 'post-Western' Europe (Delanty, 2003, 2006b). Of the three principal civilizational constellations in Europe, those of Western Christendom and the Russian and Ottoman Empires, the Western one has been dominant through-out the modern period, reinforced by twentieth-century

Atlanticism and a project of European integration which began 'in the West of the continent and initially roughly matched the contours of the Carolingian Empire. Further East, the Western referent becomes by definition more attenuated, as does the European one for, in particular, Turkey. The Europe of the early twenty-first century remains of course 'Western' in the sense of modernity and to some extent geopolitical attachment, while its centre of gravity has shifted East within Europe itself. What however remains uncertain is whether, or how long, Europe's representation of itself will continue to be shaped by the East–West polarity. The salience of these polarities can change, as illustrated by the no longer 'wild' West of the US or the no longer backward South of Germany.

This chapter is primarily concerned with contemporary Europe, but it is instructive to look at the way in which long-standing patterns, whether real or imagined, continue to shape perceptions of East–West differences. Stefan Auer, in his excellent book on Central European nationalism, rightly problematizes the common differentiation between 'Eastern' and 'Western' variants. One standard formulation is this one by Anthony Smith (1992: 61):

> The Western model of the nation tended to emphasize the centrality of a national territory or homeland, a common system of laws and the importance of a mass, civic culture binding the citizens together. The Eastern model, by contrast, was more preoccupied with ethnic descent and cultural ties.

Smith stresses that 'The contrast between these two concepts of the nation should not be overdrawn, as we find elements of both at various times in several nationalisms in both Eastern and Western Europe.' Liah Greenfeld, author of an influential book published in 1992, takes a similar line that despite such overlaps and mismatches (Greenfeld, 1995: 18) one can distinguish between 'Western, less Western and anti-Western nationalism in Europe and elsewhere' (Greenfeld, 1995: 22). Auer (2004: chapter 1) argues convincingly that such contortions are misleading, and reflect dubious dichotomies traced equally in relation to forms of transition (Vachudová and Snyder, 1997) and of political culture (Carpenter, 1997). The terms of the comparisons may vary, but in each case the contrasts simplify and over-interpret a more complex and unpredictable reality. The rapid transformation of Slovakia after 1998 from pariah to EU member-state makes the point, whether or not one follows Auer's critical defence of what he calls liberal nationalism.[6] The East–West binary division was inescapable in the Cold War period, but it should be treated with caution in the postcommunist context.

It remains a fact, however, that the mid-twentieth-century East–West division of Europe cut very deep. From the point of view of equalizing existing East–West divisions in Europe, it would of course have been better if the Red Army had liberated, and the Soviet Union colonized, Western rather than Eastern Europe. (Whether, as an East German philosopher once assured me, state socialism in the West would have been incomparably more impressive than in the East because of the West's material advantages is another question.) As it was, Soviet domination held back development in many parts of the bloc, notably East Germany and Czechoslovakia, and directed it in dubious directions in much of the rest. 'Eastern' Europe, the Europe East of what Churchill aptly baptized as the Iron Curtain, was largely cut off for forty years, not of course from 'Europe', but from the mainstream of European development.

This began with the Soviet ban on what came to be called the 'satellites' accepting Marshall aid. Whether or not the offer was seriously meant, it was at least on the table, and Czechoslovakia, in particular, was keen to accept and had at the time the political freedom to do so (Judt, 2005: 92). Having been forced to reject aid from the original Marshall Plan, communist Europe in the 1990s missed out on a widely expected and badly needed, but never even seriously considered, second Marshall Plan. The rational response of the

West to its sudden deliverance from the threat of attack from the Warsaw Pact would surely have been a massive shift of resources from defence to aid, comparable with that in the late 1940s. As it was, aid from individual Western states and from the EU was extremely limited, patchy and slow to arrive. Only in Germany was there a really significant transfer of resources, amounting to three trillion dollars over the decade, and here it took place in a context already sabotaged by the abrupt currency union of 1990 which, even if it was politically unavoidable, as Federal Chancellor Helmut Kohl seemed to believe, rendered East Germany an economic disaster area. Elsewhere in the bloc, a serious aid programme would undoubtedly have achieved far more, at far lower cost, than current EU programmes. To put it starkly, the four lost decades of communism in Central and Eastern Europe were followed by a further substantially lost decade of postcommunist transition, when economic transformation was hampered by lack of resources, as well as, arguably, by neo-liberal economic policies. This is not to say that transition has failed in central Europe (the situation in Russia and Belarus is more ambiguous). It is more a matter of missed opportunities and unnecessary suffering along the way.

In retrospect it is surprising that this prodigious social dislocation produced so little violent disorder. Czechoslovakia and the Soviet Union split up peacefully, and Yugoslavia bloodily, but the widely expected break-up of the Russian Federation, with civil war as its likely accompaniment, did not take place, despite ongoing flash-points in the Caucasus and elsewhere (Pryce-Jones, 1995). There was unpleasant street violence against foreigners, Roma and others (Ladányi and Szelényi, 2006), and a general increase in crime, but most of the pain of transition was borne by individuals. Suicide rates soared, especially for men, and in parts of the bloc, notably in Russia, life expectancy rates collapsed (Therborn, 1997: 376–7; Outhwaite and Ray, 2005: 50). At the other end of the prosperity gradient, in East Germany, people benefited as individuals, even if they lost their jobs, but the society was decimated. This German pattern, which ironically recalls Engels's remark that capitalism improved individual conditions at the cost of the human species, has a wider application in postcommunist Europe.

East–West divisions in contemporary Europe can best be examined in relation to three periods:

(i)   the *annus mirabilis* of 1989/90;
(ii)   the long transition decade that followed; and which culminated in
(iii)   the EU enlargements of 2004 and 2007 and their aftermath.

(i) **The *annus mirabilis* of 1988/90.** If 1789 was, as I suggested earlier, one of the defining events of the modern political imagination, it remains to be seen what place will be given to the anti-communist revolutions of 1989. A number of commentators have stressed the absence of really new ideas in the 1989 period, especially after the rapid eclipse of civil society movements like Solidarity in Poland or Civic Forum in Czechoslovakia; Habermas (1990), for example, called it a 'catching-up' or 'rectifying' revolution: a return to democracy (and capitalism), and to the 'normal' path of post-Second World War European development. Perhaps the revolutionary period was just too fast and too peaceful to capture the world's imagination; by the end of 2001 many people in the West were giving similar prominence to an (admittedly spectacular) terrorist attack on the United States. Tocqueville (1971: 99) wrote in his *Recollections* of the 1848 revolution of the 'complete silence' regarding the former king. Within a few days he 'could not have been more out of the picture if he had been a member of the Merovingian dynasty'. Similarly, the former dictators and their associates were the object of attention only if and when they came to trial.

(ii) **The transition decade.** It is tempting to define post-communist transition out of existence, suggesting that it is either essentially over, as many in East Central Europe would argue is the case in the parts of their states which interest them, or not (yet) seriously begun, as jaundiced observers of points further East often say (Vachudová and Snyder, 1997). Either way, for this reductive view, the implications for the rest of Europe are seen as relatively limited and can be handled under the category of transitional arrangements, where 'transition', like 'convergence', now refers to the path to EU accession rather than the shift from totalitarian socialism to liberal capitalism. It is certainly true that the world-historical significance of the transition, rightly stressed by analysts like Andrew Arato, hardly seems to be reflected in the observable phenomena. Everything, so to speak, was tossed up into the air, but much of it fell down again into relatively familiar structures and patterns. But, as I suggested earlier, it would be a mistake to play down the process in this way, however inviting the euphemistic language of transition may be.

The notion of transition is doubly problematic. It suggests a teleological movement from one state to another, driven by a technocratic and unpolitical ethos of 'There is No Alternative' and the famous dentistry metaphor: 'if you don't visit the dentist for forty years you can expect some extensive and painful treatment'. Second, the implication is that once the transition is over – a point which might be taken to coincide with, for example, EU accession – the postcommunist condition is essentially over, like the colonial history of the US. Although many citizens and political elites in the more fortunate parts of the postcommunist world would indeed take this view, it is probably wrong. The postcommunist condition is substantially shaped by the postcommunist state, in the sense of the state apparatus; and the postcommunist state, even in Germany, where it arrived ready-made, is a political structure of a particular kind. The philosopher and cultural theorist Boris Groys has brought this out very clearly. In a short but suggestive book, Groys (2006: 94) points out that the privatizing state is an activist state, no less than the communist nationalizing state: the establishment of capitalism is a political project. This left part of the region, at least for the transitional period, with 'capitalism without capitalists' (Eyal et al., 1998), and a larger and less fortunate part with 'capitalists without capitalism', in other words, with compradores of privatization oriented mainly to exporting their ill-gotten capital to more secure locations.

(iii)   The EU Enlargements.   The EU Enlargement of 2004 was striking for the mismatch between the enormous importance of what happened in May 2004 and the restricted form in which it was reflected both before and after the event. On the one hand there was the sense of a momentous transition, in which the European integration process finally embraced almost the whole of the subcontinent, including a majority of the European states excluded for forty years not just from the European Community/Union but also from the postwar democratization process itself. As Étienne Balibar described the situation in 1991 (Balibar, 2004: 90):

> Following the disappearance of one of the two blocs, the struggle itself is vanishing, which in fact constitutes a great trial of truth: now or never is the moment for the dream to materialize, for Europe to rise up, renewed or revitalized. This is also the moment when the dream risks being smashed into pieces.

Alongside all this, there was a further element, the constitutional Convention, contingently related to the impending enlargement in the sense that it could (and perhaps should) have taken place well before 1989, but intrinsically linked in its mission to make a larger Union viable and in the fact that the new members were fully represented in its deliberations. Although the Convention failed to produce an acceptable constitution, in other respects it was quite an impressive deliberative assembly which may be remembered when more immediately successful ventures are forgotten (Norman, 2005). It was also one in which old and new Europe met on relatively egalitarian and open terms. As Fraser Cameron (2004: 152) notes, 'it was difficult to distinguish speakers coming from existing or future member states', though the research of Ruth Wodak and her collaborators suggests a rather more pessimistic assessment (Krzyzanowski, 2005; Oberhuber, 2005). The dominant impression of the 2004 enlargement remains that of a bureaucratic process managed in a bureaucratic manner, and tinged with arrogance on the part of the existing members. Like, some would say, the European Union itself . . .

What did this amount to in East–West terms? The Visegrad core of the 2004 accession states could, as their intellectuals had since the 1980s, invoke the idea of Central Europe. This had been an important ideological plank in their self-affirmation against a Soviet hegemon characterized as Asiatic, and could now serve as a marker of their advanced place in the accession queue. In practice, the term more often used was East Central Europe or East and Central Europe (ECE). This had the advantage of accommodating Poland and the Baltic States, though it also obscured the more dramatic fact that in a sense Central Europe had ceased to exist. As Hans-Heinrich Nolte (1997, 2003) has pointed out, the Iron Curtain sealed the fate of a Central Europe already transformed by the loss of its Jewish and German populations – the former by persecution and genocide, the latter by voluntary or forced emigration westwards. Hungary, Czechoslovakia and Poland became for forty years the West of the East; EU accession has made them, for a time, the East of the West (Nolte, 2002: 46). With the accession of Bulgaria and Romania in 2007, they have again become closer to the imagined centre.

One of the most prominent implications of this re-shaping of East and West, of course, concerns migration. With Western Europe, now even including the Irish Republic, becoming mostly a region of immigration, the flows are essentially from the South and East to the North-West. Many EC/EU enlargements have raised issues of this kind, notably the accession of Greece in 1981, the various non-accessions of Turkey over the past decades and the first Eastern enlargement of 2004, which provoked considerable excitement about possible floods of Polish plumbers. All this has the potential to ignite renewed anxieties around the EU's 'near abroad', which form part of the explanation for why '2004' came so late. It is instructive to look back at some of the surveys conducted around the turn of the century, in which existing EU citizens warmly welcomed the idea of Swiss or Norwegian (and Maltese) accession but were more lukewarm or even negative about the ECE countries (CEC, 2000) and emphatically negative in the case of Turkey. Political elites also often shared this view. For Jacques Attali, for example, writing in 1994 when he was still President of the European Bank for Reconstruction and Development, there was a stark choice between widening and deepening the European Union: 'with twenty or twenty-two members, it would be impossible to move towards the single currency or establish common economic, social, judicial and foreign policies' (Attali, 1997: 349). Instead, he favoured a 'Continental Union' of which the EU would be a member and, 'with Russia, one of the essential motors' (Attali, 1997: 354). Such attitudes partly explain the EU's remarkably slow response to 1989, which provoked considerable resentment in Poland (Blazyca, 2002: 206–7, 212) and elsewhere in the region. Melinda Kovács (2001) neatly describes this response as 'putting down and putting off'. A more cosmopolitan Union, one must conclude, would have been more responsive and understanding – not least since it had just emerged from a potentially lethal Cold War. Beck and Grande (2004: 259) rightly point to a certain 'western European racism'. As Baldwin et al. write (1997: 168, quoted in Ingham and Ingham, 2002: 15): 'Imagine how eager Western Europe would have been in 1980 to pay ECU 18 billion a year in order to free central Europe from communism and remove Soviet troops from the region.'[7]

We should of course not forget the possibility of a very different counterfactual scenario in which either the EU was even less welcoming to the East, or in which part or all of the East deliberately rejected full membership of the EU in favour of a looser attachment in the European Economic Area. On the latter question, however unlikely it may look

at present, the future prospect that an Eastern European
Norway or Switzerland might deliberately reject the option
of accession should not be ruled out. More to the point, as
Böröcz and Sarkar (2005: 158–9) emphasized, full membership has been and is to be preceded by a long transitional
period of dependency on EU regulations.

> For the entrants during the 2004 round of accessions (who will
> enjoy equal rights within the EU by 2011), this quasi-depen-
> dency status will have lasted for 18 years. For next-round
> members Bulgaria, Romania and Turkey – optimistically
> assuming only a five-year delay – it can be expected to be
> circa 23 years.[8]

If the Eastern and Central European countries were treated
for a decade somewhat like East Germans by their Western
relatives, it is also true that their inhabitants tend for their part
to have a more 'traditional' and positive ('pre-postcolonial')
conception of Europe than Westerners. Very many Western
Europeans, for example, belong to states which have had substantial colonial empires, and although they react to this past
in very different ways (compare the generally positive and
even nostalgic image of empire in the UK with the tendency
to embarrassed denial in the Netherlands) it has perhaps
given a more cosmopolitan and multicultural angle to their
thinking about Europe. Habermas (2004: 51) emphasizes
this effect of the experience of colonial rule and decolonization: 'with the growing distantiation from imperial rule and
colonial history the European powers have had the chance *to
take up a reflexive distance to themselves*'.[9] In the East, as noted
earlier, 'Europe' in general and 'Central Europe' in particular
have operated in part as tokens in a political strategy of distantiation from the 'Asiatic' USSR, as in the East German Rudolf
Bahro's now largely forgotten *Alternative* (Bahro, 1977). To
put it bluntly, Easterners, even more than Westerners, often
talk about the European heritage in upbeat language which
can provoke hostility or embarrassment in parts of the West
and the rest of the world.

The boot is perhaps on the other foot if one turns to a related issue, that of ethnocentric prejudice. The somewhat higher levels recorded in the East of Europe than in the West generated something of a moral panic, starting with skinhead riots in the East German port of Rostock in 1991. Without wishing to belittle the unpleasant character of these manifestations, and the extremely serious levels of anti-Roma prejudice in particular, the pattern overall seems to be that such attitudes are driven by specific current crises rather than linked into nationalism and extreme-right ideology, as they have tended to be in the West (Hjerm, 2003). Very crudely, however, one might say that there is an intra-European cosmopolitan multicultural tradition in Eastern and Central Europe, historically tied to local empires, including of course the trans-European Russian Empire (Sakwa, 2006), where the West has a more extra-European one: more oriented to the Atlantic and the rest of the world via the Western European world empires. Both cosmopolitan traditions, of course, are counterposed by explicit racism in the West and ethnic prejudice in the East, but the possibility of their fusion in a cosmopolitan openness to other Europeans and to non-Europeans is one of the more optimistic scenarios in play here.

We are confronted, then, with a Europe in which East–West divisions corresponding to the Iron Curtain remain extremely salient. This is in part a matter of historical memory. It is still possible, for instance, for Eastern public figures to be threatened by proof or rumours of past collaboration with the secret police, where their Western counterparts have mostly only financial or sexual skeletons in their cupboards. The older generations are shaped by different historical events: the 1968 of the Prague Spring and its extinction is different from the 1968 of Western protest movements.[10] Such East–West divisions are however weakening in the face of countervailing forces. The first of these is a long-standing one – as long as the East–West division itself. It is that between North and South.

The North–South division is in fact important to many European states, notably Germany and Italy and, in a more muted way, France, England and the Nordic countries – and to Europe as a whole. The 'wine line' running from Northern France through Germany to roughly the Czech–Polish border is one obvious division; the slightly more southerly line between the predominance of potatoes and that of pasta marks another. Religion in the modern period began with more of a division between the Catholic South and West and the Protestant or mixed North and East; majority Protestantism is now confined to Britain, Northern Germany and the Nordic countries (including Estonia and Latvia), with Orthodox Christianity dominating the Balkans (in a 'balkanized' form, with Serbian, Romanian, Bulgarian and of course Greek variants) and Russia (including Ukraine and Belarus). In terms of physical geography, Northern Europe is largely flat, apart from parts of the British Isles and Norway; the South is more of a mixture of plains and high mountain ranges. Prosperity in Europe has tended to cluster around the centre of a North–South axis, with Southern France, the Iberian peninsula, Southern Italy and the Balkans historically or continuingly poor, and the far North also poor until its abrupt advance in the mid- to late-twentieth century.[11] Emmanuel Todd (1987) has pointed to the importance of family structures and literacy in the early advance of North Central (and largely Protestant) Europe. As late as the mid-nineteenth century, the Nordic countries, along with Scotland, Germany, the Netherlands, Luxemburg and Switzerland are ahead in literacy of the rest of Europe (Todd, 1987: 30). In his view, contra Max Weber, Protestantism itself was secondary in importance to a vertically structured or 'authoritarian' family pattern with strong links of interdependency between the generations.

> Examination of the types of family characteristic of Western Europe helps to explain the continent's take-off better than Weber's categories do . . .
>   The North of Europe – where authoritarian family systems predominate – is the scene where mass literacy, Protestantism and Bible-reading all triumphed. The Protestant Reforma-

tion, indeed, is itself probably an effect rather than a cause
of the division between Europe's North and South created
by diverging growth rates. (Todd, 1987: 59–60)

The North–South division is salient, then, in Europe as
a whole and in a number of its component states – notably
Germany, Italy and France. In all three it is historically more
of an axis between a prosperous and advanced North-West
and a more backward South-East. In the German stereotype,
as expressed in a parody of the national song 'Heil Dir im
Siegeskranz', southerners are 'hard-drinking, work-shy but
loyal to the (Catholic) church' (Brückner, 1987: 13). Here,
of course, part of the 'North' became the East (the GDR).
In Italy, the most extreme political expression of Northern
prejudice is in the early propaganda of the Lega Nord, contrasting a Germanic North with an 'African' South. Rome,
roughly halfway down the Italian peninsula, is here associated with the South and its political corruption. There is a
complex issue here of the location of national capitals. Paris,
for example, is in the North of France, while London is in the
South of England/Britain. Madrid, by contrast, is in the centre
of Spain, as Warsaw is in Poland and Brussels is in Belgium,
located just into the Flemish side of the language frontier.
The more centralized the country, the more this tends to
matter; in federal Germany, for example, there is more of
an equality between Berlin, Frankfurt and other major cities
such as Cologne, Hamburg, Stuttgart and Munich, and for
the second half of the twentieth century the Federal German
capital was the 'small' Rhineland town of Bonn.[12]

Modernization in the second half of the twentieth century
substantially relativized this North–South axis. Often the
North-West lost out and became deindustrialized, while new
technology thrived in the South, as in Germany (Wehling,
1987), or in a number of provincial growth poles, as in
France. In Italy, attempts to modernize the South were less
successful, but not without effect. Here, as elsewhere in
Southern Europe, corruption and clientelism remain strong.
However, this is by no means a Southern monopoly; in the

'transparency index', based on subjective measures (perceptions by business elites and others), the North–South divison is overridden by an East–West polarization both between Eastern and Western Europe and within the East. In the 2005 survey, only three 'Western' countries, Cyprus, Italy and Greece, ranked as more corrupt than the 'cleanest' post-communist ones, and the role of corruption in the East is less a question of ingrained culture and habit and more a structural matter of state capture (Heywood and Krastev, 2006: 172–3). David Mandel (2005: 130) quotes Gleb Pavlovsky's comment that in Russia corruption is 'no longer a phenomenon, but a class'. Within Western Europe, France, Ireland and Belgium rank as the most corrupt Northern states, while in the East, 'Northern' Estonia and 'Southern' Slovenia count as the least corrupt.

The European Union has of course been active in promoting regional and inter-regional initiatives, notably in the Mediterranean region. Following the rejection of Morocco's membership application in 1987, it and the other countries of North Africa and the Eastern shore of the Mediterranean were included in 'neighbourhood agreements', upgraded in 2007 with the addition of a new financial instrument, the European Neighbourhood Policy Instrument (ENPI). The Euro-Mediterranean Partnership established in 1995 has been an important element in this. Gallant (2006: 133) argues that 'A Mediterranean identity that is simultaneously a European identity is becoming manifest.' Neighbourhood agreements also apply to the Western parts of the former Soviet Union: Belarus, Ukraine and Moldova in the North and Georgia, Azerbaidjan and Armenia in the South. The Western Balkan countries are of course prospective member-states. Within the Union itself, the Interreg programmes encourage transnational cooperation between adjacent states and regions such as East Sussex in England and Seine-Maritime in France (which currently owns the Sussex port of Newhaven, having rescued it from the consequences of British neglect).

A second trend which weakened the simple contrast between West (and North) and East (and South) is that, as in the French case, development became increasingly differentiated between high-tech cities and more backward hinterlands. This has become even more striking in postcommunist Europe, with certain towns in, for example, Russia, heavily promoting themselves as sites for foreign investment. Leo McCann's study of Kazan (McCann, 2005) shows it attempting, not very successfully, to profile itself alongside Yekaterinburg and even St Petersburg. Here the European case illustrates broader processes of the growth of 'world cities' whose reference groups become one another rather than their respective rural surroundings.

Third, there is a more general eastward shift of some European investment in search of low wage costs; in Scandinavia, the move has of course been southwards to lower-cost regions of Western Europe, as well as eastwards. Something which is still unclear is how far processes of this kind will modify the traditional image of a Europe whose productive core and consumption high-spots are located in the 'golden banana' running from England through Northern France and Germany to Northern Italy.[13]

The EU itself remains, of course, heavily skewed to the West, with all its main institutions located in the original six member-states; only if one takes the axis running from Portugal to Finland does the Brussels/Luxemburg/Strasbourg/ Frankfurt institutional cluster appear like a natural centre.[14] Of course, this may not matter, as long as the Union overcomes its Western bias and leaves behind the painful memories of a decade of relative neglect of the East, followed by its grudging acceptance on Western terms. The latter is of course a difficult area. Many of the aims of the strategy known as conditionality were laudable, such as strengthening the independence of the judiciary, reducing corruption and police brutality and so on.[15] But the circumstances under which it was done were uncomfortable, to say the least, and provoked resentments of a kind familiar from the history of German reunification.

It may be useful to take three more concrete cases cutting across East–West differences. All three are ambiguous and

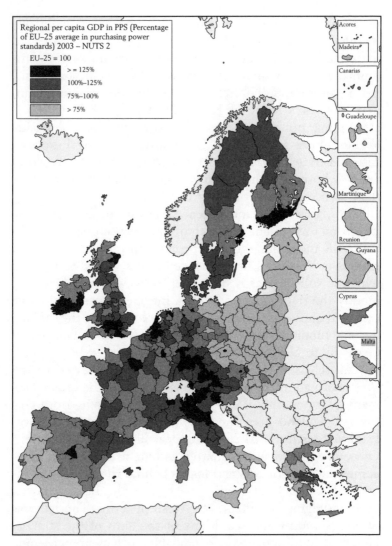

Regional per capita GDP in PPS (Percentage
of EU–25 average in purchasing power
standards) 2003 – NUTS 2

EU–25 = 100

>= 125%

100%–125%

75%–100%

> 75%

Acores

Madeira

Canarias

Guadeloupe

Martinique

Reunion

Guyana

Cyprus

Malta

Map 2.1 Regional per capita GDP in Purchasing Power
Standards
© EuroGeographics, for the administrative boundaries. Carto-
graphy: Eurostat – GISCO

to some extent remain unpredictable. The first example is again that of Germany; the second is that of Central Europe, which has been a major focus of thought and practice in Europe for centuries, and the third is the similarly long-standing axis between state socialist Europe and Scandinavia. In Germany, of course, the internal borders were rapidly effaced, and 'Western' forms extended to the whole country. A massive transformation of technical infrastructure (roads, railways, electricity and communication cables) left much of the East more modern than the West. And yet, nearly twenty years on, there remain substantial objective and subjective differences, the latter neatly captured by the expression of the 'Mauer im Kopf', the Wall in the head. A government report of 2004 traced a gloomy picture, where Chancellor Kohl at the time of reunification had predicted 'blooming landscapes'. The question whether 'we are *one people*' (Falter et al., 2006) remains moot.

To speak of Germany is also to raise the question of the whole region which, in the communist period, similarly transcended the East–West division. Central Europe or Mitteleuropa, with or without Germany, has of course a long history as a contested concept in Europe's representations of itself (Schöpflin and Wood, 1989). The postwar division of Europe might have been expected to make it no more than a geographical abstraction, but it bounced back, as mentioned earlier, in the 1970s and 1980s and remains an important way of representing the region. Links such as those between Italy, Slovenia and Austria are more than those of the merely cosmetic recipients of EU subsidies.

My third example was brilliantly marked out by Göran Therborn (1995). In his wide-ranging survey of 'European Modernity 1945–2000', he noted certain similarities between the Northern and Central parts of communist Europe and their Scandinavian neighbours.

Not only were welfare state *structures* comparably prominent, as was no surprise to anyone, but, more interestingly, *attitudes* to a number of cultural and lifestyle issues showed substantial similarities compared to the more 'traditional' parts of Europe. Despite the currently fashionable discussion of 'post-secularism', Europe as a whole remains what Therborn (1995: 274) called 'the continent of secularization' and within Europe this is particularly strong in the Nordic countries and in Eastern Europe, particularly the non-Catholic regions. This is not just an effect of communist atheist propaganda; Poland in the early 1990s also scored highest in Europe for belief in God, even above the USA, though elsewhere in the former communist bloc belief was lower than anywhere in the West apart from Sweden. Taking a different issue, that of attitudes to parenting, Therborn's analysis, based on the World Values Survey, suggested not just a sharp cleavage between North-Central Europe and South-Western Europe, as one might expect, but also within Eastern Europe. Respondents were asked, first, whether obedience or independence should be encouraged in children and, second, whether parents should sacrifice their interests to those of their children.

> There are clearly two Europes, one more individualist than most of the world, and one not. But it is not the usual line-up. *Central Europe*, except Czechoslovakia and Poland but linking up with Bulgaria, *the Baltic and the North Atlantic areas* embrace child independence and are relatively restrained in demanding parental sacrifices. Denmark and West Germany and, on the eastern fringes, Latvia, Lithuania and Bulgaria have the strongest individualism . . .
>
> The *Southwest of Europe*, from Belgium to Portugal, including the British Isles, has a distinctively collectivist cast of family values. Portugal, France and Northern Ireland, in that order, also have a marked preference for obedience over independence. (Therborn, 1995: 293)

Therborn's material derives of course from the beginning of the postcommunist 1990s, and it is therefore interesting to see how far these patterns have persisted. One particularly interesting area is that of attitudes to inequality. Survey evidence suggests a majority perception in East Central Europe that there are 'strong' or 'very strong' conflicts between managers and workers and that income differentials are 'too great', and a relation between the perception of conflict and objective inequality as measured by Gini coefficient (Delhey, 2001: 203–5).[16] Postcommunist electorates remain more egalitarian in their attitudes than Western Europeans, to a degree more closely related than in the West to the actual levels of inequality in their societies (Delhey, 2001). The traditional expression of egalitarian attitudes, in Europe and to some extent elsewhere, has been social democratic politics, but the scissor effect in the postcommunist countries of the local demise of socialist/communist political and economic policies, and the general reorientation of social democracy into third way or 'new' politics, has tended to restrict this development. I discuss these issues in more detail in chapter 5, below.

This returns us to questions of the interaction of long-term processes with more immediate events. Of the latter, the changing position of Eastern European states in what has aptly been called a regatta towards EU accession is a particularly good example. It is not long since Slovakia was seen as a remote possibility for accession in the foreseeable future; it has now been a member since 2004. The relative positions of Bulgaria and Romania, who joined at the beginning of 2007, were shifting right through the preceding years.[17] The long-term future of the poorer parts of Europe, which in practice still means the East, will be crucially shaped by the place of Europe as a whole in the emerging world economy – an issue to which I return towards the end of the following chapter.

3 THE EUROPEAN ECONOMY

Europe has been the principal site for the development of two forms of economic system: capitalism and state socialism. In both, production and exchange are organized on the basis of long-term planning, and this distinguishes them from more informal types of economc system.[1] In capitalism, plans are formulated at the level of independent individuals, families or firms, with a view to private profit; in state socialism primarily by state planning bodies operating in the public interest. This contrast is of course somewhat overdrawn, since private capitalism, if successful, provides consumers with more or less desired products and services, while state socialist systems may be substantially driven by the private or collective interests of state bureaucrats. By and large, however, the contrast holds. A state socialist economy resembles *as a whole* a capitalist firm, in that internal transactions (and even much external trade) take place on the basis of central control and planning rather than market exchange.

The origins of modern European capitalism, around the middle of the last millennium, form a major topic of historical research. As with other controversies in European history, there is a division between those who stress the distinctiveness and novelty of European developments and those who frame them in a more global developmental model, in which

European economic successes from the fifteenth to the twentieth centuries form part of a growth node in the world economy. Centrally planned economies, by contrast, have a very precise origin in the theories of the European labour movements of the nineteenth and early twentieth centuries and the political practice of the state socialist regimes, which were established in Russia in 1917 and in the late 1940s in Eastern Europe. The basic idea of the planned economy is in the works of so-called utopian socialists such as Robert Owen and in those of Marx and Engels: notably in Marx's *Critique of the Gotha Programme* and Engels's *Anti-Dühring*, in which, under communism, 'Anarchy in social production is replaced by definite social organisation.' The anti-socialist economist Joseph Schumpeter wrote in similar terms in 1921, that 'the meaning of socialisation . . . lies in the element of a *conscious* economic plan for the entire national economy'. As Schumpeter noted in his later and principal work, *Capitalism, Socialism and Democracy* (1987: 173 n.2), a number of late nineteenth- and early twentieth-century economists, notably Enrico Barone (1908), had worked out the logic of a planned economy. The detailed theoretical elaboration of this model in the 1930s (Lange, 1938) more or less coincided with its practical consolidation in Stalin's USSR. To cut a long story short, central state planning was a rough and ready way of responding to the politically defined imperatives of industrialization, arms production and eventually warfare.

When the Soviet model was imposed on the communist bloc after the Second World War its successes were in roughly inverse proportion to the degree of development of the countries concerned; it was particularly bad news for the highly developed economies of Czechoslovakia and Germany. Not surprisingly, then, much of the impetus behind initiatives to introduce market reforms came from the 'people's democracies', even if they drew also on proposals by Soviet economists. Within the Soviet bloc they went furthest in Poland and Hungary, with more cautious and discreet initiatives in ultra-loyal East Germany; only in Yugoslavia, which broke away from Soviet control, was a relatively radical form of market socialism implemented, under the slogan, and to some extent the reality, of 'workers' self-management'. These 'reforms' often made things better for consumers, but they did little to reduce the relative decline of the state socialist economies in the 1980s and the unpopularity of the regimes which presided over them. Ideas of a possible 'third way' between capitalism and state socialism rapidly evaporated in the 1990s, and by the beginning of this century the economies of Europe were almost all more or less entirely capitalist, in one form or another. There remain however significant differences between the forms of capitalism across Europe, and the rest of this chapter examines these differences and similarities, together with the European economy as a whole.

First, we must note that Europe is relatively rich compared to the rest of the world, though with a significant degree of internal inequality between its component states. Of the twenty-five richest countries in the world in per capita GDP, twenty-one are European (though some of them are very small); Western Europe's GDP is roughly equal to that of the US, though with a population of 400 as against 300 million. East–West inequalities remain significant. Taking the average GDP (at purchasing power parities) of the twenty-five EU members in 2004 as 100, only one postcommunist country, Slovenia at 78, was above just one of the pre-2004 members, Portugal at 73. The other postcommunist accession countries, with the exception of the Czech Republic at 72 and Hungary at 61, were in the 40s and low 50s. Of future candidates for membership, only Croatia (46) was in this range, while Romania, Bulgaria and Turkey were around 30 (Eurostat/Europa in Zahlen). As noted in the previous chapter, the ripe old image of the golden banana of European economic dynamism, running from England to Northern Italy and taking in the Île de France, Benelux and the Rhine, retains some value.

Despite these significant differences, reflected in the continuing tendency for some purposes to count Western

Europe, the EU-15 or the Eurozone as a measurement unit rather than EU-27,[2] it makes sense now, as it did not in the Cold War period, to speak of a common European economic system. With the (significant) exceptions of Russia, Belarus and Ukraine, and parts of the Western Balkans, there are at least formally comparable economies, whose differences do not map on to a clear East–West or North–South division.

A classic book by Michel Albert (1991), *Capitalisme contre capitalisme*, has shaped the discussion of the different forms of modern capitalism.[3] Albert, an insurance executive and former director of the French planning commission, contrasted the Anglo-American (and Irish) liberal market economy with continental European (and Japanese) systems in which the central or regional state, banks and other social institutions play a larger role. Enterprises in the former type of system, often dependent on individual or collective share-holders, will tend to be short-termist in their decisions about production, procurement and employment, hiring and firing at will, where in the latter systems longer-term relation-ships with suppliers, workers, and banks as a major source of finance tend to predominate. Legislation tends to reflect and reinforce these differences, as the UK chain-store Marks and Spencer found when it tried to close its French shops without warning. The systems can be contrasted in terms of dynamic versus sluggish or, conversely, as wild and predatory versus civilized and sustainable.

Albert's preference was very much for the continental European systems, which he called alpine or Rhenish, fol-lowing the line of the Rhine from Austria through Swit-zerland and Germany to the Low Countries, or sometimes simply German or 'German-Japanese' (1991: 13; tr. 6).[4] He suggested however that, as with 'Gresham's Law', in which 'bad money drives out good' because people hoard the sounder currency, so the more predatory and destruc-tive forms of capitalism tend to drive out the softer forms (1991: 217; tr. 191). Despite the economic and, arguably, social superiority of the Rhine model, 'it has all the charms of an old provincial spinster, petrified in her traditions, rooted in her humanistic nostalgia, encumbered by scruples and foresight' (1991: 296; tr. 256). Political debate in Europe, in its more serious aspects, tends to centre around the question whether, or how far, the rest of the continent should follow the US/UK model in order to compete in the global economy. This is of course particularly acute in postcommunist Europe, where such issues have only been on the agenda since 1989/1991. I shall return to these issues of policy at the end of this chapter.

There was not yet, Albert argued, a European economic model, not just because of the peculiarities of British and Irish capitalism, but also because of other special cases, notably those of Italy, France and Spain. The last two retained strong corporatist traditions of protectionism and of state involvement and direction, while Italy was marked by the weakness of the state and the strength of family and small-scale capitalism (1991: 24; tr. 17). France and Spain were poised between Anglo-Saxon, German and even Italian paths.

Subsequent discussion of these issues has tended to focus on the simple polarity between 'liberal market' and 'coordinated market' systems and, in one influential version, on the strategic behaviour of firms within them (Hall and Soskice, 2001). Some other more recent analysts however, notably Vivien Schmidt, emphasize the distinctiveness of a third, state-dominated model. This is found in France until the 1980s, in Japan, South Korea, Taiwan and, she suggests, Italy and to some extent Spain. Schmidt (2002: 141) concedes however that 'From traditional state capitalism, these countries' economic practices have moved at the very least to "state-enhanced" capitalism.' Despite the historical importance of this statist model, then, it is of little contemporary relevance except perhaps in Russia and some other states of the former Soviet Union. And if post-Second World War France is the model, it is not clear that this fits the much more arbitrary and politically driven interventions of the Russian state under Putin. On the other hand, the methodological point remains strong: as Schmidt (2002: 110) puts it:

the distinctive patterns of ... 'state-enhanced' capitalism tend to be lost when scholars put the firm at the centre of their analyses, with labour an important secondary preoccupation and the state only a relatively insignificant and distant third, relegated to the legal and regulatory environment in which firms act. Such an approach risks privileging countries where the state has long played only a secondary or tertiary role – that is, countries conforming to the managed or market capitalist pattern – and treating as outliers those countries in which the state has played and continues to play a larger role.

There is therefore a choice of scale between two-type models and those with three or more. The French economist Robert Boyer (2005: 20–1[5]), in an extended defence of the neo-Marxist regulation theory against more descriptive accounts of the 'varieties of capitalism', presents a four-term model:

- A market-oriented capitalism in which commercial logic, adapted by the competition supervision entities, constitutes the main organising principle for almost all coordination procedures. In this group we find all of the English-speaking countries plus Norway sometimes ...
- Meso-corporatist capitalism's driving principle is the exchange of solidarity against mobility in a conglomerate type of economic unit that is big and diversified enough to survive temporary booms and busts. Japan and Korea are two examples of this configuration.
- A strongly state-driven capitalism is characterised by an economic circuit where most of the components (innovation, production, demand, industrial relationships, credit etc.) are moulded by a myriad of public interventions occurring at a national, regional, or local level. This configuration is typical of the continental countries taking part in the European integration drive.
- Lastly, social democratic capitalism based on frequent negotiations between social partners and public authorities concerning the rules governing most of the components of social life and economic activity. The Scandinavian countries are flag-bearers for this model.

Here, then, if we ignore the East Asian case and the peculiarities of the English speakers,[6] we have a significant line of division between Scandinavia (in which, on some dimensions, we might want to include the Netherlands) and the continental mainstream. On the other hand, we lose the difference stressed by Schmidt between statist capitalisms and forms which are embedded in relations with a variety of public and private institutions, for example the German regional banks.

The British sociologist Colin Crouch (1999: chapter 6) uses a more complex model of eight dimensions (p. 170), with individual countries varying between those with 'pure profiles' and those with a mixture of different characteristics (pp. 190–3). Most of the Western European cases in 1995 display 'deviations from pure market forms' (table 6.7, p. 191), though along different dimensions:

> Austria appears . . . as primarily corporatist (with otherwise relatively free markets); Belgium, Germany, the Netherlands as concentrated; Denmark as having strong state spending but not regulation; Finland and Sweden as concentrated with strong state spending; Italy is an unusual mix of strong labour commitment and small-firm reciprocity.

Bruno Amable (2003), in one of the most ambitious contributions to this genre, also uses a number of elements to generate his five-type model.

> I start from the consideration of five fundamental institutional areas: product-market competition; the wage-labour nexus and labour-market institutions; the financial intermediation sector and corporate governance; social protection and the Welfare State; and the education sector.

Adding these in sequentially (chapter 5), he arrives at

> five types of capitalism, each characterized by specific institutional forms and particular institutional complementarities: the market-based model; the social-democratic model; the

Figure 3.1 Amable's five models of capitalism
Source: Lane (2006)

Continental European model; the Mediterranean model, and the Asian model. (Amable, 2003: 14)

The question of complementarities, of what fits with what, pervades the literature in this area, with some writers looking for a tighter degree of fit than others. Amable pushes this further by showing how, for example, product-market competition is central to the free-floating and flexible liberal market model, where firms travel light, as it were, in terms of their activities and their internal and external institutional arrangements. Short-term finance from well-developed financial markets goes along with a short-term, 'hire and fire' approach to labour, including managerial labour.[7] The other models diverge from this in varied ways.

The social democratic model is organized according to very different complementarities. A strong external competitive pressure requires some flexibility in the labour force. But flexibility is not simply achieved through lay-offs and market-based adjustments. Protection of specific investments of employees is realized through a mixture of moderate employment protection, a high level of social protection, and easy access to retraining thanks to active labour-market policies. A coordinated wage-bargaining system allows a solidaristic wage-setting which favours innovation and productivity. (Amable, 2003: 15)

The other models can be situated against this contrast. The continental European (including Norway)[8] and Mediterranean models, the latter including Italy, Spain, Portugal and Greece,[9] have stronger employment protection but less social protection than in the social democratic model. To put it crudely, you are worse off here if you lose your job and you are less likely to find another, but you're less likely to lose it in the first place. On the other hand, it is also harder in these systems to *get* a job: youth unemployment rates, in particular, are often very high. In the Asian model, there is also low state welfare provision but often high job security at the level of firms, which benefit in turn from long-term financial arrangements and state support, and from a relatively well-educated (though largely male) workforce.

Amable goes beyond much of the rest of the literature in addressing the issue of the political conditions for these configurations (chapter 2). He also addresses the issue of the elective affinities between economic and political systems not just according to the obvious left–right division, where social democracy refers to a political cluster as well as a form of economy, but also according to the division between strongly majoritarian political systems of the British type and more consensual systems characterized by coalitions, as very frequently in Germany (Amable, 2003: 181ff.).

At the back of all these models there are of course different assumptions and foci of interest. For the purposes of this discussion, it is fortunately enough to stick at a descriptive or phenomenological level and to treat them rather as photographers use filters to highlight certain aspects. For some purposes we may prefer to use the simple contrast between liberal and coordinated market economies: at other times a finer-grained analysis such as those of Crouch or Amable may be needed.[10] The theoretical assumptions bounce back however when we come to look at the possibility of combining heterogeneous elements and at the developmental trends from one model to another. Those approaches most closely tied to theoretical approaches such as rational choice theory at one end, and neo-Marxism at the other, tend to look for convergence towards a single model, whereas more descriptive institutionalist approaches stress the viability of hybrid forms (Ebbinghaus and Manow, 2001).

This is of particular importance, as I shall show in a moment, in relation to postcommunist Europe, but even in the West there is considerable disagreement about the pace and to some extent even the direction of change. There is of course a powerful neo-liberal orthodoxy, especially in the UK and, more importantly, in many EU institutions, according to which Europe should move wholeheartedly towards liberal market forms. There is however also considerable opposition to this 'Anglo-Saxon' approach in continental Europe. As Amable (2003: 238ff.) notes, the Blairite 'Third Way', which had a good ten years' run in the UK, fizzled out in the rest of Europe, after the publicity coup of an Anglo-German joint statement by Blair and Schröder (1999).[11] Whereas Blair had a substantial parliamentary majority, Schröder, the Chancellor from 1998 to 2005, had to live with his Green coalition partners and internal opposition from finance minister Oskar Lafontaine (for the first few months) and others. Even in the UK, the change of government in 1997 from Thatcher/Major to Blair/Brown was accompanied by a good deal of vapid rhetoric about 'stakeholder capitalism', though not much change in substance. While French indicative planning is indeed pretty much dead, the French state retains a very strong presence in economic life (Clift, 2006).[12]

In Germany, too, there have been policy shifts in both companies and the state towards neo-liberal forms of practice, but it is not clear that this marks a definitive rejection of the social market economy and its coordination mechanisms (Lane, 2003). As Deeg and Jackson (2006) argue, one needs to differentiate between alternative forms of change, such as formal and substantive,[13] and between the micro level (firms, etc.), meso (larger institutions and linkages of the kind focused on in the comparative capitalisms literature) and macro (e.g. forms of regulation and institutional complementarities). There is also, as I address below and in chapter 5, an important gender dimension to these issues (Warren, 2004). Very briefly, the continental European pattern of job protection will tend to benefit core workers in large-scale industry, who are predominantly male (O'Reilly, 2006).

The patterns of capitalism described above can also be seen if one focuses on the political economy of state welfare regimes.[14] Here again the scene is set by a triadic model, Gösta Esping-Andersen's 'Three Worlds of Welfare Capitalism'. Esping-Andersen (1990) distinguishes between a 'liberal' model, with means testing and a low level of benefits, where the state is seen as a modest adjunct or complement to the market, a 'conservative' model focusing on the maintenance of income and other assets of established social groups, and universalistic systems, based on social rights and egalitarian social democracy and involving the 'decommodification' of services with the de-linking of these services from contributions to the labour market or social funds.

As with Albert's models of capitalism, the liberal model is found in the UK and Ireland, as well as in North America and Australasia. Conservative regimes are found in the rest of Western Europe and also Finland, while the universalistic social democratic model is more or less confined to Scandinavia. The implication of Esping-Andersen's analysis is that the three types also map out increasing levels of seriousness and generosity in welfare provision, and if one takes the extremes of the USA and Sweden this seems clear enough.

There is however a universalistic emphasis in, for example, the UK, despite its miserably low level of benefits: although 'National Insurance' is technically distinct from taxation, and appears as a separate item deducted from UK wages and salaries, the system is essentially tax-based and independent of contributions. Similarly, the UK's health service is still substantially free at the point of use, where many other European systems outside Scandinavia are based on upfront payment by the patient and partial reimbursement. Some commentators have therefore distinguished between the generosity of provision and the extent to which it is universalistic and decommodified (Bonoli, 1997; Hill, 2006). Another issue is the extent to which welfare systems presuppose a (male) breadwinner family model or a more disaggregated one (O'Reilly, 2006).

There are also questions here about how far welfare systems have redistributive effects, given the capacity of the better off to grab a larger share of collective provision. As Julian Le Grand (1982) argued in the case of the UK, middle-class patients and parents have, for example, the time-flexibility to visit doctors and schools combined with the social capital and pushy social skills to get proper attention.[15] Some liberal systems aim to achieve a degree of redistribution through means testing and targeted benefits, notably in Australia and New Zealand and to some extent in the UK and Ireland (Castles, 2004, 2007; Hill, 2006). Castles (2004: 26–7) shows, on the basis of OECD data, that there is not so much a single European social model as a cluster of four 'families': English-speaking, Nordic, continental Western European and Southern European.

In 1960, continental Western Europe was the area making much the greatest welfare effort, with little to choose between the English-speaking and Scandinavian countries in the middle of the distribution, and with Southern Europe, Italy excepted, in the rearguard. By 1980, however, this clear hierarchy of spending had collapsed into two broader groupings, with the Scandinavian and continental Western

European countries spending around a quarter of GDP for social policy purposes and the English-speaking and Southern European countries around 15 per cent. Finally . . . hierarchy was restored, but along lines rather different to those of the early post-war era. By 1998, the Scandinavian countries had become outright welfare leaders, with average spending levels of just below 30 per cent of GDP. The countries of continental Western Europe followed close behind, with Southern Europe now somewhat ahead of an English-speaking rearguard.

In 1998, then, the OECD average for social expenditure was 23 per cent, with 'family means' for the four clusters ranging from 18 per cent for the English speakers and 21 per cent for Southern Europe to 26 per cent for Western Europe and 29 per cent for the North. Riding roughshod over diversities and variations in the composition of these totals in different countries and families of countries, we might think in terms of a bipolar distribution between the generous (or spendthrift) and the mean (or careful). As a foretaste of Eastern data not yet available in the same form, we find the Czech Republic right on the OECD mean of 23 per cent, and its Slovak 'ex' appearing as an honorary anglophone country with a score of 19 per cent. More broadly, it can be argued that the failure of the European social model to establish itself in the East is explained by the absence of the sort of compromise between capital and labour found in Western Europe after the Second World War (Bohle and Greskovits, 2005). But whereas we may reasonably expect the East and South to become more generous as they become richer and more anxious about their low fertility rates,[16] the English-speaking countries of Europe, even (and particularly) nouveau riche Ireland, seem firmly rooted in a cheapskate (or, if you prefer, realistic) pattern of expenditure, or rather non-expenditure.

Drawing together this discussion with the broader and overlapping issue of forms of capitalism, it is easy to see the outlines of a possible future European model which remains distinct from the US/UK pattern. This might involve a reorientation of continental European employment and welfare

policies in a more Scandinavian direction, which would preserve greater flexibility in a changing world environment,
with a more user-focused set of welfare services. Anthony
Giddens's recent work on the European social model points
in this direction of a shift to flexicurity and from negative to
positive welfare. Giddens (2007: 106–7) tellingly cites the
study by Leisering, Leibfried and Veit-Wilson (2001: 8), in
which social security officials 'took no interest in the lives
of applicants, or what had led them to apply for benefits'.[17]
As Amable (2003: 265) notes, there might be a significant
body of support for such a strategy, coming partly from
manufacturing employers irritated at the intrusion of increasingly predatory and speculative market pressures, and partly
from European Commission officials concerned with the
long-term viability and sustainability of European capitalism rather than the maximization of short-term profits. It
would however require a much more active Europeanization of social policy than has previously been seen in the
EC/EU, where, apart from the indirect and uneven effects
of the Common Agricultural Policy and a few feeble efforts
in the area of regional policy, there has been little but the
very modest formulations of the European Social Charter,
and even that was too much for the British. These economic
issues therefore point forward to the discussion of the European polity in chapter 4.

It is a curious feature of the comparative capitalism literature that, although it mostly dates from 1990 or later,
it has until recently contained relatively little discussion
of postcommunist Europe.[18] While this reflects a more general
tendency among Western social scientists to regard Eastern
Europe (and even, for West Germans, Eastern Germany)
as a *chasse gardée* for specialists in communist and/or 'transition' studies, it is odd that the more or less simultaneous
creation from scratch of more than twenty capitalist economies should not have attracted more attention. It was
of course hard to get reliable data from this part of the
world, and to make sense of a confused and contradictory
picture.

By the end of the twentieth century, however, a set of reasonably clear patterns was emerging. As for individuals under postcommunism, so for countries there were degrees of success or failure, in what David Dyker (2004: 314) has aptly called 'the transition pecking order'. The division between winners and losers roughly follows the East–West division, though with surprises at the extreme North (the ex-Soviet Baltic republics) and in Yugoslavia, whose head-start in the transition to a market economy was effaced (except in Slovenia, which managed to get out of the Federation in time) by the break-up of the country in a bloody set of civil wars. Two differences in initial conditions shaped the early years but then faded into the background. One was the nature of the political and economic regime in 1989, with, for example, Poland's or Hungary's substantial private sector and relatively pluralist political and intellectual environment contrasting with the absence of both in Czechoslovakia. This made for a smoother initial transition, though in the case of the private sector such differences were quickly effaced. In 1990 the contribution of the private sector to GDP is estimated at 5 per cent in Czechoslovakia as against 16 per cent in Hungary and 31 per cent in Poland; by 1995 the respective shares were 75 per cent (for the Czech Republic), 70 per cent in Hungary and 65 per cent in Poland (Williams and Balaz, 1999: 172, table 7.2).

Initial differences of this kind were fairly soon overlaid by the second factor: the severity of the policies followed by the new elites. Germany provided the extreme case which might have suggested caution elsewhere: despite massive transfers of funds to the East, the immediate imposition of a market economy and a massive privatization programme led to the loss of three-quarters of *all* jobs and massive economic and social dislocation. Poland adopted a relatively radical programme, while Czechoslovakia (and, after 1993, the Czech Republic) talked tough but was more moderate in practice.

Everywhere, however, it was assumed that the emergent forms of economy would be in line with the then dominant neo-liberal orthodoxy.[19] And as the US economist

Jeffrey Sachs, one of the architects of postcommunist transition, wrote at the beginning of the process, it was really a question

> about the means of transition, not the ends. Eastern Europe will still argue over the ends: for example, whether to aim for Swedish-style social democracy or Thatcherite liberalism. But that can wait. Sweden and Britain alike have nearly complete private ownership, private financial markets and active labour markets. Eastern Europe today has none of these institutions; for it, the alternative models of Western Europe are almost identical. (Sachs, 1990: 19)

What transition meant in practice was of course extremely variable. Ostensibly similar policies, such as 'voucher privatization'[20] in Czechoslovakia and Russia, led to dramatically different outcomes in the two cases: something which could just about pass for a property-owning democracy in the former, and a chaotic shift of resources to predatory oligarchs in the latter. In Poland, which adopted a more cautious and indirect form of privatization via holdings, the minister responsible, Janusz Lewandowski, had earlier explained that 'privatization is when someone who doesn't know who the real owner is and doesn't know what it's really worth sells something to someone who doesn't have any money' (Stark and Bruszt, 1998: 95).

We still lack an adequate sociology of privatization, either in a Western or in an Eastern context.[21] The issue has tended to be discussed either in narrowly political or economic terms or with reference to a political philosophy of anti-statism derived from neo-liberals such as Friedrich von Hayek. Both in the West in the 1980s and the East in the 1990s, the privatization process throws up interesting issues to do with property claims, and in many ways confirms earlier managerialist theses about the relative unimportance of ownership, as distinct from control, of enterprises. Against a bewildering background of mergers and break-ups, Western consumers have largely lost any sense of who is the ultimate owner of the corporations with which they have to deal. In the post-communist world, it was often astonishingly difficult even for experts to find out information of this kind. Nor would this information necessarily tell one much about the fine detail of the operations of those enterprises, however important it might have seemed both to those who retained a traditional Marxist assumption of the importance of property rights and to the neo-liberals who saw privatization as a panacea (cf. Sakwa, 1999: 43). As David Dyker (2004: 351) has shown, privatization by itself explains little:

> Why is rate and level of privatisation such a poor indicator of restructuring performance? Not, of course, because privatisation does not matter, but rather because privatisation *per se* defines neither the extent and nature of the private sector nor the manner in which that sector is organised and managed.[22]

The three most relevant models in discussion of Eastern Europe are the Polish sociologist Jadwiga Staniszkis's concept of political capitalism, the 'new class' model of Szelényi and his collaborators and the institutionialist model of Grabher, Stark and Bruszt. The first of these has perhaps the greatest relevance to the postcommunist bloc as a whole; the second and third fit best the Central European postcommunist countries in the first (2004) wave of accessions, while the third meshes most closely with the Western-focused literature on comparative capitalisms and 'embeddedness'.

Staniszkis's (1999) model of 'political capitalism' is grounded in the blurred property relations that marked the final stages of state socialism in many of the more advanced economies of the bloc. But this also, Staniszkis points out, parallels the processes described by Marx and Max Weber in the early stages of European capitalism, in particular the 'divided ownership' characteristic of late feudalism, 'when the king, vassal peasant cooperative and direct users made claim to the same object (e.g., a piece of earth)' and a mercantilist policy 'in which the state, in promoting the

new economic mechanism, tried to use it for its own ends
(stabilize the system, increase the pool of goods and services) and in this manner satisfy needs which could not
be satisfied by the state sector alone and decrease political
pressure on changing the system' (Staniszkis, 1999: 71).
The 'transfer from mercantilism to real political capitalism . . . [occurs] . . . where the actors of the enfranchising
nomenclature . . . began at the same time to use their position in the mercantilist structures to promote their own ends'
(1992: 72). Along with the growth of what she calls meta-
exchanges such as those involving futures markets (the kind
of process symbolized by Marx in the shift from M-C-M^1 to
C-M-C^1) this led to 'a point of no return accelerating the end
of communism' (1992: 73) and what she calls a 'managerial
revolution' at the level of 'organised political capital', which
itself becomes increasingly distinct from and antagonistic to
small and medium private capital (pp. 80–1).

> It seems that not only the beginnings of the market economy
> were based on the combination of competition, cooperation,
> political redistribution and status-regulated interconnections.
> Similar characteristics appear also in organized mature capi-
> talism with symptoms of state capitalism. The characteristic
> feature of capitalism that emerges from communism is the
> parallel existence of the early forms (when market rules are
> not universal, but aimed at the maintaining of the privileged
> position of one particular set of actors from the old regime,
> and when personal interconnections are a substitute for the
> still non-existent institutional market structure) and the pres-
> ence of mature forms of organized capitalism. (Staniszkis,
> 1992: 82–3)

As with the original development of European capitalism,
some societies pass fairly slowly through the early stages
while others start later and skip them, in what has been
called the late development effect (Gershenkron, Dore, cf.
Staniszkis, 1999: 131). In a familiar rule of thumb, the
further one goes East or South from the North Atlantic
axis, the less economic relations correspond to an ideal-type

of mature capitalism, and the more they are 'embedded' in other social networks of personal acquaintanceship, political patronage and so on.[23]

An approach of this kind is taken in one of the most important analyses of East Central Europe, that by Eyal, Szelényi and Townsley (1998). In this book, the authors continue a line of argument which one of them had first developed in the mid-1970s, that 'in the industrially backward agrarian societies of Eastern Europe the intelligentsia, organized into a government-bureaucratic ruling class, has taken the lead in modernization, replacing a weak bourgeoisie incapable of breaking with feudalism' (Konrád and Szelényi, 1979: 10). Thus despite the persecution of independent intellectuals, from which the authors themselves suffered, and the broader tensions between technically qualified members of the elite and the central authorities, which erupted from time to time in the 1950s and 1960s and eventually undermined the regimes, the intelligentsia could be seen, they argued, as the dominant class in state socialist societies.

Szelényi (1990) suggested that the process, to which they and others (notably Ludz, 1970) had drawn attention, of the 'intellectualization of the bureaucracy', had explained the weakness of the regimes in resisting pressures for reform, and even their willingness to embrace these initiatives. But the intelligentsia had not yet succeeded, contrary to some Trotskyist analyses, in constituting itself as a fully fledged bourgeoisie, and was left holding the capitalist baby which, whether premature or overdue, certainly needed intensive care. Thus in opposition to theories of political capitalism and nomenklatura privatization, which they concede may better fit the situation in Poland and the former Soviet Union, Eyal, Szelényi and Townsley suggest that there was a considerable change of ownership and control from the old nomenklatura. The new managerial elites of East Central Europe are defined more by their possession of cultural capital than by economic capital, diverted from the state and/or accumulated in the old 'second', grey or informal sector, or by social capital taking the form of 'old' social networks deriving from nomenklatura positions. (New networks, based on membership of the opposition movements or on postcommunist NGOs or educational institutions, are a different matter.) In an important early analysis of postcommunism, published in the same year and based on detailed analysis of Bulgaria, Czechoslovakia and Hungary, Jon Elster et al. (1998) offered 'A stylized description of East European capitalism' focusing on two specificities: an 'uncivil', black or grey set of economies, and the dualism between the new private sector and the old state or semi-privatized sector, including banking. These two sectors existed in an unhealthy symbiosis, with the former plundering assets from the latter which in turn inhibited productive growth in the former. 'As state-owned enterprises have attracted large shares in state expenditure and bank credit, private enterprises have often been crowded out' (Elster et al., 1998: 198). Ten years on, this description still fits.

The approach closest to the institutionalist analyses of Western capitalism is in the work of Grabher, Stark and Bruszt. Grabher compared the German and Hungarian cases and, with David Stark (Grabher and Stark, 1997), edited a volume on the construction and reconstruction of networks in postcommunist societies. Stark and Bruszt (1998) provided a comparative analysis of Germany, Hungary and the Czech Republic, based in part on Stark's notion of 'recombinant' property, mixing private and public in new combinations. Hungary and Czechoslovakia, they suggested, demonstrated the value of networks of the kind which in Germany had simply fallen apart and had to be reconstructed . In an argument which parallels Streeck's (1997) in relation to Western capitalism, they stress the value of the resultant checks and balances on central power:

> in the Hungarian case, we find relatively few constitutional and institutional limitations on concentrated executive authority. As a consequence, policies are neither coherent nor sustainable as they swing from extreme to extreme. By contrast, in the Czechoslovak (and, later, Czech) case, where

central executives' room for maneuver is more limited by societal deliberations and by intrastate checks and balances, the resulting moderated policy course has been more coherent and sustainable. Germany ... is an intermediate case in which ... relatively extreme policies ... were later moderated after federal and corporatist institutions took root in the *Länder* of eastern Germany. (Stark and Bruszt, 1998: 169–70)[24]

This approach has clear parallels with the institutionalists' support (despite their occasional protestations of neutrality) for coordinated market economies. It tends, however, as Dorothee Bohle (1999) immediately pointed out, to neglect the exposure of these societies to external pressures, notably those of the world market into which they were increasingly closely integrated, of the IMF and increasingly of the EU (Bohle, 1999: 17). The Czech crisis of 1997, together with the earlier shift in Hungary in 1995 to a more neo-liberal programme, suggest that these institutions, however important, are not perhaps as robust as they might seem. (Streeck and Thelen (2005), in their introduction to an edited volume focused on the West, trace the variety of institutional transformations in an overall process of liberalization; their analysis can usefully be read back into the postcommunist context.) However, this is not to say that there is no freedom of movement – a mistake to which neoliberalism, early globalization theory and some neo-Marxist theory are prone (Stark and Bruszt, 2001). As these authors point out in a subsequent article, a number of Eurozone countries have responded to EU pressures towards greater flexibility by 'preserving, and in some cases strengthening, various nonstate institutions of economc governance at the national, sectoral, regional, local and workplace levels' (Bruszt and Stark, 2003: 77).

How far we should continue to look for a distinctive postcommunist form of capitalism within Europe, as opposed to talking about residues of various kinds from communism and the transition decade(s), remains a moot point. The 2004 EU accession states tend to fall within the European range (leaving out the extreme case of the UK) on most of the relevant dimensions such as government spending (and welfare), employment protection and formal links between employers and trade unions (Gough and Reed, 2004; Riboud et al., 2002). Although Hungary and Estonia[25] tend to come out at the more 'liberal' end on some dimensions, neither is anything like as extreme as the UK, though policies such as flat taxes go further than anything seriously suggested in the West.

One of the most systematic discussions so far of these issues is by David Lane (2006). As an expert on the USSR and state socialism, Lane cautions against a hasty assimilation of these countries to the Varieties of Capitalism paradigm. It is clear that, almost everywhere in the former Soviet bloc, state socialism is dead, but less clear what has replaced it. 'Whether these countries have moved to a modern capitalist system is open to question' (Lane, 2006: 33). In the West, capitalism emerged from the diverse forms of pre-capitalist economy and state in early modern Europe, and these continue to shape the different national styles, such as a long-established tendency to statism in France, but the post-socialist situation is distinct from these:

> In the transformation of the post-socialist societies, non-capitalist features are taken from quite a different mould . . .
>
> In post-communist economies, as well as other developing ones, many components of capitalism are compromised by alien features – non-market economic relationships, the absence of a complementary ideology, of classes of entrepreneurs and capitalists. They are 'transiting', as it were, to capitalism. Analysis, then, must grasp not only the *type* of capitalism, but the *extent* to which capitalism has been constructed. (Lane, 2006: 20–1)

Running through a range of topics such as privatization, stock market capitalization, global 'openness' and income inequalities, Lane emphasizes both the unevenness of the transition process and its incompleteness. He offers a typology of three basic models. The first consists of two sub-groups: the Eastern and Central European countries, plus Estonia and Slovenia, and a somewhat less advanced sub-group of EU accession states and candidate countries made up of the other two Baltic states and Romania, Bulgaria and Croatia.[26] These are closest to the Western European capitalist societies, though with relatively low rates of internal accumulation, diverse degrees of international openness, and an important role played by states and major international companies.

> A second model is that of a hybrid state/market uncoordinated capitalism. This is a relatively economically poor group which has had an unsuccessful period of transition: Russia, Ukraine, Kazakhstan, Georgia, Turkmenistan, and Moldova. These countries have exceedingly high income differentials, and high levels of poverty and unemployment. They have the characteristics of low-income, primary sector exporting countries, with a very low integration into the global economy...While they have pursued privatization and market monetary exchange, they lack the psychological, political and societal preconditions necessary to support modern capitalism...
>
> Reliance on the state is probably the only way these societies may develop a modern industrial society. (Lane, 2006: 35–6)

Lane's third model (p. 36) is represented by those countries – Uzbekistan, Belarus and Turkmenistan – which 'have not made the breakthrough to a capitalist system...They are likely to remain statist economies. These last two groups of countries still preserve major elements of state bureaucratic control, and may be moving in the direction of a form of state capitalism.'

Lane's grim but judicious assessment suggests a number of lessons. First, there is the obvious point that much of the literature on postcommunist 'transition' has tended to concentrate on the West of the region, the triad of Hungary, Poland and Czechoslovakia, with Germany, Slovenia and the Baltic states as optional extras.[27] As Larry Ray and I suggested in our book (Outhwaite and Ray, 2005), it made sense to concentrate on places where the transition was going ahead fastest and where the most reliable information was to be found, but this inevitably skewed the discussion of postcommunism. The EU enlargement of 2004 reinforced this trend, with subsequent attention then extended to the new candidates for accession, Romania and Bulgaria, and only secondarily to the rest of the Western Balkans (a new term which emerged around this time) and the former Soviet Union. The prospect of further enlargement, or the reality of increasing dependence on Russian gas and other resources (and, one should remember, investment capital),[28] has perhaps tended to push policy-oriented research in a more optimistic direction which others might call wishful thinking. Second, the varieties of capitalism literature, though not always firm-focused as in the Hall and Soskice version, something which Lane (2006: 16–18) criticizes in particular, has so far tended in its extension to the East to rely on sophisticated manipulation of quantitative data, at the risk of overlooking the real economies of the less favoured parts of the postcommunist world.[29] Finally, however, one has to remember that these are fast-changing situations: just compare the lists of countries considered to be likely EU accession candidates in the literature of the late 1990s, with the subsequent 'promotion' of Slovakia, Lithuania and Latvia and, after a time, Romania, Bulgaria and now Croatia. This suggests that, whatever one makes of the confused situation in Ukraine and the current stasis in Belarus, the geographical location of these two states and the resultant interest in the EU (from both inside and outside) may push them into a more 'Western' pattern of development. As 'constructivist' approaches in International Relations theory have stressed, ideological constructs can be real in their effects.[30]

Henryk Domański (2000: 165) writes at the end of his discussion of social stratification in East Central Europe:

> Given the prospects of a far-reaching uniformity enforced by the market economy, we should be careful about proclaiming further divergence in coming years ... It may well be that, several years hence, the concept of East Central Europe will

preserve only its geographical connotations. Then the label 'postcommunist' will have become an item of historical philology, a vestige of a rapidly vanishing past and devoid of any reference to distinct patterns of stratification.

The point is well taken, but so is its restriction to East Central Europe (and the rest of the current EU). Its possible applicability to the rest of the postcommunist world remains an open question. From the Western Balkans to the Russian Far East, the prospects of a prosperous future seem bleak for all but a minority.

Convergence?

This brings us to the question of European convergence and Europeanization.[31] The original notion of convergence has, as we have seen, been problematized in much of the literature on varieties of capitalism or comparative capitalisms,[32] and the comparative discussions in chapter 2 and in the present chapter have explored these persisting differences and inequalities. There remains however the question of how far we can talk about a European economy in the singular. David Dyker (1999: 1) was committed by the title of his edited volume, *The European Economy*, to an affirmative answer, but he immediately stressed the heterogeneity even of Western Europe, let alone the East.[33]

In EU parlance, regional disparities are addressed under the heading of cohesion, while the term convergence tends to be reserved for macroeconomic issues in the context of accession or monetary union. These now overlap, of course, since all accession states from 2004 onwards are required to commit themselves to Eurozone membership; the 'Northern opt-out' for the local currencies of Denmark, Sweden and the UK ('two crowns and a pound') will not, barring accidents, be extended. The convergence in a narrow sense required for entry into the Eurozone is expected to lead to convergence of business cycles, prices and other elements, though the experience since 2002 of an EU monetary zone running, with gaps, from Portugal to Finland has shown that this may be a slow process. Although the Eurozone is increasingly looking like a unit, the expected coordination of capitalist economic cycles has not been achieved, nor the harmonization of tax rates and consumer prices which might have been expected to be a natural consequence.

These political uncertainties also affect, par excellence, the prospects for redistributive transfers from richer to poorer regions. As we saw in chapter 2, the safest prediction to make is that they will not amount to even the modest level achieved in Germany in the Federal redistribution mechanism between states, the *Länderfinanzausgleich*, let alone the very substantial transfers following German reunification. Within the European states themselves, the history of regional policy is on the whole a history of failure, where development takes place anywhere other than where it was intended. This has further negative implications for the likelihood of regional specialization of production.[34]

However, this raises a more fundamental question of Europe's place as a whole in the world economy. Except perhaps for the construction industry and food and tourism, most economic activities can currently be pursued more cheaply outside Europe, and even these could mostly be carried out by non-European firms using non-European labour. This is not just a relative decline in the place of Europe in world production, as other regions such as China and India develop their productive capacity, but the (for Europeans) alarming prospect of a Europe which no longer has *any* substantial comparative advantage. The Goldman Sachs Report of 2004, which predicted that by 2041 the Chinese economy would have overtaken the US as the world's largest, attracted a good deal of attention. It forms the centrepiece, indeed the basis of the centrefold, of a recent popular book by a *Spiegel* journalist. Steingart (2006) extrapolates the figures backwards to 1820 and forwards to 2050. In 2005, Western Europe and the US have roughly equal levels of output, just below and just above $12 billion respectively. China's roughly comparable figure is $9.4 billion; this however reflects a massive increase from $1.6 billion in 1990; by

2050 China is way out ahead, with 45 billion as against 35 in the US and 19 in Western Europe; India has arrived halfway between the two, at 28 billion. More to the point, however, is the shift of Western production and jobs to China and other low-wage economies, notably software engineering and consumer services to India. Second, there is the growing Chinese presence in Europe and the US. Chinese firms have recently bought up, for example, car, computer, perfume, TV and household electric companies in the US and Europe, and are clearly poised to extend from these bases. India, too, is increasingly active, with the 2007 takeover of the largest remaining fragment of the UK steel industry by an Indian firm. Thus, even if Europe and the US adopted Steingart's suggested emergency strategy and formed an effectively protectionist free-trade area charging large consumer taxes, the Chinese economy, largely privatized but still state-directed, would remain a dominant presence.

These prospects need to be seen in the longer-run historical context of the development of the world economy. Like Will Hutton, who had earlier (2002) given an up-beat account of Europe and has recently written on China (2006), Kees van der Pijl (2006b: chapter 9) takes a calmer, though hardly irenic, view of the recent Eastern challenge, locating it in a historical sequence in which the hegemony of the English-speaking North Atlantic countries, the 'heartland', has been challenged by 'contender states' (France in the late seventeenth to the early nineteenth centuries, imperial and Nazi Germany, Japan and the USSR in the twentieth, and now China in the late twentieth and twenty-first). 'The Napoleonic state provides us with the outlines of the general contender state model: concentric development driven from above, using the state as a lever; a "revolutionary" ideology mobilising the social base; and a foreign policy backing up the claim of sovereign equality with a powerful military' (van der Pijl, 2006b: 12). He stresses (his emphasis) that '*most contender states in history were on a course of overtaking the heartland, had their economies not at some point run aground in political crisis entailing geopolitical confrontation*' (p. 328).

In the Chinese case, of course, the prospect of political disorder is already at hand, with an ostensibly still communist political dictatorship confronting not just a small dissident minority but an increasingly restive rural population. Internal political disorder is only one way in which China might destabilize the world; a more short-term alternative, which it could adopt tomorrow, would be to shift its massive dollar holdings into euros or possibly yen, thus precipitating the long-overdue collapse of the US dollar and perhaps of the US economy and the world economy more generally. An intermediate possibility would be the likely development of a more aggressive geopolitical and military posture to match its economic power. One way or another, it is clear that the old 'triad' model of the US, Europe and Japan (Ohmae, 1985) is now acquiring at least two further elements (China and India) and possibly more, Russia and Brazil being the currently most prominent candidates.[35] And it is clear that relative marginalization of Europe, predicted a century and a half ago by Tocqueville, is now a fact. Europe's shrinking share of world population and output is bound eventually to be matched by a corresponding geopolitical and perhaps also cultural marginalization, though the US is clearly first in line to be cut down to size, with its massive foreign debt and still overvalued currency (see, for example, Brenner, 2005).

Nevertheless, the US remains attractive to many of the world's inhabitants, including those suffering most from its foreign, economic and environmental policies. Jeremy Rifkin (2004) has suggested that the American dream has been supplanted by the European dream, in an interesting counter-argument to those, common in the English-speaking countries, to the effect that Europe has not yet learned the necessary lessons of neo-liberalism. The economic logic may well suggest Gresham's Law, in which bad, predatory, capitalism drives out good, but there are political countercurrents, drawn from the heritage of European social democracy, which retain considerable force at the level of EU policy-making. The next chapter explores European state forms and the emergent polity of the European Union.

4 THE EUROPEAN POLITY

I began the previous chapter by presenting the two types of economic system which were substantially developed in Europe: capitalism and state socialism. In the political sphere, too, we have experienced two characteristically European state forms: the capitalist national state, becoming democratic or dictatorial in the twentieth century, and its always dictatorial Marxist-Leninist variant. We have also had, for the past half-century, a third form which we might more appropriately call a polity rather than a state: the EC/EU.

By around the middle of the last millennium, there was a discernible shift within Europe from a pattern dominated by feudal territories, empires and city-states to one of emergent monarchies prefiguring the national state. The Holy Roman Empire survived into the beginning of the nineteenth century, and the Ottoman and Russian Empires (the latter only formally established in 1721) till the end of the First World War, followed in the Russian case for another seventy years by the USSR. But what are sometimes called the 'new monarchies', such as England, Scotland and France, became more common and set the pattern for the future. These were territorial states with an increasingly centralized and bureaucratized administration. By the mid-sixteenth century, for example, the French 'royal domain' included most of the present French territory; England, which lost its continental foothold in Calais in 1558, had its current borders and a well-established Tudor state bureaucracy. The revolutionary republican regimes in the Netherlands in the late sixteenth century, and in England in the mid-seventeenth, embodied ideas of popular rule which came into their own in the American and French Revolutions and the democratic movements which followed. Self-determination now came in two overlapping versions: democracy, which gradually advanced from an extremist doctrine to a unquestioned *acquis* (except for the extreme right and parts of the extreme left) and the 'national principle'.

Nationa*lism* as a doctrine which could reinforce a state or, alternatively, push it towards fragmentation or subsumption in a larger national unit was a largely nineteenth-century creation.[1] In the West of Europe, it tended to strengthen existing states, though on the peripheries it also encouraged separatist movements in Wales, Ireland, Scotland, Brittany, Catalonia and the Basque Country. In the centre, it inspired the creation of unitary states in Italy and Germany, while further East its role was most often to subvert multinational states such as the Austro-Hungarian or Ottoman Empires. Despite socialist internationalism and the charge that 'state nationalism', as we might call it by analogy with 'state terrorism', was the 'father of war', the end of the First World War led to the creation of a slew of new states, ostensibly national but in practice containing significant minorities. Nazism was in large part an enterprise of recuperating German minorities in other states or taking over those states to 'protect' them, expelling or murdering Jews and others defined as non-German, and clearing the ground for settler colonies far into Russia. The end of Nazi rule saw a similar though much less bloody ethnic cleansing in reverse, as well as the effective colonization of half of Europe (and a third of what was left of Germany after the 1945 boundary changes) by the USSR.

Soviet Marxism-Leninism was ostensibly *inter*nationalist and, unlike fascism, not a statist doctrine. In principle, it expected the withering away or dying off of the state in its internal aspect,[2] and the gradual consolidation of a peaceful world community of socialist peoples. In practice, the interests of socialism turned out to mean the geopolitical interests of the Soviet Union: the 'people's democracies'[3] kept their national identity and de jure independence,[4] while de facto being subordinate to control from Moscow or from the local Soviet Embassy. After the invasion of Czechoslovakia in 1968, this was formalized in the 'Brezhnev doctrine' of the limited sovereignty of socialist states. The Marxist-Leninist state was distinctive not so much for its internal structure, which followed the forms of parliamentarism and often even of multi-party democracy,[5] nor for the fact that this was a sham to conceal the dictatorship of the ruling party, but for the fact that this party-state was responsible for directing virtually all economic, political and cultural activity.[6]

As well as the ill-fated 'people's democracies', the postwar years also saw the revival of the European integration process. The jury is perhaps still out on the question of whether we should see this as the beginning of a postnational constellation (Habermas, 1998) or the rescue of the European nation-state (Milward, 1992). Either way, it is clear that any discussion of contemporary forms of the European state has to take into account their relation to the EU, whether as member-states of the Union or of the European Economic Area, as potential members or as neighbours.

Even in Western Europe, there is a striking diversity in forms and ideas of the state. Although England developed a quite advanced state bureaucracy under the Tudors, it escaped (through the dramatic expedient of a revolution and a brief republican regime) the continental path of absolute monarchy and remained what Dyson (1980: 36–44) called 'an aberrant case'. The very word 'state' has negative associations in English and tends to be avoided where possible; we have 'British Railways' or, now, 'National Rail', not 'Ferrovia dello Stato'; studies of 'political arithmetic', political science or 'government', not 'Staatswissenschaft', and so on. The Irish Republic, having established its own state, is less coy about using the term, whereas it is more or less taboo in the

US, where some combination of 'federal' and 'government' is preferred.

It would, however, be misleading to draw too sharp a historical contrast between a statist continent and a society-centred island. The Netherlands, like Britain, had a republican experiment in the seventeenth century which continues to influence its political culture, while Scandinavia displays a combination of powerful states with a wide scope of activity and considerable local activism, with surveillance of, rather than just by, government. If these examples are seen as peripheral, there is also the case of Poland, where central state power was traditionally restrained by a powerful nobility and where of course the state territory itself was repeatedly rebordered and, for a time, obliterated. The German and Italian states were latecomers on the European scene, and only half a century after unification were pioneering a particularly vile form of totalitarian statism. After this aberration, they now stand out in Europe, along with Spain, as examples of large decentralized states. In the early twenty-first century, it is tempting to think that the dust has settled after the processes of state formation which dominated the twentieth, yet in the past fifteen years we have seen the extinction of three European states, the USSR, Yugoslavia and the GDR, and the separation of the Czech and Slovak Republics.

Even in Western Europe, there is a reasonable chance that Belgium, the UK and Spain will split apart in the coming years. Fifty years after the European rescue of the nation-state, Europe may be incubating what regional nationalists might also call a second rescue of their territories from centuries of alien rule. Here the specific contribution of the EU is that it makes viable states which were previously not viable, or at least where the costs of independence seemed to outweigh the benefits. Independent statehood within the EU is statehood lite, without many of the entry costs previously associated with it. Conversely, of course, regional nationalists may settle for devolved government within the EU, since independent statehood is not what it was and regions get taken seriously within the EU's multi-level format. Either way, however, the status of the national state is problematized in new ways. Faced with all these recent and prospective changes, the borders of America and perhaps even Africa, most of them arbitrarily drawn by earlier Europeans, look relatively stable.

The European national state has always been something of a confidence trick, even as it wielded the power of life and death over its own and other citizens. As Kenneth Dyson (1980: 29) writes:

> The emergence of the idea of the impersonal, abstract state, which controls a consolidated territory and possesses a system of offices that is differentiated from that of other organizations operating in the same territory, was a ramshackle affair, and neither identical nor simultaneous in different countries. . . . The characteristics of the modern state were acquired in a complex flux of disintegration of old political units as forces of particularism or provincialism engendered revolts against the Empire and the Papacy, and of efforts at territorial integration.

The modern sense of the word 'state' emerges gradually from the background notion of a state of affairs, a status quo or the social status, as we would now call it, of particular authorities. State remains an abstract concept: the British government is substantially located in some offices in central London, but the British state is not so geographically circumscribed. This is not the place to trace the details of state formation and of what, paraphrasing Cornelius Castoriadis, one might call 'the imaginary institution of the state', but it is important to remember that what Benedict Anderson (1991) labelled the 'imagined community' in nationalism can also be applied to non-nationalist forms of political imagination.[7] There are also of course material processes in play, of surplus extraction, the growth of bureaucracies and armies, policing and warfare. What I mean by a confidence trick is that the element of display and bluff, so prominent in the early modern European state, remains a feature of much more developed states in the nineteenth century. In Charles Tilly's vigorous image, European states have mutated:

> from wasps to locomotives ... Tribute-taking states remained fierce but light in weight by comparison with their bulky successors; they stung, but they didn't suck dry. As time went on, states ... took on activities, powers and commitments whose very support constrained them. (Tilly, 1992: 96)

But this development took longer to get underway than is often believed.[8] Prussia is a good example. Usually associated with centralism and rational bureaucracy, the Prussian state was in fact remarkably decentralized (Clark, 2006). The Africanist Gerd Spittler (1981, 1983) has pointed to the similarities between the French colonial state in Mali and the eighteenth-century Prussian state.

As Peter Baldwin (2005: 17) argues, the conventional contrasts between weak and strong states need to be rethought:

> Take, as examples, two fields in which the supposedly laissez-faire British state of the nineteenth century appears to have been stronger than its Continental counterparts: taxation and public health. Despite its flexible and, in some sense, amateurish tax collection system, the British state was able to extract a far higher percentage of GNP than the French. It also implemented direct income taxation earlier and more thoroughly than France or Germany.

Similarly, in the case of epidemic disease, Britain had better sanitary infrastructure and a more extensive system of health surveillance.

For all this, however, there remains a contrast between relatively centralist and/or statist societies and those whose governance was more devolved or informal. Having looked in the previous chapter at the way in which this structured economic activity and welfare, it is worth exploring some further dimensions of state activity.[9] England, for example, had a state Church headed by the monarch and represented in the parliament from the sixteenth century, but lacked a standing army until the eighteenth century (whereas France had the beginning of one in 1445 – see Finer, 1975) and still lacks a written constitution, unless one counts the EU treaties and a few bits and pieces of European human rights legislation incorporated into English law. Germany, as Marx and Engels famously remarked in *The German Ideology*, missed out on the French Revolution and therefore diverted its revolutionary energies into the realm of ideas. France tended to shape the European political imaginary, having achieved territorial consolidation at an early stage and finally, after the Dutch and English prototypes, putting the idea of the secular republic on the European map. The ideology of republican citizenship continues to shape the policies of the French state across a whole range of issues, from welfare to the headscarf. Something of the same can be found in Switzerland, though with a strong localist twist and a much more consensual political culture.

Sometimes the differences seem like a simple matter of path dependence. To be a monarchist in France or Italy or a republican in Britain is to be a political eccentric. In the second half of the twentieth century, it was quite normal to be a communist party member in Italy or France, very unusual in Britain and, in West Germany, illegal from 1956 to 1968, when the DKP was founded as a substitute for the still banned KPD, and subsequently, following the 'radicals decree' (*Radikalenerlass*) of 1972, still liable to exclude you from state employment as, say, a teacher or train driver.

Other differences are more fundamental. Dyson differentiates between 'state societies' and 'stateless societies', in which the kind of conception which he is concerned to analyse is either absent or present in such a muted form as to generate a difference of principle.

> 'Stateless' societies display, above all, a pronounced continuity of medieval feudal ideas and institutions, including a diffusion of power, and find their coherence in a conception

of the customary requirements of an ordered society, in an appeal to heritage and social practice rather than to rationally ordered principles and technique. (Dyson, 1980: 52)

He appears to include in this category only the UK and, outside Europe, the English-speaking democracies. Within the category of state societies, however, he provides an interesting classification in relation to party political democracy.

The character of continental European politics has been shaped by the different patterns of accommodation of the idea of the state and democracy in 'state' societies. It is possible to identify three major patterns. First, there is the French pattern, in which representative institutions and state institutions are seen as two different and coexisting conceptions of how the democratic notion of the sovereignty of the people is to be expressed. This 'solution' preserves a considerable distance and tension between the two sets of institutions, and because the question of the appropriate balance between them is left open means that fundamental constitutional argument remains at the centre of politics. A second pattern is the Dutch and Swedish, where the representative and executive institutions are seen as the two 'poles' or 'powers' of the state. While there remains a distance between both institutions, a co-operative working relationship is emphasized by an extensive view (in institutional terms) of the state which subsumes both. Finally, there is the Austrian and West German pattern, which involves a more complete merging to produce 'public-service' democracies in which a large presence of officials in the composition of both parties and parliaments is complemented by a party 'penetration' of the bureaucracy. They are viewed as 'party states'. The parties are the agencies of integration of the idea of the state and democracy and perform a more elevated, moral and didactic role than is suggested by the British notion of 'party government'. (Dyson, 1980: 279)[10]

Can we relate this classificatory model to other aspects of these political systems? These types, which one might for convenience label agonistic, cooperative and corporatist respectively, can usefully be mapped on to Amable's distinction, mentioned in the previous chapter, between strongly majoritarian 'winner-takes-all' political systems of the British type and more consensual systems characterized by coalitions (Amable, 2003: 181ff.). At first sight all the continental systems seem to fit the latter category, but in view of the strongly presidential system of the French Fifth Republic, as well as its often majoritarian electoral system,[11] it seems more appropriate to include it with majoritarian Britain. Even under conditions of 'cohabitation', where the president and the parliamentary majority are from opposing parties, the French president retains a huge range of powers. The Federal Republic of Germany is very much the land of coalitions, having been ruled by them for most of its history, including 'grand coalitions' of the two opposed but leading parties, SPD and CDU/CSU, in the late 1960s and from 2005 to the time of writing.

Together with the country's federal structure, this produces what has been aptly called a consensual democracy or 'democracy of negotiation' (*Verhandlungsdemokratie*).[12] The UK, as we shall see later, is harder to categorize, with its move in the late twentieth century, contrary to the general European pattern, towards greater centralization and statism (Schmidt, 2006). This Thatcherite development was not really reversed under Blair's decade (1997–2007), with the important exception of devolution to Scotland, which has its own parliament and government, and Wales, which has a slightly more limited form of devolution. But despite shifts of this kind, the *longue durée* of European state formation continues to impact on current political structures and practices. Britain may be statist in comparison to German federalism or Italian regionalism, but it retains important aspects of a more decentralized past, in areas as diverse as the law (except in Scotland, whose very different legal system is itself an element of diversity in the UK) and the education system, which has only recently been subjected to state control through the 'national curriculum' and various forms of supervision of higher education.

As in the previous chapter, we have begun our journey in Western Europe, with a number of guides who explicitly confine their attention to this half of the continent. How does all this look in the East? The usual representation is one in which a centralized and authoritarian state dominates an atomized society. This is a reasonable approximation to the situation in imperial and Soviet Russia and in twentieth-century Stalinist Europe, but we need to look further back to understand the current shape of the state in Eastern and Central Europe. Gramsci's powerful image of the Russian state dominating an atomized civil society may fit the imperial Russian situation well enough, but it hardly fits neighbouring Poland or Hungary. George Schöpflin (1993: 5) stresses the familiar theme of backwardness, where this means both an economic lag behind the West and the relative weakness of East European societies in relation to the persisting empires of Prussia, Austria, Russia and Turkey.

> There was much in the history of Eastern Europe that over-lapped with the history of Western Europe. . . . To a greater or lesser extent, especially Central Europe, where Eastern Europe had adopted Western Christianity, these societies shared in aspects of feudalism, medieval Chistian universalism, the Renaissance, the Reformation and Counter-Reformation and the Enlightenment. Yet each one of these was shared slightly differently, less intensively, less fully, with the result that East European participation in the European experience was only partial. (Schöpflin, 1993: 11)

The relative weakness of civil society in Eastern Europe meant that politics tended to take an etatist form, whether at the hands of bourgeois modernizers or of revolutionary socialists or nationalists who rejected the status quo. During the Cold War, these historical patterns were indeed of largely historical interest, given the massive fact of the Stalinization of the region. Stalin the person was of course gone by 1953, but the system persisted until 1989. It was of course possible to argue that the abandonment in Poland of forced agricultural collectivization in the 1950s reflected long-term patterns of relatively weak central authority, but the more obvious explanations were short-term ones about the position of the Polish communist party in a more than usually anti-Russian country.

After 1989, of course, all this was again up for grabs. On the one hand, the new power-holders might be expected to resume a statist modernizing project; on the other hand, the new ideological climate favoured a more neo-liberal conception of the role of the state. This is a state actor's perspective: do you, for example, try to manage privatization from above, as in Germany or to some extent Hungary, or do you stand back and let it take its course, as (in very different ways) in Czechoslovakia or Russia? From a more external and structural perspective, what stands out is the weakness of the postcommunist state, as in Poznanski's analysis of 'the crisis of transition as a state crisis':

> at the outset of the transition, the economic system was really the state. The state was the formal owner and coordinator, while markets were submerged and undefined. Neglecting this reality, the radical reformers instantly caused too much damage to the state, and thus to the [economic] system. (Poznanski, 2002: 64)

Where does this leave the postcommunist state? Even those who see postcommunist transition as essentially complete, at least in the new member-states of the EU, would not deny that the experience of the communist and postcommunist decades continues to shape political reality across the former bloc. The very terms 'state' and 'security', to say nothing of their conjunction, are inevitably charged in a way that they are not in most of Western Europe.[13] More generally, as Schöpflin (1993: 283) writes, 'Under communism, the individual regarded the state as hostile, state regulations as arbitrary, unpredictable and predatory and as a resource to be exploited, whether through the second economy or through theft.' Despite all this baggage,[14] one has to recognize the 'normality' of much of political reality in postcommunist Europe. As Jan Zielonka (2006: 30) notes, 'no widespread public rebellion against the programme of economic transformation took place in any of the ten countries'.[15] More positively:

> When we look at democratic institutions across the enlarged EU there is no clear East–West divide, at least from the formal point of view. All new members are either parliamentary or semi-presidential republics. . . . They all have constitutions providing checks and balances between different branches of power. Citizens' basic rights and freedoms are guaranteed by law. True, laws on the media in the new member states are in constant flux, with government officials trying to manipulate television broadcasting in particular. However, in this sense the situation is not as bad as in some old EU member states such as Italy. (Zielonka, 2006: 79)[16]

The 'Italian test' can be applied more widely. Populist politicians like the Kaczynski brothers may seem scary, but hardly more than the ghastly Berlusconi and his governments supported by neo-fascists. And while it is true that postcommunist party systems have not yet stabilized along the lines familiar in the West, the characteristic postcommunist pattern of a rebadged ex-socialist party confronting a right which combines neo-liberal economics with relatively progressive social views is increasingly familiar in the West as well.[17]

Three dangers confronting Eastern European polities might be mentioned. First, and most importantly, their economic base remains fragile, as does their popular legitimacy. A striking example is the 2006 riots in Hungary, following the publication of the prime minister's admission that he and his party had systematically lied about the economic state of the country in order to be elected. More optimistically, of course, one could point to the fact that the riots fizzled out and were not repeated elsewhere. The second danger is of a slide from parliamentary to presidential power of the kind familiar from Russia and some of the former Soviet republics and of course, further west, from Serbia and Slovakia in the recent past. Under communism, presidents had of course been figureheads, though they also often had a senior party role. In East Central Europe and the Baltic states their role now tends to be limited, certainly as compared to the states making up the former Soviet Union (Colas, 2002: 239–42). Presidentialism in the literal or extended sense is of course not new in the West, whether in the French Fifth Republic, German *Kanzlerdemokratie*, Berlusconi's prime ministerships or the rise of prime ministerial power in the UK, culminating in Blair's long and increasingly autocratic reign.

A third, complementary danger concerns the role of parliaments. These were of course ritual bodies of appointees under communism; under postcommunist conditions, while they have not generated the kind of instability which dogged the French Fourth Republic, it can be argued that their deputies have become over-dominant in political life and detached themselves too much from their notional 'base'. Attila Ágh (1998) speaks in this context of the 'overparliamentarisation of politics'. Again, this is something that has also caused concern in the West, with parties increasingly marginalizing their sometimes embarrassing activists and relying more heavily on focus groups and media campaigns. And while it might seem paradoxical to accuse the EU of being over-parliamentarized, given the miserable weakness of the European Parliament, it is clear that MEPs, especially those elected on party lists, are also too rooted in their peripatetic parliamentary home rather than the member-states whose populations they notionally represent.

The European Union

This brings me to the final issue to be addressed in this chapter: the emergent European polity composed of the EU and the states which are members of it, or closely associated with it. The boundary issue is important because the EU's borders, however closed they may be to many travellers from the outside, are open in both a synchronic and a diachronic sense. Diachronically, because the outside tendentially becomes the inside, with each new enlargement; synchronically, because at any given time certain non-member-states are included in one or another EU regime, and conversely certain member-states are excluded or exclude themselves from certain areas of participation.

At present, for example, the 'Schengen' area of uncontrolled travel across national borders includes EU non-members Norway, Iceland and now Switzerland but not the British Isles. Several of the new member-states' currencies are pegged to the euro, while Denmark, Sweden and the UK retain their old independent currencies. This 'variable geometry' is mirrored in a whole range of different degrees of participation or homogeneity within the Union. To some extent these are geographically determined: the UK and Belgium will never have a joint border one can walk across. Others are more a matter of social structure, such as the participation of countries with substantial agricultural regions in the Common Agricultural Policy or of poorer regions in various aid schemes. Others again are politically determined, such as the British and Scandinavian opt-outs over even such crucial issues as the common currency and, in the former case, freedom of movement across national borders.

What sort of polity is the EU becoming? The shift in nomenclature, from the original 'European Communities' (Coal and Steel in 1951, the European Economic Community and EURATOM in 1958) and their fusion in 1967, to the European Union from 1993, suggests progress towards the official goal, as stated in the treaties, of 'ever closer union', and there has indeed been such progress. But rather like the development of social democracy in the twentieth century, the positive achievements tend to go alongside a scaling-down of the ultimate goals (Shore, 2000: chapter 1). European federalism, like socialism, now seems to many Europeans either unattainable in the form in which it was originally conceived, or anyway undesirable. Many commentators would see the failure of the European Constitution of 2003–4 as the last feeble gasp of a failed project, which henceforth must be conceived in a different and more modest way.

We should, however, begin by asking what a European federation or confederation would be, and why Europeans might have wanted it in the second half of the twentieth century (Stråth, 2005). The idea has of course a much longer history, marked by early thinkers such as Kant, Saint-Simon and Renan, and by many more in the twentieth century. For present purposes, however, it is enough to start with the end of the Second World War, since one important motivation for the project of European integration was in fact to prevent such a war happening again. Two-thirds of a century later, this aim seems quaint, and the idea of achieving it by, as a first step, coordinating the production of coal and steel between the former axis powers and some of their victims seems a roundabout route. Yet this is what happened, and it substantially shaped later developments.

It was also of course possible to want integration for its own sake, on the basis that, as Willy Brandt once said of divided Germany, 'what belongs together should grow together'. Europeans have the basis for the sort of solidarity aspired to, and often achieved, by its national states and this calls for an institutional expression of a similar kind, as in the great nineteenth-century projects of German or Italian unification. Somewhere between these two poles one can locate views about the need to form larger economic units, to solve economic and other problems for which the national state was too small – and Europe has of course some extremely small states which have tended, for obvious reasons, to be the most enthusiastic supporters of integration.

Postwar European integration began, then, with a fudge between motives of these kinds – an ambiguity which persists to the early twenty-first century. Institutionally, it is interesting to see how the original model of the Coal and Steel Community has shaped the whole subsequent evolution of the Union. There was a 'high authority' of nine members, so that each of the six states could nominate one, and the larger members a second one. There was a council of ministers, with one from each member, and a parliamentary assembly with seventy-eight members of national parliaments. Finally, there was a court and an advisory committee of what we would now call stakeholders. The assembly and the court subsequently had their scope extended to the EEC and EURATOM. We now have a larger European Commission, a larger set of councils of ministers as well as the European Council of heads of state and government, a larger court and a ten times larger directly elected parliament with substantially extended, though still very limited, powers.

Whatever the merits of this design, it is clearly not the most obvious for a federation or confederation, where one would expect the executive authority to be subject to parliamentary control and for legislation to be passed by the parliament, this typically consisting of a combination of elected representatives of the citizens as a whole and representatives, elected or not, of the component states, along the model of the US Senate or the German Bundesrat. This federal structure would then be replicated at lower levels with executive authorities, national or regional parliamentary assemblies, supreme courts (at least at state level) and so on. Something like this was in fact proposed in the drafting of the European Constitution, and the downgrading of the Council of Ministers was probably the proposal least acceptable to many member-states. In this, of course, they could justifiably claim to be following the majority views of their electorates whose main focus of attention and loyalty remains the national state.

Put in these terms, it may seem that the European federal project has failed; Anderson (1996: 147; quoted in Rumford, 2002: 65) has called this 'arrested federalism'. Alternatively, one can argue that it is still on the agenda, however often it is deferred. Or, finally, in an increasingly fashionable response, one can suggest that what we've ended up with is pretty well good enough, and that there is no need to go much further, nor of course to go backward.[18] As Delanty and Rumford write:

in the 1990s integration was fast becoming a worn-out concept, undermined on the one hand by the prospect of massive enlargement featuring the former communist countries of Eastern and central Europe, and on the other by the idea that EU integration, understood in the conventional sense, had reached a plateau after the Maastricht and Amsterdam Treaties. (2005: 166)

The teleological associations of the term 'integration', like those of 'transition', indeed suggest abandoning it, though it has the merit of drawing attention to the moving, processual aspect of developments in Europe.[19] An alternative term like 'polity-formation' (Chryssochou, 1998, cited by Delanty and Rumford, 2005: 165–6) may be preferable, though this simply returns us to the question of what sort of polity is being formed.

Or should we just bite the bullet and call the EU a state, perhaps with a qualifying adjective such as 'network' or 'regional'? As Vivien Schmidt writes:

Although it began as a regional trade association of nation-states, the EU has gone much further than any such association toward a formal governance system with jurisdiction over a wide range of issues and areas. Among regional trade associations, only the EU has developed a single currency, a single market, a single voice in international trade negotiation, a single anti-trust authority, common policies on environmental protection, worker safety and health, a common foreign and security policy, and even the beginnings of a common defense policy.

[Thus] While the use of the term state may ... be difficult for classically trained IR theorists, there is no other word that does justice to the growing power and developing sovereignty – however contingent – of the EU. (Schmidt, 2006: 10–14)

Schmidt's preference is for the term regional state; the focus of her book is on the impact of the EU on member-state polities (see also Katenhausen and Lamping, 2003; Jacquot and Wolf, 2003; Schimmelfennig and Sedelmeier, 2005a). Clearly, one has to think of the EU polity or state as significantly constituted by its interrelations with national and sub-national levels. This is not really the case with national states, whose internal structure, unified, decentralized, federal or whatever, will only sometimes be of importance for analysis. It may be much more relevant to know whether or not they are EU members, though even here the variety of association agreements means that this difference, too, may not be so significant. For some purposes, the same is true of the EU. When it acts in trade negotiations, its interlocutors do not need to know the details of its membership or internal constitutional arrangements. More often, however, Union policies are ratified by national ministers and implemented, often in differently modulated ways, via the agency of national governments, local courts, public officials and so on. In this sense, 'multi-level governance' is simply a fact. To invert Marx's phrase: 'Europe has changed; the point is to understand it.'

Attempts to understand the European polity are however bound up with arguments for particular institutional designs, and it may be helpful to look at three of these. One of the boldest recent contributions is the political philosopher Glyn Morgan's defence of *The Idea of a European Superstate* (2005). Morgan deliberately takes the strongest and most provocative term in the 'Eurosceptic' vocabulary, demolishes some of the arguments for and assumptions about the desirability of a European state and then, in a startling volte-face, argues that we need it after all because only a unitary European state can provide the best available guarantee of security.

> It is no accident that the nation-state emerged as the dominant type of political unit in the modern era. It is no accident that the world's sole global power, the United States, is a nation-state. If Europe is to play any comparable role, then it must adopt a comparable type of polity. Europe must, in short, become a 'superstate'. Those who refuse to accept this conclusion are either deluding themselves or they are prepared to see Europe remain a weak and dependent power. (Morgan, 2005: 161)

This is, I think, a realism too far.[20] Are there not, or could there not be, more economical ways of dealing, on a multilateral basis, with such threats to world peace as Bush II-style US foreign policy, international terrorism and hypothetical challenges from rising powers like China and India as well as declining but still powerful ones like Russia? A Europe which is, as was said of West Germany, an economic giant but a political dwarf, will always be a significant force in the world. There is, however, a nugget of historical truth behind Morgan's argument. It was always a rule of thumb that the speed of European integration at a given time was the vector sum of the perceived degree of prosperity and the perceived intensity of the Soviet threat. With the latter gone and the former looking a little fragile, European federalists, despite the largely successful enlargement of the EU, are over-dependent on complicated and contingent claims about economic benefits and the need to preserve a 'European social model' which is already heavily eroded by neo-liberal 'reforms' and a difficult demographic environment of ageing populations. To call for a European social policy that would be as efficient and economical as the Common Agricultural Policy is hardly a way to get votes, which hardly anyone can be bothered to cast anyway. Morgan (2005: 162) suggests that 'a federalist European superstate is further from being a viable option today than at any time in Europe's postwar history'.

An obvious alternative response is to abandon the already stalled integration project or to wind it back in an intergovernmentalist direction. A comparably bold proposal on these lines is offered by the historian John Gillingham (2006). Gillingham's strategy of 'hibernation' and downsizing goes so far as to propose half-seriously the sale of some of the EU's real estate in Brussels. Without the CAP and related policies on fisheries, aid and so forth, 'the 18000 grey-suited functionaries at the Berlaymont [the European Commission's headquarters RWO] could . . . be reduced to about 300' (Gillingham, 2006: 226). Gillingham, who has written major books on European integration, is devastating about some of the misconceived and wasteful policies of the EU, but it is odd to see him fixating on the size of the central Commission bureaucracy, which is actually relatively small; most EU policies are implemented by member-states (Spence and Stevens, 2006: 178–9).[21] And, while it is possible to imagine a Eurosceptic majority launching an enterprise of this kind, it is hard to see it succeeding, for all the reasons Max Weber pointed to in his classic analyses of bureaucracy nearly a century ago. A rather more likely scenario, which may be what Gillingham really wants, would be limits to the expansion of EU activities and a future of stagnation. Whether the EU bicycle, in Walter Hallstein's memorable image, could stand up without moving forward, is another matter.

There is however a third way, suggested by a growing body of literature which is accommodated to the EU in something like its present state. John A. Hall (2006) invokes the old Gaullist slogan of 'l'Europe des patries' in his argument for a steady state. Drawing on Ernest Gellner's image of 'Megalomania versus Ruritania', he warns that an excess of integrationist zeal may produce a nationalist reaction. 'The EU is made up of co-operating nation-states. Little should be done to change something that is working' (Hall, 2006: 121). For Rainer Lepsius (2004: 5), too, the national state remains the 'central political object of identification'; the EU lacks the 'interactive density and linguistic homogeneity' required to make it an appropriate site for working out economic and cultural conflicts; and 'The integrative capacity of a society organised as a national state cannot be replaced by the new European structures'.

Hall and Lepsius are historical and political sociologists, but, not surprisingly, much of this literature is produced by interdiscipinary legal experts such as Joseph Weiler. Weiler (2001: 70), in a classic discussion of Europe's *Sonderweg* or special path, writes that 'Europe has charted its own brand of constitutional federalism. It works. Why fix it?' Weiler's argument echoes in a curious and no doubt deliberate way

Ernest Renan's account of national sentiment, grounded in a common past and a constantly renewed affirmation of belonging together, 'a daily plebiscite'.

> Constitutional actors in the member states accept the European constitutional discipline not because as a matter of legal doctrine, as is the case in the federal state, they are subordinate to a higher sovereignty and authority attaching to norms validated by the federal principle, the constitutional *demos*. They accept it as an autonomous voluntary act; endlessly renewed on each occasion of subordination, in the discrete areas governed by Europe, which is the aggregate expression of other wills, other political identities, other political communities. (Weiler, 2001: 68)

Weiler's focus here is on constitutional law, but his view seems to be shaped by the relatively smooth operation of European legal integration as a whole. The primacy of European law has been largely unquestioned,[22] and Court decisions almost always accepted, despite the Court's lack of bailiffs or other means of enforcement.

It is at the democratic end of the European polity that matters become more problematic. The attention of European citizens is primarily focused on national or regional, rather than European, politics, and the transfer of power to the European level has mostly not been stressed by member-state governments, except when they are seeking an excuse for unpopular policies. Where the policies are popular, national governments tend, not surprisingly, to take the credit themselves. Vivien Schmidt (2006: 33), in an exceptionally innovative study of the interface between European and national politics, concludes that 'while the EU has *policy without politics*, the member-states end up with *politics without policy* in EU-related areas. And this makes for major problems for national democracy.' The democratic deficit, in other words, is not only in the relatively unpolitical spheres of EU policy-making,[23] with their confusing interplay of parliamentary, executive and legislative entities, but back home in the member-states themselves, and in non-members like Norway, who participate in the European Economic Area, Schengen, etc., without even a formal place in EU non-politics.[24]

> National elections tend to be focussed on substantive policy issues that increasingly can only be fully addressed at the EU level, such as immigration, food safety, environment, or economic growth, while European Paliamentary elections tend to focus more on general polity issues that can only be resolved by nationally based actors, such as how to reform EU institutions – where, that is, they are concerned with EU issues at all. (Schmidt, 2006: 33)

This is not so much a 'joint decision trap' as what, borrowing from Bachrach and Baratz (1970), one might call a 'non-decision trap' – at least from the citizen's point of view.

To speak of the European polity, then, is to address not just the EU and the individual member states (including close associates like Norway and Switzerland) but, crucially, the interplay between them. Schmidt shows how essentially unitary states like the UK[25] and France interact differently with the EU from more decentralized ones like Germany:

> Europeanization ... has been more disruptive to simple polities with unified structures like France and Britain, where the traditionally powerful executive has given up significant autonomy and control, as a result of the diffusion of decision-making upward to the EU, downward to more autonomous regional authorities, and sideways to more independent judicial authorities.
>
> Compound polities with federal structures like Germany, Belgium, and Austria, instead, have largely maintained an equilibrium between executive, legislature and judiciary as well as between centre and periphery – although not without some renegotiation of powers. The impact has been mixed with regard to regionalized states such as Italy and Spain, where the EU has served to reinforce executive power and regional autonomy at one and the same time – although not without a struggle between center and periphery. (Schmidt, 2006: 54–5)[26]

Schmidt's diagnosis may seem worrying, but her conclusion is relatively optimistic. As long as we recognize that the EU should be seen as a regional state and do not try to democratize it according to the model of national democracies, we can live with something like its present arrangements: 'Its "federal" checks and balances, its voting rules ensuring supermajorities, its elaborate interest intermediation process *with* the people, and its consensus politics go very far toward guaranteeing good governance *for* the people' (Schmidt, 2006: 222–3). All that is needed is for the member-states to recognize this and adapt their political discourse and practices accordingly.

In a related approach, Jan Zielonka and others have presented a vision of the EU as a kind of empire, more specifically a neo-medieval one in which political authority is divided and multiple, not clearly nested as in idealized descriptions of feudalism, but a messier picture of competing sovereignties, statuses and rights. This has a particularly compelling quality in relation to the status of citizens in the EU; if anything, the analogy is with the Roman Empire, in which being able to say *civis romanus sum* conferred some immunity from local jurisdictions, just as being a European citizen now confers rights of movement and employment denied to those known in Italy as *extracomunitari*. Rome also had, of course, a common currency, language, army and legal system (Zielonka, 2006: 17). The crucial difference is that it was based on conquest and central rule rather than voluntary accession and democratic representation. Zielonka's book is substantially concerned with Eastern enlargement, since 'it is the European integration project that needs to be adjusted to enlargement, and not the other way around' (Zielonka, 2006: 89; see also Verdun and Croci, 2005).[27]

Claus Offe and Ulrich Preuss (2006) adopt a similar answer to 'The Problem of Legitimacy in the European Polity'. They start from a similar point to Schmidt: 'the problem is not primarily that the *EU* must become democratic; it is that *member states* must *remain* democratic'. Following Philippe Schmitter's model of a *condominio*, 'an entity which unites

elements of a federal state (*Bundesstaat*) and of a confederation (*Staatenbund*) without strictly conforming to either of
them',[28] they suggest the deliberately paradoxical image of
a republican empire:

> The European Union is the first spatially extended union of
> a great number of highly distinctive peoples that is governed
> as a republican regime. It reconciles the main attribute of
> an empire – multinationality – with an essential quality of a
> republic, political freedom, the latter resulting from the volun-
> tary character of the former. (Offe and Preuss, 2006: 195)

The appeal of a model of this kind is its flexibility, which
Ulrich Beck and others have linked to a cosmopolitan vision
which transcends old-fashioned oppositions between inside
and outside, us and them (Beck and Grande, 2004; Lavenex
2004). A cosmopolitan Europe is also reflexive not just in
the sense of responding to humanly generated risks (the sense
of reflexivity which Beck had stressed in his earlier work),[29]
but also in that it relativizes conceptions of inside/outside,
self/other, Europe *or* the nation-state: 'Europe is another
word for variable geometry, variable national interests, variable concern (Betroffenheit), variable internal and external
relations, variable statehood, variable identity.' As Beck and
Grande argue at length, a reflective and cosmopolitan conception of Europe can to some extent escape the dilemmas
of in/out, us/them, nation-state/federation.[30]

Cosmopolitan democracy arguably requires a degree of
informality and imprecision, given the difficulties of constituting formal assemblies to deal with the problems of
massive territories. Deliberative democracy in close contact
with a multiplicity of intersecting European public spheres
(Peters et al., 2005) is an attractive vision. What it lacks,
of course, is the notion of a process by which clear-cut
political choices can be presented to an electorate for decision. Individual lobbying groups may enjoy an enhanced
sense of efficacy, but European citizens as a whole are even
more estranged from the European Parliament than from

their national assemblies. The negative votes on the European Constitution in France and the Netherlands, two states involved from the beginning in the integration project and generally reckoned among the most favourably inclined to it, carry a powerful lesson. Kees van der Pijl provides a damning indictment which puts an analysis like Vivien Schmidt's analysis in a broader context:

> There is a European Parliament, and there are various channels of interest articulation at the level of the EU, all institutions which one will not find at the Atlantic level, or NAFTA or ASEAN. Hence political mobilization and class struggle or compromise *could* always develop at the EU level, however unlikely this may now seem. But compared to the clear separation between national politics and transnational economy in the original homeland, which reserves the transnational space for capital whilst containing democratic aspirations within each separate state, a 'European politics' is best characterized as a contradiction that could go either way – that is, it could re-nationalize politics entirely, leaving only a regulatory infrastructure in place at the EU level ... or else press forward to develop a full-fledged politics at the EU level. The 'only' problem here is that the populations of Europe have been *doubly disenfranchised*, both by the general restriction of democracy in the neo-liberal reform drive, and by the specific displacement of key prerogatives of national parliaments to European structures in the economic domain. (van der Pijl, 2006a: 36)[31]

The problem, in other words, is that it may be impossible to democratize the EU without undermining the democratic states which make it up.[32] Yet other federal polities manage this, with only occasional grumbles in Bavaria, Texas or the Valais about goings-on in the national capitals. Klaus von Beyme (2005) has sketched out some ways in which federal structures accommodate differences in, for example, the size of their component states. But to speak like this, Euro-realists would say, is to fail to grasp the reality of the EU, where legitimating structures are inevitably embedded

at national level and the pursuit of a stronger European identity is a dangerous diversion (Weiler, 2001; Scharpf, 2004).
Philippe Schmitter's 'Why Bother?' (Schmitter, 2000) rings
out over the subsequent debates, and the debacle of the Constitution keeps the echo going. Offe and Preuss suggest that
the representation of European citizens in the parliament
could become more genuinely 'direct' and less a reflection
of national political formations, but this modest suggestion
remains imprecise and very limited. Their basic message is
one of caution:

> Democratizing Europe after the model of the nation-state will
> not increase but undermine the capacity of the Euro-polity
> to allocate rights and claims in a 'nation-blind' manner. Even
> the most robust national democracy (or, rather, precisely the
> most robust national democracy) does not help here, as it will
> function as an obstacle to, rather than a promoter of . . . an
> institutionalized form of solidarity. (Offe and Preuss, 2006:
> 197–8)

If, then, the problem of the EU polity is essentially that of
its decoupling from society, which reproduces in spades the
alienation of the national political sphere diagnosed by Marx
in the nineteenth century and by Régis Debray (1981) in the
twentieth,[33] we are returned to the neglected theme of European society and its global context. Delanty and Rumford
(2005: 163) point to the similarities between European and
global politics: 'In Europe, as in the world polity more generally, cultural control is exerted by those who are seen to work
for the common good rather than self-interest, framing their
calls for development, progress, standardization, and rational
organization in terms of the potential benefits to everyone.'
The European polity thus displays in microcosm the tension
between the stylistic democratization of modern politics,
marked by the informal style of leaders like Blair and Bush,
and the increasing alienation of marginalized and excluded
populations, which in the European context tends to be
expressed at best in hostility to the European project and at
worst in a generalized xenophobia (Bale, 2003). The pursuit

of European integration was always, in a phrase also applied in a different way to fascism, an 'extremism of the centre'. In its well-meaning but arrogant elitism it has now generated an anti-European extremism which may be spreading from the extreme right to the mainstream. As Cas Mudde (2006) writes, 'Europe is currently experiencing a populist *Zeitgeist*, in which populism is prevalent in politics as well as in many other aspects of life'.

One possible response to this situation is for the European Union to ride rather than resist the populist waves, by more and bolder initiatives for the visible benefit of European citizens. The reduction imposed in 2007 on exorbitant charges for transnational mobile phone calls, or the fine imposed on Microsoft for abuse of its dominant position, are good examples of what can be done. A Europe which delivered rapid and effective remedies, above the heads of member-state governments, would be better placed to attract the support of European citizens. The problem is that the European origins of many achievements in fields such as equal opportunity legislation tend to be forgotten in the course of the local, national implementation of European legislation. What does seem clear is that the future of European democracy will be necessarily multi-levelled, with local, regional, national and European politics forming a complex web of decision-making. The difficulties of expanding democracy at the European level should not be taken to suggest a retreat to the primacy of national politics.

5 SOCIAL DIVISIONS AND SOCIAL IDENTITIES

In the last two chapters I have been examining two relatively differentiated sectors of European society: the economy and the polity. It is now time to relate these to other aspects of European society. Modernity involves a complex set of orientations to, and representations of, social relations, of which the concepts of 'the' economy and 'the' state are two. Society, whether national, regional or European, can also be represented in a holistic way or in terms of particular social entities such as classes. Most accounts will look at both dimensions, stressing consensus or conflict according to theoretical preference or perceived relevance. Functionalists and evolutionary theorists will tend to stress the harmonious integration of the component parts of the societies they describe; 'conflict theorists' such as Marxists stress the instability of any temporary equilibrium in the battles between opposed social forces. At the European level, too, realists in International Relations stress power politics, conflict and the primacy of national interests, while others offer a more peaceful vision of the gradual realization, in both senses of the term, of European unity.

The trio of class, gender, and 'race' or ethnicity has become a commonplace of social analysis since the late twentieth century. The temporalities of these concepts are of course different. Class has been solidly on the agenda since the mid-nineteenth century in Europe, whereas feminist analyses of gender relations were relatively uncommon until the 1970s, despite prominent exceptions such as that of Simone de Beauvoir (1949). As for race, ideas of racial conflict were firmly discredited by Nazism, and, although there were important analyses of race in the US, such as Gunnar Myrdal's *American Dilemma* (1944), followed by studies in the UK and the rest of Europe of ethnic relations in the wake of postwar immigration, race-critical theory did not really become established until towards the end of the century, in conjunction with postcolonial analyses. (As with feminism, there were of course important precursors such as Frantz Fanon.)

Additional bases of division such as sexual orientation or disability are only now being addressed in the same theoretical terms. What is clear is that any of these bases of social division needs to be theorized in relation to the others (Anthias, 2001; Klinger and Knapp, 2005; Payne, 2006). Second, analyses of these social divisions *within* European states need to be combined with an analysis of inequalities *between* them (Mau, 2004).

The temporality in the conceptual bases of the analysis of social divisions is compounded by the East–West split. There are excellent recent comparative studies of class in Western Europe but far fewer for the East, although some of the best theoretical and empirical work came historically from there, notably the classic book by Stanislaw Ossowski (1956). The radically different conditions for the development of feminist thought in East and West meant that the analysis of gender relations was similarly delayed, as was that of issues of 'race', in a part of Europe where people of non-'European' origin were a rarity.[1]

In the case of class analysis, a further time-line must be borne in mind. From the 1950s, a number of contributions questioned the continuing relevance of class as a basis of social division or asserted the need to reconceptualize it. Political parties such as the West German SPD and the British Labour Party attempted to reformulate their programmes. In the German case this mutation from workers' socialist party to *Volkspartei* was accomplished in 1958; in Britain it took Blair's creation of 'New Labour' in the mid-1990s to complete the transition. In between, there was a revival of academic Marxist class analysis in the 1970s, alongside the rise of feminism. The theme of postindustrialism flourished in the late 1960s and early 1970s, then went into eclipse for a while in the face of sceptical critiques by Krishan Kumar (1978), Jay Gershuny (1978) and others. It bounced back in a sharper form in the 1980s and onwards with a negative focus on de-industrialization and a positive one on the information society and the 'weightless' economy (Leadbeater, 2000).

In the East, accounts of state socialist societies can be roughly categorized according to whether they endorsed the Marxist assertion that class conflicts are central to all (or at least all developed capitalist) societies and whether, if so, they made the same claim about socialist societies. Official accounts of Soviet-type societies were tied to the orthodox view that there had been a history of this kind but it was now over. With minor variations, to do with the distinct status of collective farmers and intellectuals, these societies portrayed themselves as essentially classless or on the way to classlessness, and characterized by harmonious and cooperative, rather than conflictual, relations between their component strata.

Western Marxists with Trotskyist or Maoist leanings, however critical they were of Soviet-type societies, often argued that the nomenklatura elite was not a fully fledged (state) bourgeoisie and that the 'degeneration' of these 'workers' states' could be remedied by a merely political as distinct from a social revolution. Other Western theorists, such as Frank Parkin (1971) and Anthony Giddens (1973), along with some more unofficial accounts from writers based in or emigrated from state socialist societies (Djilas, 1966; Ossowski, 1963; Konrád and Szelényi, 1979; Bahro, 1978; Voslensky, 1984), identified class antagonisms similar to, and/or different in various ways from, those in capitalist societies.

As things turned out, the regimes collapsed in a series of essentially political revolutions, involving state collapse rather than any challenge posed by the very diverse oppositional forces. The metaphor of implosion has been much used to describe 1989, and with good reason. In class terms, the most striking characteristic of the anti-communist opposition movements was that they transcended both class differences and differences of political orientation, bringing together these diverse forces in a single-issue movement to get rid of 'them'.

Despite the fundamental differences between East and West, there are substantial parallels between the developments in class structure over the Cold War period. Welfare states were further developed in both parts of Europe, though more slowly after the capitalist economic crisis of the mid-seventies. With the transformation of agriculture after the Second World War the peasants who had been 'nationalized' in Eugen Weber's sense in the late nineteenth century (Weber, 1977), or collectivized in most of the Soviet bloc in the 1950s, were increasingly displaced into manufacturing or service occupations. In France, Henri Mendras (1970) wrote of 'the end of the peasants', and there was a similar exodus in Portugal, where the proportion of male farm workers dropped by nearly a third from 1960 to 1991 (Crouch, 1999: 137). In West Germany, by 1980 it had dropped to near the UK level (4 per cent as against 3 per cent) (Pratt, 2003: 188). Agricultural policy, one of the key domains of the European Communities, came to look more like a disguised social policy to support the vestiges of rural life and an increasingly threatened natural environment, though it was not until the twenty-first century that the latter goal was made explicit in policy discussions.

The petty bourgeoisie, too, was squeezed by capitalist concentration (in the West) and state policy in the East. Self-employment, as Colin Crouch (1999: 82–4) stresses, is an ambiguous categorization, linking a number of distinct forms of occupation. Overall it declined in Western Europe in the early postwar decades; it rose again from around 1975, as other forms of employment became more precarious and more employees took early retirement or were made redundant. In a countervailing postwar development, stronger in the West than the East, white-collar work expanded massively in the postwar boom, and, despite the rise of information technology, which led to a shake-out in, for example, bank counter staff, white-collar or 'white-blouse' occupations were overall better protected than manual (especially unskilled manual) jobs. This impacted significantly on the sexual composition of the workforce, though less on the traditional gendering of work. Here the East was far ahead in establishing very high female participation rates in the workforce, backed up by very substantial, if not always very good, childcare and other welfare regimes. Women were employed in many occupations seen in the West as still a male preserve, though they were rarely admitted to the highest political office.

Marx's class theory is of course grounded in his theory of modes of production, and in thinking about the relevance of Marxist class theory or post-Marxist theories such as Bourdieu's to postcommunism we need first to ask whether there is a distinctive postcommunist form of production. Marx wrote in the *Grundrisse* of 'forms which precede capitalist production', and perhaps we can identify at least a family resemblance between 'forms which (also) come *after* state socialist production'. More speculatively still, perhaps Marx and Max Weber's analysis of the emergence of capitalism in early modern Europe might help us to understand late twentieth- and early twenty-first-century capitalism in the postcommunist world.

How might a postcommunist capitalism be expected to differ from Western models? These economies had often very substantial productive resources but lacked markets and market-related institutions such as stock exchanges, commercial banks and structures of commercial law. They also lacked a bourgeoisie. Opinions differ of course on whether this latter lack is an important one and whether it is likely to persist. Managerialists will tend to argue that managers are managers, whether they are notionally responsible to individual capitalists, to collectivities of shareholders, to state ministries and/or party officials or, for that matter, to criminal organizations.[2] If Western capitalism has become increasingly managerial, the East can start and stay that way.

But even if a bourgeoisie is functionally dispensable in a modern capitalist economy, students of social structure will still want to know whether one is developing or not, and this will determine, or at least affect, other aspects of societal development. Along with the de-collectivization of agriculture and the emergence of a petty bourgeoisie, this (where it is happening) is the third major social structural transformation of postcommunism.[3]

A 'modern' industrial bourgeoisie can develop in various ways. One path is via the conversion of agricultural property, as evidenced in early modern England and as described by Barrington Moore (1966).[4] Another is via the gradual expansion of existing artisanal and/or merchant activity; a third is by syphoning off resources made available by positions held in a state or Church hierarchy. In postcommunist transition, the third of these has rightly attracted the most attention, under the slogan, whch seems to have been invented in Poland, of nomenklatura privatization (Ray, 1995: 452–7; Stark and Bruszt, 1998). In a (for the beneficiaries) ideal scenario, existing state managers were able to reconfigure themselves as shareholders in newly privatized enterprises, in what in the West would be called a management buyout but was here often more of a handout. Even where, as in Russia, there was officially a more egalitarian distribution of shares, they were often bought up by existing management or local magnates.[5]

It should be clear that any emergent capitalist class in postcommunist societies is going to be a rather different animal from that found in the West.[6] One should note, first, that what counts as capital or a productive resource is extremely unpredictable, and, second, that ownership and control of such resources are bound up with complex processes of justification and social valorization. As well as capital in the conventional economic sense, then, we should also be thinking of Pierre Bourdieu's concepts of cultural capital and social capital and the related concept of social capital developed by James Coleman, Robert Putnam and others. (On these, see Grix, 2001.)

To cut a long story short, whereas Putnam's analyses of Italy and the US tend to treat social capital as a public good, and something which unproblematically conduces to social development,[7] Bourdieu's focus is closer to Marx in looking at the way in which these forms of capital and the ways in which they are used by their bearers reinforce social inequalities and antagonisms between classes. Bourdieu (1983) distinguished three forms of capital: economic, cultural and social. His concept of cultural capital has some analogies with the economic notion of human capital but this, Bourdieu argued, pays insufficient attention to the detailed structures in which such forms of capital are deployed and to informal educational resources in the family and elsewhere, which largely determine the rate of return of educational investments. 'The structure of the field, i.e., the unequal distribution of capital, is the source of the specific effects of capital' (1983: 49).

Thus, for example, in the postcommunist context, the ability to speak or teach English may be a positional good of some importance in virtue of its rarity. Bourdieu defines social capital as 'the aggregate of the actual or potential resources which are linked to possession of a durable network of more or less institutionalized relationships of mutual acquaintance and recognition' (1983: 51). And in a sentence designed to illustrate the shift to ostensibly more meritocratic forms of social selection in Western societies but which also has considerable relevance to the postcommunist context, Bourdieu wrote: 'the more the official transmission of capital is prevented or hindered, the more the effects of the clandestine circulation of capital in the form of cultural capital become determinant in the reproduction of the social structure' (1983: 55).

In the USSR and Eastern Europe, of course, there was officially no capital until the later stages of the communist period, and even then only in parts of the bloc. Although people often held substantial stocks of cash, the more useful resources were foreign currency and informal connections, which provided access to scarce goods.[8] To revert to the example cited earlier, an ability to speak foreign languages, acquired in special schools or through service in the tourist industry, state security, etc., may be far more marketable than formal educational qualifications, and personal connections may carry more weight than ownership or control of formal economic or material resources. An ironical expression of this is the practice, quite common for a time in Russia, in which people got together, set a money value on their collective expertise and asked banks to match this with loan capital. Once again, processes of this kind present in a somewhat crude and exaggerated form something which was by no means unknown in Western capitalism during the dot-com mania at the beginning of the twenty-first century. More optimistically, social capital can be viewed in a way which owes more to Putnam (1993) than to Bourdieu, as a collective resource rather than part of a competitive game. The point is that it is always both.

Without looking in detail at the empirical support for a social capital model of the kind advanced by Eyal, Szelényi and Townley (1998), as opposed to one of political capitalism, since this would have to be argued out in a much more regionally and sectorally differentiated way,[9] and related to the broader discussion of elite continuity (Higley and Lengyel, 2000), one can see in the critical responses to Eyal, Szelényi and Townsley a general tension between a Bourdieu-influenced model and a more orthodox Marxist one. Michael Burawoy, who has conducted some of the most fundamental research on communist and postcommunist industry, brings out, in an important review symposium in the *American Journal of Sociology* (Burawoy, 2001), the differences between an approach which focuses on the strategies of class members, in this case of an elite class, and a Marxist class analysis, which he favours, grounded in antagonistic relations tied to conflicts at the point of production.

The authors of the book reply, reasonably enough, that there is little evidence of action on the part of a 'demobilized' working class.[10]

Stratification patterns in communist and postcommunist societies, too, may seem more open to Weberian, Dahrendorfian or Bourdieusian models than to a simple opposition between exploiters and exploited grounded in the social relations of production. Weber's model of 'classes, status groups and parties' as phenomena of the distribution of *power* may seem particularly relevant in a context where, as a recent discussion of Russia argues, the relation to state power has been the principal source of privilege:

> Overall the shift from czarist to socialist planned economic and now to capitalist market economic power structures did not much affect the extraordinary importance of *authoritatively distributed privileges* as a central basic principle for unequal positions in the Russian social order. (Hölscher and Dittrich, 1999: section 4.2)

This is not the place to systematically examine the substantial amounts of evidence for both the intelligentsia and the political capitalism hypotheses. Both are explicitly presented as analyses of transition to an essentially open future. As Eyal et al. (1998: 186) put it:

> The social structure of Central European societies is still in flux. From this point of view the most important issue pending is whether a domestic propertied *grande bourgeoisie* which could challenge the hegemony of the current power bloc will emerge and, if it does, on what basis it will exercise power and which actors will comprise it. We believe that the answers to these questions will depend on the balance of social forces and the contingent outcomes of their social struggles.[11]

To repeat a point made earlier, there are substantial differences between states and regions. Patterns of ownership are also diverse across the region, with banks, investment

companies, and holding companies like the German Treuhandanstalt and its successor playing very different roles
in different countries. The authors of a study ten years
ago of new entrepreneurs concluded that 'the creation in
eastern Germany of a *class* of new entrepreneurs who will
provide a social basis for capitalism still has a long way
to go' (Koch and Thomas, 1997). This may of course not
be the right way to phrase such questions, to the extent
that Russia and Eastern European capitalism is owned and
even managed by foreigners. (In Germany, of course, the
'Wessis' (Westerners) are not even officially or identifiably
foreign.) Hungary was in the forefront of this process, though
comparing their 1993 data with a 1996 survey Eyal et al.
(1998: 154) note 'a massive increase in the proportion of
firms reporting ownership by domestic individuals'. Nevertheless, the globalization and/or Europeanization of Eastern
European capitalism means that discussion of class relations necessarily takes on an international dimension which
is more familiar in development studies than in the class
analysis of advanced industrial societies. EU enlargement is
undoubtedly giving a further push to the Europeanization
and globalization of managerial elites, though the German
prologue suggests that the pace of such changes may not be
particularly fast.

I have already mentioned the issue of class politics in
Western Europe. Malcolm Waters and others, in an extremely
creative series of contributions, have developed a historical
model of class societies which culminates in their supersession.
Their model is based on three categories. First, a classical model of what they call 'economic class society', in which
economically based classes with strong subcultures conflict
within the framework of 'a weak or liberal state' (Waters,
1997: 30). Second, an 'organized-class society', in which
classes are incorporated in political and other structures into
a stronger state dominated by a political-bureaucratic elite.
Their formal political and institutional representation in a
sense compensates for their internal differentiation and the
decline of strong occupational subcultures.

Social classes take on a new lease of life despite market fragmentation and a progressing division of labour. The politi-
cal-organizational superstructures of class, trade unions and
political parties take over the dominant social-structuring
role. (Waters, 1997: 32)

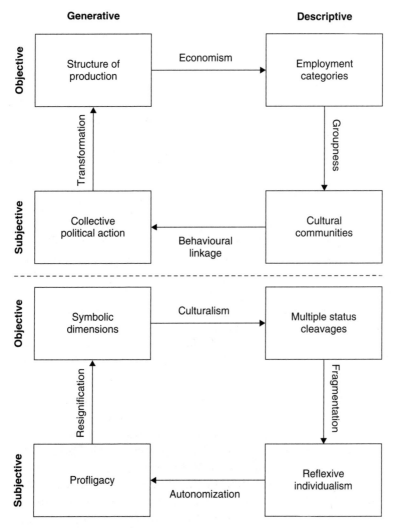

Figure 5.1   Sociology after postmodernism
Source: Waters (Sage, 1996)

Finally, in an emergent post-class or 'status-conventional' society, illustrated in figure 5.1 in the section below the dotted line, 'stratification is sourced in the cultural sphere. The strata are lifestyle and/or value-based status configurations' (Waters, 1997: 33). Intellectual property, mobile and fluid, tends to displace land and capital as the basis of social differentiation. Politics ceases to be class-based, and identity, lifestyle and issues politics become more important than the large blocs of left and right. Post-class societies remain differentiated, unequal and conflictual, but along shifting and unpredictable lines.

These three typical patterns could respectively be roughly identified, in Western Europe, with a short nineteenth century beginning in the 1840s, a social democratic/welfare state in the twentieth century, petering out in the 1980s, and a post-welfarist 'third way' twenty-first century just beginning. Whatever one thinks of this overall conception, the model of organized-class society strongly recalls the world of state socialism. The nomenklatura elite, the officially defined and celebrated working class, its alliance with the collective peasantry and the Mickey Mouse political parties representing different classes and sometimes, in the people's democracies, approved ideological differences, fill out the picture of an organized-class society par excellence, or even one in which, as Pakulski and Waters (1995: 45) themselves argued, 'political ranking displaced class division'. The short-term volatility of postcommunist politics, its failure so far to settle into what had been, though was arguably ceasing to be, the left–right class-based Western European pattern of the earlier part of the century, can be explained by the removal of these organizing structures. At the same time, however, as noted above, postcommunist electorates remain more egalitarian in their attitudes than Western Europeans, to a degree more closely related than in the West to the actual levels of inequality in their societies (Delhey, 2001). The traditional expression of egalitarian attitudes, in Europe and to some extent elsewhere, has been social democratic politics, but the scissor effect in the postcommunist countries of the local demise of socialist/communist political and economic policies, and the general reorientation of Western social democracy into third way or 'new' politics, has perhaps prevented what would otherwise have been a natural development. Overall, the effects of social structure on political preferences are not, or not yet, particularly significant in postcommunist Europe. As Szelényi and his colleagues (Eyal et al., 1998: 212) suggested, ideological issues tend to predominate in the earlier period of transition, with class issues tending to emerge only some time later.

Mateju et al. (2005: 233–4) identify a similar shift from political attitudes polarized between 'winners' and 'losers', or people perceiving themselves as such, to a more objectively determined interest-based politics:

> In the early periods of the transformation, the role of subjective factors (subjective mobility, relative deprivation, perception of change in life-chances, and so on) in the determination of voting behaviour is likely to be stronger than the role of objective class. As the new post-socialist class structure emerges and the politics of symbols is transformed into the politics of interests, however, objective class is becoming a more and more important factor in voting behaviour.

However this situation changes in the coming decades, with EU enlargements again focusing attention on the issue of who sits where, in which supranational groupings, in the enlarged European Parliament (Hix, Noury and Roland, 2006; Lewis and Mansfeldová, 2006), the postcommunist party landscape is of particular interest to students of class or post-class politics.

A third analytical approach, developed by Ulrich Beck, offers a further perspective on these issues: less classical than the post-Marxist Bourdieusianism of Eyal, Szelényi and Townsley, and less postmodern/culturalist than that of Waters et al. Beck's analysis develops an insight of Reinhart Kreckel (1992: 140), cited in Crouch (1999: 424), that modern capitalism is characterized by a 'class relation without classes', *Klassenverhältnis ohne Klassen*: 'To put it in Marxist terms, we increasingly confront the phenomenon of a capitalism *without* classes, but with individualized social

inequality and all the related social and political problems'
(Beck, 1992: 88).

Max Weber had already suggested, contra Marx, that class
relations are less likely than status group memberships to
form a basis for common consciousness, and it could be
argued that this underlying logic has became clearer in the
later twentieth century with the erosion of occupational
communities and the decline of class-based (and socialist
party-based) forms of association. In postwar Europe, Beck
(1992: 95–101) suggests, we find an 'individualized society
of employees':

> the unstable unity of shared life experiences mediated by
> the market and shaped by status, which Max Weber brought
> together in the concept of social class, began to break apart.
> Its different elements (such as material conditions dependent
> upon specific market opportunities, the effectiveness of tradi-
> tion and of pre-capitalist lifestyles, the consciousness of com-
> munal bonds and of barriers to mobility, as well as networks
> of contact) have slowly disintegrated. (Beck, 1992: 96)

If class relations tend less than in the past to generate
class identities, we must ask if other identities have replaced
them. One way of describing modernity in its current form
might be indeed to say that roles have tended to be replaced
by identities, in the sense of flexible and open-ended dis-
positions rather than firm expectations. Nationality, for
example, is more likely to be conceptualized in cultural and
lifestyle terms than in terms of duties, let alone 'blood and
soil'. Even if we wanted to, we are too diverse to appeal to
descent, and too mobile to appeal to place.[12] Even national
cultures can only be credibly characterized in stylistic terms,
rather than common values or a dominant culture (the ill-
fated *Leitkultur* touted for a time by the German Christian
Democrats). The great Polish sociologist Stanislaw Ossowski
developed a model in the 1950s of what he called non-egali-
tarian classlessness, and this is still relevant today. Classes
and class positions are forming, though not classes *für-sich*
or as political actors. Resentment of class inequalities does

not seem to be confined to nostalgic socialists – especially if one looks further east to the obscene wealth of some of the 'new Russians'.

The fact that no postcommunist proletariat has developed into a class for itself (even where, as in Poland in 1993 and 1995, there was something of a communist backlash) does not mean that class politics is dead or that East Central Europe has overtaken the West on the way to an American future. Survey evidence suggests a majority perception in East Central Europe that there are 'strong' or 'very strong' conflicts between managers and workers and that income differentials are 'too great', and a relation between the perception of conflict and objective inequality as measured by Gini coefficient (Delhey, 2001: 203–5). And although many managers may see themselves as managing enterprises under difficult conditions for the public good, this is not necessarily how their efforts will be perceived.

Subjective representations of the class structure also display an interesting contrast, remarkably stable through the 1990s, between East and West. Eastern German respondents offered a sharply pyramidal model with a tiny upper stratum, while Westerners discerned a 'spinning-top' model with much larger upper and middle strata, the latter outnumbering the working class by two to one.

How far one can detect a shift to a more lifestyle-based pattern of consumption and social differentiation is still somewhat unclear. It has, however, formed a major emphasis of recent German work on Germany itself (Geissler, 2000; Hradil, 2001; Hradil and Schiener, 2002) and on Russia (Hölscher and Dittrich, 1999). The model of social milieus, based on value orientations and lifestyles, was developed by the market and electoral research institute Sinus in the 1980s and taken up by a number of social scientists in the 1990s. In a comparison drawn in 2000, Sinus identified two specifically 'Eastern' milieus, a conservative bourgeois-humanist one oriented to old Protestant virtues, and a 'GDR-rooted' one, encompassing dismissed or retired members of the former East German elites whose attitudes remain strongly distinct

Table 5.1 The Sinus-Milieus® new model 2005 for Germany

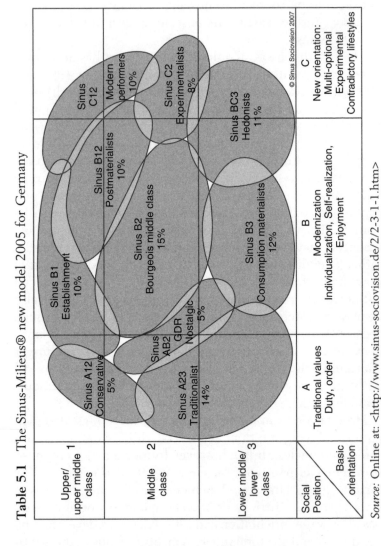

Source: Online at: <http://www.sinus-sociovision.de/2/2-3-1-1.htm>

from those of West Germans. Other Eastern milieus (such as left-intellectual, career-oriented, and traditional worker/peasant) were characterized as 'converging' with corresponding milieus in the West. More recent surveys by Sinus Sociovision itself still identify nearly four million Germans (6 per cent) of 'GDR-nostalgics' in the 'traditional' (left-hand) side of the model.

Gender

The twentieth century saw a gradual process of emancipation of European women from the household-based occupations to which they had been increasingly confined in the nineteenth century, as advances in productive technology and changes in attitudes restricted factory work first by children and then by women. Family-based agriculture remained of course a major element of women's work, with domestic service another major sector until the 1920s. However, it was only in the last third of the century that Western European women were genuinely independent in the job market and formal occupational segregation ended. The postwar British welfare state, which was widely admired but not imitated for some considerable time on the continent (Therborn, 1995: 92), was still predicated on the idea of the family and the family wage, and welfare payments continue to be structured according to patterns of marriage and cohabitation. Married women were excluded from schoolteaching in Britain until the 1940s, and in Ireland they were excluded from public service until EC accession in 1973. In some European societies married women until recently required their husband's formal consent for certain legal transactions. Formal legal equality between husband and wife, which until 1929 was confined to the Nordic countries, the UK and the USSR, was not achieved until 1983 in Greece and 1984 in the Netherlands and Switzerland (Therborn, 1995: 108).

It sometimes seems as if 'postfeminism' and neo-traditional practices such as lavish weddings, often held abroad, are becoming entrenched before the implications of 1970s feminism have really taken hold. On the other hand, Therborn (1995: 63) suggests that variations in women's labour market participation result more from economic opportunities than from traditional cultural attitudes or institutional constraints.

> Regions of heavy industry and of latifundian agriculture tend to have low rates of female labour force participation. On the

other hand, the two most Catholic *Länder* of Germany, Saarland and Bavaria, constitute the two extremes of gendered labour markets in the old Federal Republic. While the more strongly Catholic Southern Italy has a low participation rate, by national as well as European standards, the deeply Catholic northern Portugal has a female labour force participation far above the EC average.[13]

It may be that something like the process we identified in relation to class can also be found in relation to gender: a powerful structuring factor but with very different impacts according to household patterns. The 'normalizing' effect of heterosexual partnership and/or child-rearing compounds the background differences in assumptions about gendered behaviour. Young women who had enjoyed relatively equal opportunities in education, work and social life may find themselves abruptly tipped into child-rearing, housebound activity and a heavily gendered division of domestic labour. Class analysis, in other words, needs to go together with an analysis of gender relations.

The Western feminist movements of the 1970s were accompanied by movements for gay liberation, and sexual orientation has become another focus of contemporary attention on processes of discrimination. At the time of writing, for example, Catholic adoption agencies in the UK have been resisting their legal obligation to facilitate adoption by same-sex couples; there had been similar controversies over discrimination by private hotels. Despite exceptions like these, homophobia has rapidly come to be treated, officially at least, as on a par with racism, though again with lags in parts of Southern and Eastern Europe, notably in Poland. On the whole, however, as in the case of racism, official attitudes and regulations seem to have changed with impressive speed over the past couple of decades.

The legal proscriptions on racist behaviour are, however, found in very different forms in individual European states. Monitoring practices vary widely even in the three European countries – the UK, the Netherlands and France – which were among the first to introduce legislation against racism and to develop systems of ethnic monitoring to identify under-representation of ethnic minorities; the development of European initiatives is only just beginning. These legal provisions also sit oddly with a Europe which fortifies itself against immigrants and which has only partially succeeded in integrating its populations of non-European origin.

Long-standing migratory flows within Europe from East to West largely dried up with the establishment of communist rule in the East. In their place the postwar boom drew in two intersecting movements: a mostly long-distance one from colonies or ex-colonies to France, Britain, the Netherlands and Belgium, and more often short-distance intra-European movements from East and South, particularly Italy, Yugoslavia and Turkey, into Germany and Switzerland. Much of this migration was state-sponsored and based on active recruitment. There were also politically rather than economically determined movements such as those of exiles from the post-fascist dictatorships of Spain and Portugal, and of European settlers from Algeria and elsewhere after independence. Specialists tend to differentiate between race and ethnicity by grounding the former in relations of descent and the latter more in cultural processes (Banton, 1983; Carling, 1991), though this usage is only gradually spreading outside the English-language area (White, 1999: 214). In any case, in practice the most marginal ethnic differences, such as those between Swiss and Southern Italians, easily become racialized under conditions of immigration. On the whole, however, 'those who have been seen as most significantly different are those from outside the social construction of Europe' (White, 1999: 213).

Russell King and Marco Donati (1999: 136, 143) neatly contrast the Mediterranean 'migration divides' in the 1960s and 1980s/1990s. Whereas in the sixties it ran horizontally through Europe between North and South, in the early twenty-first century it follows the Southern and Eastern Mediterranean coastline, with only former Yugoslavia (except Slovenia), Albania and Turkey on the 'sending' side of the line.

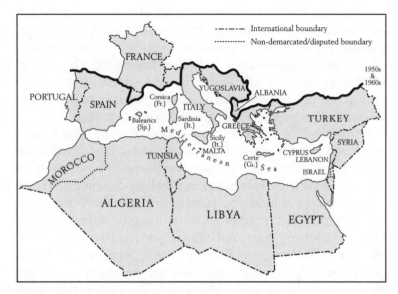

Map 5.1   The migration divide in the 1960s
Source: King, Russell and Donati, in Ray Hudson and Allan Williams (eds) (1999)

White (1999: 218–19) usefully distinguishes four typical forms of exclusion from which racial and ethnic minorities may suffer. First, there may be legal restraints such as those on long-term foreign residents for whom it is difficult to become citizens, as is the case notably in Germany and Switzerland. Many countries also, bizarrely, prevent asylum seekers from working while their cases are under consideration. Second, explicitly racist attitudes expressed by extremist parties and movements, or present more diffusely in native populations, may question the right of foreigners to remain on the national territory; a typical strategy is to point to the numerical relation between unemployment figures and those for 'foreign' populations. Third, White identifies 'the failure to provide for group-specific needs', such as education and information in minority languages. Finally, there are forms of economic and social deprivation intersecting

with, and reinforcing, the other forms of exclusion; the stig-
matization of entire urban districts, in France and elsewhere,
illustrates this. Within the EU, deflationary policies associated with the adoption of the euro arguably exacerbated
this. Most recently, the panic reaction to militant Islamism,
itself in part a response to disastrous interventions in the
Middle East by some European countries, notably the UK,
has hardened attitudes on both 'sides'. All this means that
the development into a comfortable multiculturalism now
seems far less probable than in the 1980s, and the term itself
has been criticized not only from the right, but also from
the left, where it has been seen as reinforcing the isolation
of minorities and sometimes the subordination of women
and children.

In Europe, however, the term 'ethnic minority' tends to
suggest populations of substantial ethno-territories, for whom
migration is something lost in the mists of time. A surprising number of these sustain regional autonomist movements
with varying degrees of militancy. Crouch (1999: 294–5)
situates these in relation to state 'cores' such as the home
counties in England, and Paris and the Île de France. Running
together his categories of 'soft', 'hard' and 'separatist' subcultures, and leaving out some at the 'soft' end, yields the
following list:

Belgium: Flanders, Wallonia; German-speakers in the East
Finland: Swedes and Lapps (also in Norway and Sweden)
France: Brittany, 'Occitania', Corsica, Normandy
Germany: Bavaria, Sorbs in Eastern Germany
Italy: Alto Adige, 'Padania' (according to the Lega Nord)
Netherlands: Friesland
Spain: Catalonia, Basque country, Galicia
UK: Wales, Scotland, Northern Ireland, perhaps Cornwall
   To this we should add, from the East, at the very least:
Romania: Hungarians
Slovakia: Hungarians
Baltic states: Russians

There is also, of course, the Roma subculture throughout Europe, but particularly in the East.

From the above list, the following have significant regionalist movements:

Flanders *and* Wallonia
Brittany, Corsica, Occitania
Alto Adige and the North
Friesland
Catalonia, Basque country, Galicia
Wales, Scotland, republicans in Northern Ireland
Hungarians in Transylvania

As noted earlier, the break-up of Britain (Nairn, 1977, 1981, 2003), and also of Belgium and Spain, is not at all improbable.

All of this raises important questions about national, regional and European identities. Very crudely, these can either be seen as nested, in the form of concentric circles, or as excluding one another. You can see yourself as Scottish *and* British *and* European, or Basque *and* Spanish *and* European, or just as one or two out of the three. In both these cases, the form relating to the national state is in decline. The British Social Attitudes Survey suggests that from 1995 to 2005 those expressing claim to British identity dropped by 8 per cent to less than half. In an ICM poll of November 2006, 59 per cent of English respondents supported Scottish independence, while 68 per cent favoured the creation of a parliament for England. In Spain, according to a recent survey by the Spanish Centre of Sociological Investigations (CIS), 44 per cent of Basques identify themselves first as Basques (only 8 per cent first as Spaniards), 40 per cent of Catalans with Catalonia (20 per cent identify first with Spain), and 32 per cent of Galicians with Galicia (9 per cent with Spain). On the whole, the more decentralized the state, and the stronger the regional identities as opposed to nation-state identities, the greater the willingness to identify with Europe. Italy is a good example where the relative inefficacy of the national state may also be a contributory factor; rule from Brussels may be more attractive if you are discontented with rule from Rome. In the UK, by contrast, although state power has been decentralized to Wales, Scotland and, on and off, to Northern Ireland, the dominant English core remains very centralized and what is euphemistically known as 'Euroscepticism' is unusually strong. Green (2000: 302–3, table 15.2) provides a useful summary of research on the interrelations between identities.

Before returning to the idea of a European identity, it may be helpful to look more closely at national identities. These substantially developed or were constructed in the nineteenth century (Eley and Suny, 1996; Greenfeld, 1992, 2006), and underpinned the mass wars of the twentieth century as well as a huge variety of political movements across the continent. Nationalism is one of Europe's arguably most successful and most destructive exports, along with the musket, the bomb and the motor car. The Second World War, not surprisingly, somewhat discredited nationalism, which remains pretty much a dirty word in the former Axis countries in Europe, yet it has remained an exceptionally powerful force in Western Europe and emerged intact from cold storage in the Soviet bloc. Even here, renegade Soviet-type regimes like those of Yugoslavia, Albania and later Romania were substantially driven by nationalist appeals, which in the Yugoslav case later tore the country apart. In the Western European form of Cold War dissidence, best represented by Gaullist France within NATO, nationalism was again an important motivation and appeal. We should of course distinguish the mature nationalism of established national states from the nation-building impulses which sustained the big unifications of Italy and Germany in the nineteenth century and from a host of separatist nationalisms in the twentieth.[14]

Why might the existence or strength of a European identity be important? One answer is that it is essential to sustain civil society at the European level. Discussion of European civil society necessarily hangs between the two poles of questions about broadly conceived European cultural identities,

Table 5.2 Explaining variance in levels of European identification: summary of hypotheses and findings

Hypothesis	Finding
Attributional Hypotheses	
Socio-economic status: Elites will tend to identify with Europe more than non-élites.	Strongly supported
Cosmopolitanism: Cosmopolitans will tend to identify with Europe more than non-cosmopolitans.	Largely supported
Generational: Younger cohorts will tend to identify with Europe more than older.	Supported by quantitative data Not supported by qualitative data
Gender: Men will tend to identify with Europe more than women.	Supported
Attitudinal Hypotheses	
Post-materialism: Post-materialists will tend to identify with Europe more than materialists.	Supported
Ideology: Those in the centre will tend to identify with Europe more than those on the right or left.	Not supported as hypothesized Those on the left identify more closely with Europe Those on the right are less likely to identify with Europe
Non-traditionalism: European identification is associated with a wider set of non-traditional attitudes.	Not supported
Integration support: European identification is driven by support for the integration project.	Most powerfully supported, but direction of causality?
Normative: European identification is driven by universalist, pacifist, and other normative values.	Strongly supported
Social Psychological Hypotheses	
Political Efficacy: The more efficacious will tend to identify with Europe more than the less efficacious.	Mostly supported

Hypothesis	Finding
Instrumentalism: Identification with Europe is driven by perceptions of personal or national benefits to be gained from integration.	Strongly supported for country benefit. Mixed support for personal benefit
Minority refuge: A European identity provides a refuge for excluded national minorities.	Not supported
Socialization: European identity is the product of parental or peer socialization.	Not supported
Leadership: Europeans take identity cues from leaders they admire.	Some support, but direction of causality?
Political Cultural Hypothesis	
Nationality: European identity levels vary according to nationality.	Supported. Countries with high levels of European identity: France, Italy, Spain, Portugal (and Austria – appearing in one survey only) Middle/ambiguous cases: Luxembourg (probably high), Belgium, Germany, and Greece Countries with low levels: Netherlands, Denmark, Ireland, Britain (and Sweden – appearing in one survey only)
'Primordialism': European identity increases with the country's years of membership in the EC/EU.	Not supported. Opposite is true
Size of country: People in smaller countries will be more likely to identify with Europe.	Not supported
Wealth of country: People in wealthier countries will be more likely to identify with Europe.	Supported
Catholic culture: People in Catholic countries will be more likely to identify as Europeans.	Generally supported, but depends on dependent-variable question format
Second-World-War effect: People in former Axis countries will be more likely to identify as Europeans.	Not supported
Regional culture: European identity levels vary according to region.	Supported. Those in southern countries identify more closely with Europe

Source: Green (2000): 302–3, table 15.2

on the one hand, and European-level economic and political institutions and practices on the other. As Habermas wrote in his 1974 lecture, in an early reflection on the possibilities of social identities not tied to territorial states and their membership, a collective identity can only be conceived in a reflexive form, in an awareness that one has opportunities to participate in:

> processes of communication in which identity formation occurs as a continuous learning process. Such value and norm creating communications ... flow out of the 'base' into the pores of organisationally structured areas of life. They have a subpolitical character, i.e. they operate below the level of political decision processes, but they indirectly influence the political system because they change the normative framework of political decisions. (Habermas, 1976: 116)

This in turn is seen as an essential to formal European politics and the reduction of the 'democratic deficit'.

A second answer is in terms of the need to sustain social solidarity at the European level in order to legitimate redistributive and other social policy initiatives.[15] Europeans who feel little or nothing in common with those from other member-states are unlikely to be willing to make sacrifices for them. Habermas has contributed to developing this answer too. In a relatively little-noticed essay, Habermas (1991: 70) argues that an ethics of justice needs to be augmented not, as John Rawls had suggested, with benevolence or other aspects of private morality, but by solidarity, where justice and solidarity are seen not as two distinct but complementary elements, but as 'two aspects of the same thing' (p. 70).

> From a communication-theoretical perspective there is ... a close connection between concern for the good of one's neighbour and an interest in the common good: the identity of the group reproduces itself by means of intact relations of reciprocal recognition. Thus the complementary perspective to individual equal treatment is not benevolence but solidarity ...

Justice refers to the equal freedoms of unrepresentable and self-determining individuals, whereas *solidarity* refers to the good of the good of the consociates (Genossen) united in an intersubjectively shared form of life – and therefore to the preservation of the integrity of this form of life itself . . .

It is above all in the reciprocal recognition of accountable subjects, who orient their action to validity claims, that the ideas of justice and solidarity become real (gegenwärtig). But these normative obligations do not *of themselves* extend beyond the boundaries of a concrete lifeworld of family, tribe, town or nation. These limits can only be broken through in discourses, so far as these are institutionalised in modern societies. (Habermas, 1991: 71)

Claus Offe (2000), at the beginning of a rather pessimistic analysis of the state of contemporary postcommunst societies, provides a similarly broad account of solidarity as a global feature of well-functioning societies:

The 'horizontal' phenomena of trust and solidarity (linking citizens to each other) are preconditions for the 'vertical' phenomenon of the establishment and continued existence of state authority . . . In simple terms, this means that before citizens can recognize the authority of the state, they must first mutually recognize each other as being motivated by – and hence reciprocally worthy of – trust and solidarity . . . Trust in one's fellow citizens provides the cognitive and moral foundations for *democracy*, the risks of which no one would reasonably accept otherwise. The solidarity citizens feel toward one another, or to which they allow themselves to be obligated through their representative institutions, is the moral basis of the *welfare state*. Thus, both democracy and the welfare state are dependent upon the prior existence of binding motives, which in turn are tied to the form of political integration found in the nation-state. (Offe, 2000: 5)

Or, one might add, the postnational federal state. Some commentators, like Offe (2005), would see solidarity as the source and animating spirit of the European welfare state or, more broadly, social model. For Hartmut Kaelble (Kaelble and Schmidt, 2004: 40–1):

> The development of the modern welfare state gave the European national state a new legitimacy. New civic duties, the contributions to social insurance, arose like new civil rights on the basis of the achievements of the welfare state. A national solidarity was thus established between the economically active and the old, between the healthy and the sick, between workers and the unemployed... The welfare state stabilized the then discredited national states in the second half of the twentieth century in a way which could hardly have been imagined half a century earlier.[16]

As Joe Weiler (2002: 569–70) puts it: 'Europe prides itself on a tradition of social solidarity which found political and legal expression in the post-war welfare state.'[17] Wolfgang Streeck (1999) conceptualizes the EU's developing social model as 'productivist-competitive solidarity'. As we have seen, however, the Europeanization of social policy has barely got beyond first base, despite its obvious importance as a policy goal, even from a narrowly economistic perspective focused on the removal of impediments to the free movement of labour.

A third answer is cast in terms of cosmopolitan democracy, where Europe is seen as a test-bed or springboard for the development of more globalized political structures (Schwengel, 1999). Once again, Europe is pioneering a mode of governance, this time transnational rather than national: one which gives some practical embodiment to the current extension of democratic thinking into conceptions of cosmopolitan democracy (Held, 1995), a development perhaps as important as the earlier extension of liberal democracy into social democracy. As Habermas has stressed, if the liberal democratic nation-state has few internal enemies, it is increasingly seen as inappropriate to the contemporary reality of global processes and challenges as well as to the desire of many citizens for more local autonomy. In this postnational constellation, as Habermas (2001 [1998]) has called it, the progress of European unification, combined as it is with attempts to strengthen regional autonomy under the slogan of 'subsidiarity', becomes a crucial external determinant of the internal reconfiguration of many European states.

It is perhaps only to be expected that a European identity will be less substantial than state-centred or regional identities, but these are all constructed and reproduced through increasingly mediated and reflexive practices. Some regions, for example in Italy, may have very substantial historical roots and be marked by, for example, highly distinctive dialects; others however will be more a by-product of administrative operations, such as the 'North-East' of England or Humberside.

The question then, as noted earlier, becomes whether identities are nested or orthogonal to, and in conflict with, one another. A Welsh or Catalan nationalist may or may not affirm a European identity, but is likely to reject a British/ Spanish one. A supporter of the unified British or Spanish state (or a 'Unionist' in Northern Ireland) will tend to play down a Scottish or Basque identity, or at least see it as a harmonious component of the state-centred identity. As Balibar and Wallerstein (1991: 94) wrote:

> All identity is individual, but there is no individual identity that is not historical or, in other words, constructed within a field of social values, norms of behaviour and collective symbols. The real question is how the dominant reference points of individual identity change over time and with the changing institutional environment.[18]

Among the determinants of the strength of these identities one can identify some positive and some negative factors. To begin with the positive, it is clear, as Michael Bruter (2005: 138–9) emphasizes, that a sense of European identity increased almost everywhere in the EU over the last three decades of the twentieth century; the only exceptions are countries like Germany and Luxemburg, where it was already strong at the beginning of the period. There is some evidence that a European in the sense of EU identity tends to be strongest in states whose membership of the EC/EU is longest, even if this is distinct from, and not always particularly closely related to, support for European integration (Bruter, 2005). As in the case of national identity and nationalism, it is possible to distinguish between broadly cultural and more specific civic versions of European identity.

A broader European identity may be strengthened by cross-border interaction (Grundy and Jamieson, 2005, 2007; Wallace, Datler and Spannring, 2005), which in much of mainland Europe is also a common feature of everyday life.[19] Additionally, there may also be a contribution to at least a European awareness by the presence of major European institutions. In Luxemburg, Strasbourg or Brussels, for example, it is impossible not to be aware of the latter, whereas in London there is only the European Bank for Reconstruction and Development, and no EU institution apart from an obscure pharmaceutical agency. Moreover, travel from the UK to the mainland, despite or because of the overpriced rail link, involves substantial planning and expense. A national-state or regional identity may similarly be strengthened either by a central location in the national or regional capital or, conversely, by a frontier location. Regionalist identity may be expected to be stronger the greater the distance from the national capital, though this can cut both ways: Scottish islanders, for example, may feel too remote from Edinburgh to identify strongly with the government there. A European identity may be affected negatively by hostility to the EU or positively by dissatisfaction with the national state, and both these identities may be strengthened by dislike of the regional language or politics. A study by Sue Grundy and Lynn Jamieson (2005) is of exceptional interest here, because they compare metropolitan and regional sites, though apart from the Madrid/Bilbao difference mentioned above (n. 19) they found relatively little evidence for the notion that disaffection from the nation-state leads to stronger European or global identities. Compared to Manchester, however, 'a consistently somewhat larger proportion of the target sample[20] from Edinburgh strongly identified with Europe' (2005: 9.3). Overall, one is struck by the complexities of measuring the quality of expressions of identification and of the specific situations in the sites studied.[21]

Some of these complexities come out even in more quantitative approaches, such as the excellent overview by Antonia Ruiz Jiménez et al. (2004). It is a mistake, the authors suggest, to treat national and European identities as competing with one another in a zero-sum game:

> these two identities are compatible because they are of different order and endowed with different meanings ... attachment to national identity is largely 'cultural', while attachment to a European identity is primarily 'instrumental'[22] ... [but] ... the particular configuration of national identities in each country gives rise to distinct dynamics and historical inertias that have an impact on the emergence and configuration of a European identity. (Ruiz Jiménez et al., 2004: 18)

In particular, the authors subtract the number of respondents admitting only to national identities from those affirming both national and European identities. Comparing the two extreme positions represented by Britain and Greece on the one hand, with figures of −28 and −20, with Spain (22) and Italy (28) on the other, they suggest that a European identity may be conceived in more civic and forward-oriented terms in the latter cases, and more historically traditionalist terms in the former. The result, where a close or very close attachment to nation is pretty much shared by all Europeans,[23] is that Greeks and Britons are peculiarly low in the degree of their attachment to Europe and the EU. There is clearly much more to be done in exploring differences of this kind. In particular, it will be important, as the authors of *The Civic Culture* (Almond and Verba, 1963) found half a century ago, to pay close attention to the way in which particular phrases translate from one language and political context to another.

What is clear is that there has been a very substantial attempt to inspire and nurture a pan-European identity focused on what we now know as the EU and developed, as Wiener (1997: 538–9) notes, in connection with the ultimately rather half-hearted introduction of a European citizenship:

> a paper on 'European identity' was issued at the 1973 Copen-hagen summit. It broadly defined European identity as being based on a 'common heritage' and 'acting together in rela-tion to the rest of the world', while the 'dynamic nature of European unification' was to be respected. This . . . idea of Community development was then approached by a citizen-ship practice that included the adoption of the two policy objectives of 'special rights' for European citizens and a 'pass-port union' . . . The notion of citizen thus turned into a new informal resource of the *acquis communautaire.*

As Bo Stråth (2002) has suggested, the appeal to identity has in some ways replaced appeals to the notion of integra-tion as a self-evident good. How far these centralized initia-tives amount to the creation of a genuine European identity, assuming such a thing is anyway important (Kantner, 2006), is of course open to question.

What, then, is distinctive about Europe in relation to these issues? Clearly not the mere *fact* of class divisions, any more than that of gender or ethnic divisions. All these are however modulated in specific ways in the European context. Schumpeter (1951) wrote about social classes 'in an ethnically homogeneous environment', and although such environments might not be so common in a strict sense, especially in his homeland of Central Europe, the phrase points to the characteristically European pattern of class conflict *within* the boundaries of the national state. Marx and Engels and their followers wanted the 'proletarians of all countries' to transcend these boundaries, but the limited success of this appeal was shown by the general mobiliza-tions of the First World War. Coinciding with the moves to universal suffrage, the rise of the European labour move-ment produced workers' parties across the continent which retained their identity, though not their radical ideologies, throughout the twentieth century. Europe's pattern of a left/right political axis was also primary outside Europe, for example in postwar Japan; it seems such an obvious feature of political life that we are aware of it only when it is largely absent, as in the US.

Europe also pioneered ideas of women's emancipation – admittedly in a context where women were less independent than in many black African and Caribbean societies. The idea that access to economic opportunities and lifestyles should not be skewed by gender or sexual orientation seems to be a relatively distinctive feature of modern Europe, with origins in the work of Wollstonecraft and others; homophobia is no longer acceptable, despite occasional backlashes from reactionary politicians. Again, this is not to say that feminist ideas have been fully assimilated, even in Eastern Europe where a particular idea of women's emancipation had been part of the socialist package. As Barbara Einhorn (2006: 188) writes:

> In practice, the gendered inequalities produced by ostensibly egalitarian state socialist ideology are matched by those induced by the individualist liberal meta-narrative . . . the neo-liberal agenda of democratization within market-driven policies of economic restructuring has a major impact on the potential for gender justice, in East and West, North and South.

What has changed is that 'glass ceilings' and other obstacles to women's achievement are no longer officially sanctioned; in relatively backward states, including the UK, European equal opportunities legislation rapidly swept aside local legal obstacles.

Ethnicity and race are a more problematic area. On the one hand, as we have seen, the formal outlawing of ethnic and racial discrimination preceded, and formed the model for, that of gender discrimination. Anti-racism was sometimes mocked for 'political correctness', but it was not systematically belittled and trivialized as feminism was. On the other hand, racism and 'racially' based disadvantage remain pervasive in all European societies, reinforced by a panic response to sporadic terrorism. Islam, the third great religion in Europe of Middle Eastern origin, is again an object of suspicion for many Europeans as it was in the heyday of Christianity. Such attitudes and prejudices continue to undermine any celebration of European achievements and of the project of European unification.

6 CONCLUSION: EUROPE IN ITS PLACE

It has been argued in this book that Europe needs to be put in its place in at least two senses. First, in its place in the world, which for too long it aspired to dominate. Here the demographic marginalization of Europe is beyond doubt (Therborn, 2004, 2006: 39–41; Outhwaite, 2006a: 153). 'In 1900 Europe housed a quarter of the world's population, in 2000 one-eighth, and in 2050 it is predicted to harbour only one-fifteenth of the human beings of the earth' (Therborn, 2006: 39). The European population is also ageing:

> By 2000, there were already more people aged 65 and older than there were children under 15 in Japan, and in Germany, Greece, Italy and Spain. In 2015 this seems likely to be the case over the whole of Europe. (Therborn, 2006: 40)

The implications for Europe's place in world production are not perhaps so clear, though one may expect it to decline. Geopolitically, European hegemony until the mid-twentieth century was followed by the bipolar opposition between a European/Asian superstate, the USSR, and a former European settler colony, the USA, and their respective 'allies'.[1] The demise of the Soviet Union in 1991 has not yet given rise to a lasting alternative pattern. US hegemony is probably not politically or economically sustainable, but the likely future configuration of the current second-rate powers (Russia, China, the EU, etc.) is not yet clear.

To treat the EU as something like a state in this way is to problematize Europe in a second sense, in which the project of European integration has not yet found its place among a variety of alternative national, regional and global projects. One of these is of course Gillingham's radical downgrading of the EU to an intergovernmental association – something which is not inconceivable, however unlikely. At the opposite extreme is the suggestion that the EU might transform itself into a much larger organization, encompassing the whole of the affluent world and perhaps even most or all of the world as a whole. In between these alternatives, there are a number of intermediate possibilities. Attali's notion, which now seems a little quaint, that the EU in its previous shape might itself become a member of a larger regional grouping, is one of these. Of the various ways to cooperate with Russia, huge in territory though no longer particularly large in population,[2] some sort of federation with the EU is perhaps as promising as many others. As Richard Sakwa (2006: 215) neatly puts it, Russia is 'too big to join the European Union but too important to be left out'. Another alternative is Steingart's suggestion of a free-trade area made up of the EU and NAFTA, united against the 'threat' from China and India. In this scenario, presumably, Russia and South America might jump either way, choosing to be poor Europeans with at least a US-level welfare state or, alternatively, relatively rich allies of Asia.

Behind these alternative scenarios of the political form of Europe is the more speculative question of what we take to be the identity, not of Europeans in various geographical and social locations across Europe, but of Europe itself. As we saw in chapter 2, the subcontinent has tended for the past few hundred years to be represented largely in terms of its North-Western core. The spread of this core has shifted from time to time, centred on Italy in the Renaissance, on France and Germany in the Enlightenment and on the North-West (Britain, Belgium, Northern France and

North-West Germany) in the long nineteenth century of industrialization. Following the Second World War, the East–West polarity was dominant in Europe and in the world as a whole; the process of European integration was begun in the Carolingian core, spreading eventually, in 1981, as far East as Greece but still with a discernibly 'Western' emphasis.

Only with 2004 and the subsequent Eastern enlargements did Europe's predominant political structure become more or less co-extensive with the subcontinent as a whole. Whatever political delays may intervene, the extension of the EU to cover the Western Balkans, Belarus, Ukraine, Moldova and Turkey is firmly on the agenda. This means that Europe has become post-Western in at least two senses: an obvious one in which its political expression is no longer confined to the West of the continent, even if its main political institutions remain located in a small corner of the North-West; the second, more interesting, sense in which Europe may now be thought of as post-Western is that a Europe which stretches politically so far to the East is also inevitably shaped by its links to points further East still. The EU already borders directly on a part of Russia, and Russia in turn borders on Japan. If the borders of Turkey become part of the borders of an enlarged EU, it will border on Syria, Iraq, Iran and the former Soviet republics (and likely candidates for EU membership) of Georgia and Armenia, to which we should probably add nearby Azerbaidjan. A Europe configured politically in this way is no longer only European, but politically as well as geographically part of Eurasia. It also, of course, has historical and ongoing links with Africa, both Northern and Central/Southern.

It is of course in Russia that the idea of Eurasia has been most fully explored, from the early nineteenth century to the present. Much of this discussion is best left to historians and to those with a particular interest in the fringes of contemporary Russian politics. As Richard Sakwa (2006: 215) has shown, however, it raises issues of cosmopolitanism which are or should be at the centre of European thinking.

In geographical and cultural terms Russia appears to have an innate cosmopolitanism in that its very existence refutes narrow definitions of East and West, Europe and Asia, nation-state and empire, modernity and backwardness. Russia's multiple identities transcend dominant narratives of what it means to be 'Western', while not always sure of the nature of the alternative that it seeks to embody.

This is not just a Russian problem, since Russia's uneasy relation to cosmopolitanism is paralleled by that of the EU (Outhwaite, 2006c). Sakwa (2006: 222) cites the foreign policy-maker Sergei Karaganov, for whom relations with Europe are central. On the one hand, 'A new post-European civilisation, and the first relatively successful pro-totype of world government, are taking shape today.' On the other hand, 'Russia was moving towards the Europe of De Gaulle, Churchill and Adenauer, and when it got closer, it saw the Europe of the Brussels bureaucracy and political correctness.'

Many Europeans further West would of course share these sentiments. In the case of the former Soviet Union, Sakwa (2006: 226) concludes:

> Russia is already a microcosm of a cosmopolitan state, and the nation-state may not be the natural political community in Eurasia . . . The innate features of cosmopolitanism mediate between traditional state building and the transformation of international relations in Eurasia and beyond.

Despite the uniqueness of the Russian situation, it has rel-evance to Europe as a whole. The other former communist countries in the European Union have also seen their eastern outlook fundamentally transformed. Migration, which used to mean almost exclusively the departure of their own citizens to the West, now denotes substantial flows of transitory or permanent immigrants from Asia and elsewhere. As noted earlier, these countries have moved from being the West of the East to being the East of the West: their own political future is settled (barring accidents), while that of Russia and the Middle East is, to say the least, not.

Europeanization, then, as Gerard Delanty and Chris Rumford (2005) understand it, is a broad social process, located in a context of modernity, globalization and cosmopolitanism. The Europe which is emerging is in a sense post-European in its increasingly circumscribed place in the world, its hybrid diversity and openness, just as the EC/EU extends beyond its relatively homogeneous Central Carolingian heartland on an Eastern trajectory which has no obvious end-point this side of Vladivostok. The EU is of course a major part of the story, but it is not, as Delanty and Rumford insist, the whole story.

And to be a European is not to be a Français(e), Deutsche(r) or Brit writ large, just as the emergent EU polity is not a replay on a grander scale of Italian or German unification. A polity, Delanty and Rumford stress, is not the same as a state: 'defined as the institutional structure of a political community through which society constitutes itself ... it does not presume a unity between territory, society and political organisation'. This more abstract conceptualization fits a corresponding model of European society which must be seen in the cosmopolitan terms of international society and world society (Delanty and Rumford, 2005: 161). This in turn, the authors suggest, implies rethinking the concept of civil society, where this is seen as a domain of associational life relatively independent of state apparatuses and market processes: 'The dominant approach to viewing European civil society, which sees it either as the aggregation of national civil societies or the pet project of a European supra-state, is ... deeply flawed' (Delanty and Rumford, 2005: 180–1). To say that Europe has to be seen as a world region might seem obvious enough, but there remains a long-standing dislocation between a literature in International Relations (and its elder sister, Sociology) focusing on global processes, and a European Studies literature relatively isolated from these concerns. A theory of European society (Delanty and Rumford, 2005: 154; Outhwaite, 2006a: chapter 8), must do justice to the interpenetration of the local, the national and the global, in Europe as elsewhere.

What are we to compare Europe with? As we saw in chapter 1, it is traditional to stress the diversity of Europe, though compared to Asia, as Therborn (2006: 28ff.) notes, it is in fact relatively homogeneous. Within Europe, as Colin Crouch (1999: 404–5) has pointed out, in relation to the North–South divide:

> it is notable that it is the 'northern' Europe of the welfare state, muted social inequalities, and rather regulated capitalism that most contrasts with contemporary North America. However, these are the very parts of Europe that in other respects most resemble the USA: for example, a high level of general education, technological sophistication, increasingly egalitarian gender relations. The Southern Europe that contrasts with the USA on these points is more similar to the latter country on questions of social inequality, weak welfare state development, and relatively small manufacturing sectors.

The point is of more general application. We tend to compare Europe with the US, but in some ways we should be looking also at the other export-European societies of America and Australasia to see, for example, the mutations of European practices of political mobilization. It is useful to see, as Sombart (1976 [1906]) asked, why there is no socialism in the United States, but also why there *is* in Canada, Latin America and Australia.

Within Europe, there are clearly tendencies both towards homogenization and to differentiation and division, which are probably best analysed according to models of regional development within states. The European Union is inevitably a terrain par excellence of unintended consequences or perverse effects, such as the way a policy which aimed to preserve small-scale agriculture also channelled funds to highly capitalized agri-business. Policies of this kind often seem to produce paradoxical outcomes: even if Western Europe *had* launched a serious Marshall Plan II in the 1990s, it is not impossible that it would have had the same perverse effects as the massive transfers from West to East

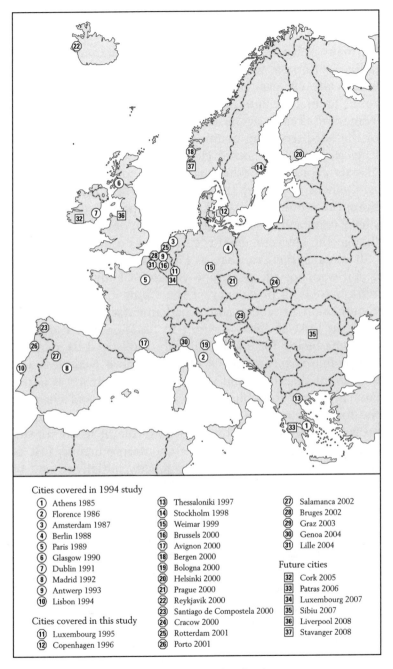

Cities covered in 1994 study

1. Athens 1985
2. Florence 1986
3. Amsterdam 1987
4. Berlin 1988
5. Paris 1989
6. Glasgow 1990
7. Dublin 1991
8. Madrid 1992
9. Antwerp 1993
10. Lisbon 1994

Cities covered in this study

11. Luxembourg 1995
12. Copenhagen 1996

13. Thessaloniki 1997
14. Stockholm 1998
15. Weimar 1999
16. Brussels 2000
17. Avignon 2000
18. Bergen 2000
19. Bologna 2000
20. Helsinki 2000
21. Prague 2000
22. Reykjavik 2000
23. Santiago de Compostela 2000
24. Cracow 2000
25. Rotterdam 2001
26. Porto 2001

27. Salamanca 2002
28. Bruges 2002
29. Graz 2003
30. Genoa 2004
31. Lille 2004

Future cities

32. Cork 2005
33. Patras 2006
34. Luxembourg 2007
35. Sibiu 2007
36. Liverpool 2008
37. Stavanger 2008

Map 6.1 European cities and capitals of culture
Source: Online at: <http://ec.europa.eu/culture/eac/sources_info/ studies/pdf_part1.pdf> p. 234

Germany. What this means for a serious social and regional policy in Europe, which at present of course hardly exists, is radically unclear. Much depends on whether Europeans come to migrate internally as freely as North Americans. There are already significant flows of retirement migration to the Mediterranean countries, as documented by Russell King and others. Another clear trend is to the promotion of state capitals and other major cities to world city status, symbolized in part by the EU's increasingly eclectic list of European cultural capitals. Air travel is projected to grow to a level comparable with North American domestic networks, though the environmental costs may put a brake on this.

It remains the case that, as Henry Kissinger complained, if you want to talk to Europe you don't know who to call. With a rotating presidency of the Council, a marginalized Commission president and a parliamentary system which tends, at least at election times, to function as a European sounding-board for local political conflicts, it is perhaps remarkable that the EU is not even more leaderless and incoherent than it is. And yet it moves, and grows: as in the French Fourth Republic, apparent instability and chaos at the top can coexist with considerable stability and gradual progress underneath. A too vigorous attempt to coordinate and centralize might indeed be counterproductive, just as some of the EU's cultural and publicity initiatives tend to over-reach themselves (and are deliberately watered down in more Eurosceptical regions such as the UK).

The question which has not perhaps been asked often enough is what would have happened to Europe over the past half-century if it had not embarked on the integration project and had remained a site of intergovernmental cooperation under the umbrella of NATO and the Council of Europe.[3] Alan Milward's term 'rescue' suggests a rather drastic alternative if the rescue had not taken place; perhaps a better term might be recovery, though in the sense of EuropAssistance for a stalled car rather than resuscitation. The Second World War, it seems safe to say, would not have re-started; to that extent the founding fathers of European integration, like the proverbial generals, were indeed fighting the previous war (in this case against it). Economically, the costs of 'non-Europe' are impossible to calculate reliably, since even the costs and benefits of the common currency are controversial. And this is anyway surely beside the point. European integration seems, to me at least, a politically worthwhile project in a region where an alternative or complementary project, that of socialism, seems to have run into the sand or, to put it more complacently, stretched out for a time on the relatively comfortable sand of the European social model and a reasonable level of affluence.

The integration project is of course flawed and suspect in many ways. The US midwife's motives were suspect; the EU's neo-liberal economic agenda has always sat uneasily with its centrist political corporatism; its unconcern for the economic consequences in the rest of the world of an anyway misconceived agricultural policy were hidden behind the fig-leaf of a very modest development policy (Karagiannis, 2004). For all this, however, the emergent European polity remains, I think, an exceptionally promising cosmopolitan political project in a part of the world which developed an attractive political theory of cosmopolitanism, as well as a number of practices catastrophically at odds with it. The incoherence of current European policy in the world is partly, of course, the result of Europe's structurally uncoordinated state, but also of a self-limiting modesty grounded in experience. Here too, as well as in its internal social and political organization, Europe's most realistic, most effective and most attractive future may be something like a Scandinavian one. From Rome to, say, Stockholm is not so far, even when you have to go via Brussels.

NOTES

CHAPTER 1   EUROPEAN CULTURE AND SOCIETY

1   Norman Davies (1996), for example, rightly criticizes the Western bias of many histories.

2   See however Teschke (2003) for a critical assessment of the myths associated with the Peace of Westphalia.

3   As Beck and Grande (2005: 282–3) have noted, the contrast between Francis Fukuyama's peaceful vision of the end of history in a convergence towards European- and US-style liberal democracy and Samuel Huntington's alarming fantasy of a 'clash of civilizations' in many ways replays the Valladolid conference of 1550, between universalistic inclusionism (they too can become Christians) and particularistic rejection of the 'savages'.

4   As Peter Calvacoressi (1991: 17) wrote, 'German industrialists were casting around for *Ergänzungsräume*, supplementary zones of economic activity such as Great Britain and France had acquired by colonization beyond Europe ... *Ergänzungsräume* became *Lebensraum*: the latter term, with its additional demographic implications, appeared in serious academic parlance about 1900.'

5   Similarly, in a review of Kwame Anthony Appiah's book, *In My Father's House: Africa in the Philosophy of Culture*, Richard Rorty writes that Appiah insists 'that "African culture" is the name of an important project rather than of an available datum'. This is also of course a problem for so-called national

cultures. Cf. Theodor Adorno (1985), Walter Abish's novel, *How German is it?* (1983), and James Donald, 'How English is it?', in Donald (1992).

6 As Therborn (2002: 293–4) writes, in a comparative discussion of flows of people, ideas and so on in Europe and East Asia: 'Over the past 500–600 years, Europe has been more open to intercontinental flows than East Asia ... and in the last 500 years Europe has been the initiator of many intercontinental flows.'

7 For a historical and critical discussion of this concept as applied to Europe, see Müller (2004).

8 Interestingly, this aspect of European culture was already stressed by Machiavelli; see Hay (1957: 122). Göran Therborn (1995) has good material on these issues.

CHAPTER 2   EUROPE: EAST, WEST, NORTH, SOUTH

1 Somewhat Eurocentrically referred to by Braudel (1987: 338) as 'les Europe d'Amérique qui en découlent directement'.

2 The expression was invented by Peter Schneider in 1982, in his classic novel *Der Mauerspringer*, in which he correctly predicted that it would take longer to demolish than the visible wall (Schneider, 1982: 117; see also Neller, 2006).

3 As Étienne Balibar (2004: 24–5) has suggested, 'we should resist the illusion of believing ... that some national traditions are open, tolerant, and "universalist" by "nature" or on account of their "exceptionality", whereas others, still by virtue of their nature or historical specificity, are intolerant and "particularist"'. Balibar was referring to national traditions and to their attitudes to foreigners, but the point has a more general application.

4 It should be noted that the term 'Occidentalism' has an entirely different meaning. It is modelled on Said's concept of Orientalism and has been used to refer to similar attitudes of suspicion and contempt, this time directed at the 'West' (see Carrier, 1995; Buruma and Margalit, 2004; Delanty, 2006b: 268).

5 Russia's land empire was, as noted earlier, a classic case of European 'internal colonialism', the securing of control over peripheries.

6   For a related line of argument, made with special reference to the Spanish context, see Pollack (2000).

7   This figure was a current estimate of the likely cost of enlargement; the European Currency Unit (ECU) is of course the forerunner of the euro. See also Outhwaite (2006).

8   In the event, of course, Turkish entry was further delayed, and Romania and Bulgaria entered alone in 2007. On further impending accessions, see also, for example, Bechev (2005).

9   In a much more critical approach to this question, Böröcz and Sarkar (2005) see the EU as in some ways a continuation of Western European colonialism in another context.

10 See Stockmann (2005: 45); there is a fuller discussion of political generations in Germany in Blech (1995) and Arzheimer (2006).

11 Sweden, with its substantial industry from the nineteenth century onwards, is of course something of an exception. More fundamentally, as Colin Crouch (1999: 405) points out, 'the central core of Western Europe can neither be allocated to north or south nor be turned into a region of its own. This analytical difficulty is caused by the complex politico-religious histories of France and Germany, the distinctive patterns of the smaller countries of the region, and the unusual position of the UK.'

12 As it was called by John Le Carré (1968).

13 As Therborn (1995: 189, 194–5) notes, this 'city belt' roughly corresponds to the Lotharingian centre of the Carolingian Empire in the middle of the ninth century.

14 EU propaganda tries to disguise this by listing the most obscure agencies along with the main institutions.

15 See, for example, Pridham (2005); Grabbe (2006); Schimmelfennig (2007). A book edited by Mary Kaldor and Ivan Vejvoda, including contributions from most postcommunist countries in Europe (Kaldor and Vejvoda, 1999) is an early example of an attempt to address issues of the *quality* of political democratization.

16 The Gini coefficient measures the percentage difference between a hypothetical model of perfect equality (the Lorenz curve) and actual income inequality – so higher Gini coefficients indicate greater income inequality.

17 The postcommunist region displays, in a particularly interesting way, some of the difficulties of causal analysis in history

and the other social sciences, as I hope to show in future work.

CHAPTER 3   THE EUROPEAN ECONOMY

1   In the terminology of Bernard Chavance (1999) and regula-
    tion theory, they are salary-money systems (SMS). See also
    Motamed-Nejad (1999b).
2   The new member-states are of course, with the exception of
    Poland, all small or very small; the 2004 entrants made up a
    mere 16 per cent of the enlarged Union's population, and only
    5 per cent of its GDP. All new members are expected in due
    course to join the Eurozone, with only Denmark, Sweden and
    the UK allowed to remain outside indefinitely.
3   As Johann Arnason (2005a: 230) notes, 'it was only after the
    disappearance of anti-capitalist challenges that the question
    of variations within the capitalist universe became acute'.
    There had, however, been earlier analyses along the same
    lines; Schmidt (2002) cites in particular Shonfield (1965) and
    Katzenstein (1978).
4   More precisely, he associates 'alpine' with monetary policy in
    the extended D-Mark zone including Austria and Switzerland,
    and 'Rhenish' with the Germany of Bonn, the postwar federal
    capital and the site of the Social Democratic Party's conver-
    sion in 1959 to an accommodation with capitalism. On Japan
    and Germany, see also Yamamura and Streeck (2003).
5   See also his table 5, p. 22. Boyer earlier (p. 5) refers to 'at
    least four forms of capitalism . . . for the OECD countries'
    and notes in his conclusion (p. 38) that 'This spectrum is still
    widening with the transformation of former Soviet-type econ-
    omies in Eastern Europe and in China'. He also points to the
    possibility of a model with thirty-two variations derived from
    the five institutional forms identified by regulation theory
    (p. 13; see also the useful summary on p. 7).
6   Although Boyer includes Ireland here, it is actually quite
    distinct in many respects from the English-speaking pattern,
    which itself is of course diverse.
7   On more detailed aspects of this, see recent work by Daniel
    Cohen (1999) and Richard Sennett (1998). In Sennett's anal-
    ysis, 'perfectly viable businesses are gutted or abandoned,

capable employees are set adrift rather than rewarded, simply because the organization must prove to the market that it is capable of change'.

8   Norway is included in the continental countries rather than, as one might expect, the Nordic social democratic cluster, because of a relatively distinctive position on each of the five dimensions (table 5.1, p. 173). Thus, although initially it seems closer to the social democratic model, the conjunction of them puts it closer to continental Europe (pp. 180–1). Amable (2003: 20) is undecided whether to include the Netherlands and Switzerland in continental Europe or to give them another, sixth, grouping.

9   Some authors include France in the Southern or Mediterranean category, either, like Schmidt (2002), because of the active economic role historically played by the state or, like Rhodes and van Apeldoorn (1997), on the basis of patterns of 'corporate governance', where this includes ownership structures, the role of banks and the composition of management boards (see Amable, 2003: 82). Within the Iberian peninsula, there are important differences in gender and youth employment between Portugal and Spain, deriving from the last years of the Portuguese colonial empire in Africa and the resultant shortage of young men conscripted into the army or migrating abroad to escape this. My thanks to Jacqueline O'Reilly for drawing my attention to this.

10   Amable selects a larger than usual number of dimensions; other analyses tend to concentrate on financial systems and labour markets (Deeg and Jackson, 2006: 8).

11   See also Pollack (2000).

12   As Perraton and Clift (2006: 9) write, 'The 1980s and 1990s did indeed see far-reaching policies of privatization and financial deregulation with the consequent abandonment of much of the earlier industrial policy. However, these changes were designed in detail by state authorities.'

13   See also Streeck and Thelen (2005).

14   Amable (2003: 158–9) helpfully presents a comparison of his own welfare models with others in the literature. See also, for a useful overview, Hemerijck et al. (2006).

15   See also Goodin and Le Grand (1987).

16   As Castles (2004: 40) notes, 'by 1988, Southern Europe, in general, was committing more resources to social purposes

than the English-speaking world'. See also Obinger et al. (2005), for a comparative study of Denmark, Austria, Switzerland and New Zealand.

17   See also Giddens, Diamond and Liddle (2006). For a critique of the state's more intrusive approach to the unemployed, see however Gray (2004).

18   A relatively early exception, still worth consulting, is a volume based on a conference held in 1998: Chavance et al. (1999).

19   This raises of course an exceptionally interesting historical counterfactual: what if the transition had taken place twenty years earlier, when Fordism was still a going concern and neo-liberalism had not taken root, or ten years later, when its impact has been somewhat softened? (See Bohle, 1999: 10.)

20   This form of privatization, initiated in Czechoslovakia by Vaclav Klaus, gave shares in enterprises to the workforce or to outsiders (for a detailed discussion, see Kosta, 1997).

21   For a particularly illuminating sceptical discussion of Russia, which has more general application, see Clarke (1993).

22   David Lane (2006: 31) takes a similar view: 'GDP recovery . . . is not very strongly related to the extent of the private sector or privatization'.

23   The same process can be seen within states such as Italy. These networks may of course be mobilized in an economically effective way, as Bagnasco described in the Italan case.

24   For a more detailed discussion, see Thumfart (2002), esp. pp. 433–588.

25   On Estonia, see, for example, Buchen (2006), who in fact goes so far as to describe it as 'a case of a liberal market economy'.

26   Lane's sub-division here is close to, though not identical with, that between the 2004 accession states and those lined up for accession in 2007.

27   Motamed-Nejad (1999b) is a useful exception to this tendency.

28   This reminder is superfluous for readers interested in London football clubs.

29   In its original Western incarnation, it combined this with detailed case studies of firms. In the East, such work tends to be found in Marxist ethnographic studies such as Michael Burawoy's superb work of participant observation (Burawoy and Krotov, 1993).

30 On this, see, for example, Blyth (2003: 270–2).
31 On the term Europeanization, see Cowles, Caporoso and Risse (2001); Schmidt (2006).
32 For a fuller discussion of the classical theory of convergence, see Outhwaite and Ray (2005), chapter 3.
33 Nick von Tunzelmann (1999), in the same volume, differentiates in his account of postwar growth in Europe between West, North, South and East and presents his material comparatively between the first three. This approach, which shows up some important differences, is less common than one might expect in the literature.
34 See Smith et al. (2000).
35 These things change: as the US economist Paul Samuelson said to Steingart (2006: 383; my translation), with the honesty of a ninety-one-year-old, 'If you had come to me in 1945 and asked me which part of the world will grow fastest, I would without hesitation have said Chile and Argentina . . .'

CHAPTER 4   THE EUROPEAN POLITY

1 Tilly (1992: 116) suggests that separatist nationalism of a kind 'ran throughout European history, whenever and wherever rulers of a given religion or language conquered people of another religion or language. Nationalism in the sense of heightened commitment to a state's international strategy appeared rarely before the nineteenth century, and then chiefly in the heat of war.'
2 Foreshadowed by the doctrine, announced by Khrushchev, that the Soviet state no longer represented the dictatorship of the proletariat but was a 'state of the whole people' (всенародное).
3 'Mensonge par pléonasme', as Raymond Aron neatly described the term.
4 Moscow politely declined a Bulgarian posposal that the country might become a republic of the Soviet Union.
5 In East Germany, for example, as well as the communist party (SED) and its subsidiary party for West Berlin (SEW), there was a party for Christians, one for liberals, one for farm workers, and even one for old nationalists – all linked with the communists in a coalition known as the National Front.

These 'block parties' were known sarcastically as the block flutes, because they played the same tune.

6 The intensity of this control was of course different in different societies.

7 Mark Neocleous (2003) has beautifully mapped the state images of body, mind, personality and home.

8 The same is of course true of industrialization and the development of an industrial working class in Europe; see, for example, Moore (1978).

9 Charles Tilly (1975: 636), summarizing his classic edited collection, notes 'the existence in Europe . . . of two large processes of state formation, and the gradual shift from one toward the other. The first is the extension of the power and range of a more or less autonomous political unit . . . [he cites Brandenburg-Prussia, France, England and Spain as examples] . . . [and] a second large process, consisting of the more or less deliberate *creation* of new states by existing states'. The second process, he notes, can take place in either direction: the emergence of new states out of larger ones (Portugal, Netherlands, Yugoslavia, Czechoslovakia) and the consolidation of several states into a larger one (Germany, Italy). In both cases, he stresses, there will be a combination of internal forces (such as national liberation movements) and the intervention or acquiescence of external states. In a later book, Tilly (1992: 12, 159–60) criticizes this emphasis on the model status of Britain, France and Brandenburg-Prussia, on the grounds that they constitute an intermediate path between a capital-intensive pattern of state development, represented by Venice, and a coercion-intensive one represented by Moscow/Saint Petersburg. But from a presentist perspective the pattern still holds.

10 This conception seems to be supported in the German case by Article 21 of the *Grundgesetz*, the Basic Law or Constitution, and, more recently, by the 'party law' of 2004, which begins with a functionalist definition of the role of parties: 'Parties are a constitutionally necessary component of the free and democratic basic order. With their free and lasting participation in the people's political will-formation they fulfil a public task prescribed for them by the Basic Law and guaranteed by it' (quoted in 'Parteiensystem der Bundesrepublik Deutschland', *Informationen zur politischen Bildung* 292, 2006;

my translation). It is of course possible that a trawl through comparable sources in the other countries would yield similar general statements.

11 Gaullist and post-Gaullist France has had a two-round run-off system for most of its history, except for a brief experiment with proportional representation.

12 The term was popularized by Gerhard Lehmbruch (see Czada, 2006).

13 This is reflected in some postcommunist Constitutions, such as those of Bulgaria and Hungary, which 'explicitly state that . . . no state party or ideology should be allowed' (Elster et al., 1998: 93). In the West, Spain is an example of the persistence of unresolved issues from the Civil War and the fascist dictatorship, marked in particular by the exhumation, in the early years of the twenty-first century, of victims of local pogroms.

14 Schöpflin (2003: 287) writes of 'The desert left by communism . . . ideas and values that make the smooth functioning of democracy problematical.' As he notes, p. 286, the new rulers tended to overestimate what could be expected of the bureaucracy, then turning in their disappointment to inexperienced political allies.

15 The eight postcommunist countries acceding in 2004, plus Romania and Bulgaria. The prospect of EU membership, as well as the conditionality of (other forms of) Western aid, was of course an important element in reconciling populations to the hardships of transition. For a more internal explanation in terms of a 'low-level equilibrium' between transformation in the economic and political spheres, see Greskovitz (1998).

16 Zielonka (2006: 38–43) concedes that things are less rosy in the other postcommunist countries.

17 Although Western liberal parties of the latter kind, like the German FDP, never really got anywhere, even with the help of a proportional system and a decentralized federal state, the British Conservatives are currently trying out a relatively centrist approach.

18 There are interesting echoes here of the reconciliation of social democrats with the actually existing welfare state, or of state socialist ideologues in the 1970s with 'developed' socialist society.

19   I wrote these lines on New Year's Day 2007, as Bulgaria and Romania had just joined the EU and Slovenia adopted the euro.

20   'Realism', of course, in the International Relations sense of power politics.

21   As Spence and Stevens point out, this fact also of course qualifies any counter-claims emphasizing the small size of the Commission.

22   The most substantial challenge came from the German Federal Constitutional Court, which had previously been the supreme legal authority and the guardian of the German Rechtsstaat – a role which of course it retains except where EU law has priority.

23   'National partisan politics has been marginalized. Ministers speak in the Council more in the name of the national interest than for governmental majorities. Members of the EP speak more in terms of the public interest than for electoral majorities. Citizens have more influence in Brussels when lobbying as organized interests than when voting or protesting in national capitals' (Schmidt, 2006: 2).

24   See, for example, the Norwegian Study of Power and Democracy, part of a larger series of Nordic studies, at: <www.sv.uio.no/mutr/english/index.html>.

25   As noted earlier, the UK now has substantial devolution to Scotland and to a lesser extent to Wales, and the Blair government reversed Thatcher's abolition of metropolitan institutions in London and elsewhere. Its political style however remains essentially unitary, reinforced by a strongly majoritarian voting system in which coalitions have historically been rare. This may of course be about to change.

26   The details of Schmidt's analysis of her four states do not concern us here, but her concluding recommendations give a flavour of it. 'The French need to rethink their vision of leadership in Europe . . . given that they know that France no longer leads Europe, are in crisis over national identity, and increasingly blame EU "neoliberalism" for their economic problems. The British need to develop a vision of Britain in Europe, given that the discourse of economic interest does not respond to growing concerns about sovereignty and identity, while the idea of British separateness in Europe could very well lead to

the reality of British separation from Europe ... The Germans need to update their vision of "German-as-European" in light of the changes related to unification and fading memories of World War II, especially since they increasingly question the benefits of membership and worry about the EU's impact on the social market economy. The Italians ... need to concern themselves not so much with their vision of Italy in Europe as with their implementation of European rules in Italy, since their pride in being European is likely to suffer as a result of the fact that the EU "rescue of the nation-state" is no longer enough to rescue the nation-state.'

27   The book is also a superb guide through recent literature on the EU.

28   As they note, the German Constitutional Court called the EU a *Staatenverbund*, in a somewhat desperate neologism.

29   See the collective volume by Beck, Giddens and Lash (1994).

30   See, in particular, chapter 2, section 3. Among the divisions transcended or at least relativized is that between domestic social policy and European regional policy: 'regional policy becomes European social policy' (p. 271).

31   Schmidt's analysis, though less radical, is essentially complementary to this. She writes: 'Currently, there is no consensus to increase democratic legitimacy by shifting government *by* and *of* the people to the EU level through the direct election of EU leaders or EU-wide parliamentary elections – nor would this necessarily help democratize the EU, given the lack of a collective identity or will. But this means that democratic reforms of the EU still focus mainly on improving governance *for* the people, through greater accountability and transparency, and *with* the people, through more interest-based access and a greater opening to "civil society". This does little to decrease the fragmentation of EU democracy as a whole.'

32   As David Bailey (2006) points out, studies of European integration might benefit from paying more attention to critical state theory, drawn from, among other sources, Marx and Foucault, which has consistently addressed contradictions generated by forms of governance themselves and what have been called 'crises of crisis management'.

33   More recently, see Crouch (2004).

CHAPTER 5   SOCIAL DIVISIONS AND SOCIAL IDENTITIES

1   There were, for example, some North Vietnamese *Gastarbeiter* in East Germany and small numbers of students from outside Europe. The situation in the multi-ethnic and multinational Soviet Union was of course very different.

2   For an example of large-scale criminality in postcommunism, see Outhwaite and Ray (2005: 80–5). Scandals such as the Bulgarian one described there are perhaps more common the further East one goes, but they are by no means confined to the East and South of Europe. In the Transparency International index of perceived corruption (Transparency International 2002: <www.gwdg.de>), which admittedly refers more to low-level bribery, Bulgaria appears around the middle of a scale of 101 states (the others excluded for reasons of inadequate data), and slightly less corrupt than Poland, Latvia and the Czech and Slovak Republics. It is in the nature of processes of criminalization and decriminalization like the Bulgarian case that they are hard to estimate, but we should note that it is not just money that can be laundered, but also economic and other elites and entire branches of economic enterprise. It is easy to distinguish analytically between a virtuous spiral of decriminalization of previously criminal activities and personnel, as can be traced in the history of the United States and other advanced capitalist countries, and a downward spiral of increasing criminalization. What is less easy is to judge the relative importance of the two components of this double helix and the overall trend. For Central and Eastern Europe (with the exception of parts of former Yugoslavia) we might be optimistic, whereas for Russia and most of the former Soviet Union the picture is a good deal less clear.

3   Any such bourgeoisie is likely to be a parasitic, *rentier* class rather than an entrepreneurial one (cf. Eyal et al., 1998: 171–3). There were of course important differences within the communist bloc in Europe. Poland had substantially private agriculture and a sizeable private sector, as did Hungary. Czechoslovakia, by contrast, had neither. There are also substantial differences in the transitional period. Some postcommunist economies were immediately thrown open to external investment (GDR, Hungary); others presented very considerable obstacles to it (most of Russia). In some, privatization

was not much more than a slogan; in others it described a major revolutionary process. The internal differentiation of the former bloc, to some extent papered over during the communist period, became a major theme as soon as the dust of 1989 had settled. The Visegrad group of Hungary, Poland and Czechoslovakia, arising from a meeting in early 1991, already grounded its original programme of cooperation by stressing the similarity between the (then) three relatively advanced countries and by implication their distinctness from the rest of the former bloc (Declaration of February 1991). The EU enlargement of May 2004 reinforced these differences.

4   The subtitle of Moore's classic book, *Social Origins of Dictatorship and Democracy*, is: 'lord and peasant in the making of the modern world'.

5   As the authors of a classic report (World Bank, 2002: 72–3) put it, 'Navigating between continued state ownership with eroding control rights and a transfer to ineffective private owners with an inadequate institutional framework is possibly one of the most difficult challenges confronting policymakers in charge of privatization.'

6   This is not of course to deny the very substantial differences between Western societies (for a good discussion, see Bottomore and Brym, 1989).

7   Putnam's work has been enormously influential in discussions of/in postcommunist Europe (see, in particular, Kolankiewicz, 1996). One recent example among many is a study by Badescu and Sum (2005) comparing social capital in Transylvania with that in the rest of Romania. Transylvanians score higher on measures of social capital and certain aspects of social trust.

8   János Kenedi's *Do it Yourself* (1981) is a hilarious account of his eye-opening experiences when he decided to build himself a house in the Hungary of the 1970s.

9   King (2001) is an exceptionally useful study of Hungary, the Czech Republic and Slovakia, with some shrewd evaluations of the diversity of evidence for these theoretical models. He suggests that the aggregate differences between these countries can be best explained by differences in organization and legitimation in the late communist period (see, in particular, pp. 113–15).

10   They had emphasized (p.18) that the book 'focuses on the top of the social hierarchies . . . on . . . intra-class or . . . inter-elite

struggles. This does not imply that inter-class conflicts will not be of vital importance in shaping the characters of these societies. Rather, it is to say that in this historical conjuncture, where old class and elite constellations are dissolving, and new classes are not yet formed, looking at these inter-elite struggles is theoretically and historically justified.'

11 They go on (p. 189) to differentiate various kinds of habitus: apparatchik, technocrat, and ex-dissident intelligentsia (see below). For an interesting discussion of post-1945 and post-1989 reconstruction in Germany, based on the idea of imitation, see Jacoby (2000).

12 Small societies such as Ireland may retain place of origin as a significant attribute.

13 There are historical reasons for this, concerned with migration and colonial military service under the dictatorship. Thanks to Jacqueline O'Reilly for making this point.

14 Jonathan Hearn (2007) has written in this context of the routinization (in Max Weber's sense of Versachlichung) of nationalism.

15 As the Labour former Foreign Secretary Robin Cook (2005) put it, 'It is not difficult to identify what should be the core values of a party that belongs to the family of modern European social democracy. Top of anyone's list must come solidarity – the principle that the strength of a society is measured by the extent that its rich members support vulnerable fellow citizens.'

16 My translation.

17 He goes on to say that 'the consensus around the classical welfare state is no longer as solid as before'. I have here simplified a story which I discuss in more detail in a volume edited by Nathalie Karagiannis (Outhwaite, 2007). In particular, one should note that other analysts see state-supported welfare policy as a *substitute* for solidarity, as much as for uncoordinated acts of private charity). More technical and policy-oriented discussions of the welfare state tend to avoid the term solidarity, while more reflective commentators often use it as a way of marking out certain forms of welfare state from others. The historian Peter Baldwin (1990) differentiates between solidaristic, i.e. redistributive, and more limited welfare systems.

18 See also Balibar (2004).

19   Grundy and Jamieson found a striking difference both between their representative samples and their 'target' samples (those with experience of trans-European mobility) and between relatively central and peripheral regions of Europe. In Manchester and Edinburgh, for example, over half of the 'targets' expressed strong attachment to a European identity, as against around a third of the representative sample. In Central Europe, by contrast, these differences were not so pronounced and the overall level of interest in European integration was much higher (over 50 per cent for the representative sample in Austria, with no significant difference between Vienna and the rural Vorarlberg) as against barely a quarter in Bilbao, compared with over half in Madrid, and around a third in Manchester and Edinburgh. (The high figure for Austria is interesting, given that it also scores close to the UK for hostility to the European Union.) In both Spain and the UK, the target sample scored significantly higher. Czechs and Slovaks were much more likely to speak another European language and to have visited another European state – presumably not each other's (6.3).

20   That is, those who had engaged in some significant cross-European mobility activity such as a student exchange programme.

21   In Bilbao, they suggest, it is possible that 'lack of identification with a nation state had opened the way for a rhetorical use of supra-national identity, but not identification with an actual supra-national state, the European Union' (9.5). The Spanish state, they note, is also strongly associated with the EU; 'there is no equivalent discourse in Spain to the frequently produced alignment in the British media of both Englishness and Britishness with aloofness from Europe' (5.7). The qualitative dimension is addressed in, for example, some of Willfried Spohn's research for the EURONAT project; see Spohn (2001).

22   More precisely, the grounds for the attachment.

23   The 2002 figures for 'close or very close' attachment range from 72 per cent (in the Czech Republic) to 97 per cent. There is however more divergence for 'very close attachment', with Britain way down at 14 per cent, compared to Germany, the next lowest, in the high 20s, and Hungary top again at 66 per cent.

CHAPTER 6   CONCLUSION: EUROPE IN ITS PLACE

1   The allies of the US were of course sovereign states, with the partial exception of Germany, while those of the Soviet Union were subordinate to it.
2   On current projections, a Russia of 104 million in 2050 would not be so much bigger in *population* terms than a Turkey of 86 million. By then, of course, it may also have a majority of Muslims. See Therborn (2004, 2006).
3   The EU's failures are indeed mostly intergovernmental failures, in areas such as foreign and defence policy: its successes in areas where the Commission and the Court play a larger role.

BIBLIOGRAPHY

Abish, W. (1983) *How German is it?* London: Faber.

Adorno, Theodor (1985) 'On the Question: What is German?', *New German Critique* 36 (Fall): 121–31.

Ágh, Attila (1998) *Emerging Democracies in East Central Europe and the Balkans*. Cheltenham: Edward Elgar.

Albert, Michel (1993 [1991]) *Capitalisme contre capitalisme*. Tr. *Capitalism vs Capitalism*. New York: Four Walls Eight Windows.

Allen, Matthew (2004) 'The Varieties of Capitalism Paradigm: Not Enough Variety?', *Socio-Economic Review* 2/1 (Jan): 87–108.

Allum, P. (1995) *State and Society in Western Europe*. Cambridge: Polity.

Almond, Gabriel and Verba, Sidney (1963) *The Civic Culture*. Princeton: Princeton University Press.

Altvater, Elmer (1998) 'Theoretical Deliberations on Time and Space in Post-socialist Transformation', *Regional Studies* 32/7: 591–605.

Amable, Bruno (2003) *The Diversity of Modern Capitalisms*. Oxford: Oxford University Press.

Amin, Ash (2003) 'Multiethnicity and the Idea of Europe', *Theory, Culture and Society* 21/2: 1–24.

Amin, S. (1988) *L'Eurocentrisme: Critique d'une idéologie*. Paris: Anthropos. *Eurocentrism*. New York: Monthly Review Press and London: Zed Books, 1989.

Anderson, B. (1991 [1983]) *Imagined Communities: Reflections on the Origin and Spread of Nationalism*. London: Verso.

Anderson, James (1996) 'The Shifting Stage of Politics: New Medieval and Postmodern Territorialities?', *Environment and Planning D: Society and Space* 14/2: 133–53.

Anthias, Floya (2001) 'The Concept of "Social Division" and Theorising Social Stratification: Looking at Ethnicity and Class', *Sociology* 35/4: 835–54.

Archer, M. (1988) *Culture and Agency.* Cambridge: Cambridge University Press.

Arnason, Johann P. (1993) *The Future That Failed: Origins and Destinies of the Soviet Model.* London: Routledge.

Arnason, Johann P. (ed.) (2005a) *Special Issue: East Central European Perspectives, European Journal of Social Theory* 8/4 (November).

Arnason, Johann P. (2005b) 'East and West: From Invidious Dichotomy to Incomplete Deconstruction', in Gerard Delanty and Engin F. Isin (eds), *Handbook of Historical Sociology.* London: Sage, pp. 220–34.

Arnason, Johann P. (2006a) 'Civilizational Analysis, Social Theory and Comparative History', in Gerard Delanty (ed.), *Contemporary European Social Theory.* London: Routledge, pp. 230–41.

Arnason, Johann P. (2006b) 'Contested Divergence: Rethinking the "Rise of the West"', in Gerard Delanty (ed.), *Europe and Asia Beyond East and West.* London: Routledge, pp. 77–91.

Aron, R. (1958) *Dix-huit leçons sur la société industrielle.* Paris: Gallimard. Tr. M. K. Bottomore, *Eighteen Lectures on Industrial Society.* London: Weidenfeld and Nicolson, 1967.

Arzheimer, Kai (2006) 'Von "Westalgie" und "Zonenkindern". Die Rolle der jüngeren Generation im Prozess der Vereinigung', in J. W. Falter, O. W. Gabriel, H. Rattinger and H. Schoen (eds), *Sind wir ein Volk? Ost- und Westdeutschland im Vergleich.* Munich: Beck, pp. 212–34.

Asbach, Olaf (2002) 'Verfassung und Demokratie in der Europäischen Union. Zur Kritik der Debatte um eine Konstitutionalisierung Europas', *Leviathan* 30/2, June: 267–97.

Atkinson, M. and Elliott, L. (1999) 'Where the Jobs Will Be in the US of €', the *Guardian*, 13 Feb.: 26.

Attali, Jacques (1997) 'A Continental Architecture', in Peter Gowan and Perry Anderson (eds), *The Question of Europe.* London: Verso, pp. 345–84.

Auer, Stefan (2004) *Liberal Nationalism in Central Europe.* London: RoutledgeCurzon.

Aust, Stefan and Schmidt-Klingenberg, Michael (eds) (2003) *Experiment Europa. Ein Kontinent macht Geschichte.* Stuttgart/ Munich: Deutsche Verlags-Anstalt.

Avdagic, Sabina (2006) 'One Path or Several? Understanding the Varied Development of Tripartism in New European Capitalisms'. Cologne: MPIfG Discussion Paper 06/5.

Bachrach, Peter and Baratz, M. S. (1970) *Power and Poverty: Theory and Practice.* Oxford: Oxford University Press.

Bahro, Rudolf (1978 [1977]) *Die Alternative.* Frankfurt: Europäische Verlagsanstalt. Trans. by David Fernbach as *The Alternative in Eastern Europe.* London: New Left Books, 1978.

Bailey, David (2006) 'Governance or the Crisis of Governmentality? Applying Critical State Theory at the European Level', *Journal of European Public Policy* 13/1 (Jan.): 16–33.

Baldwin, Peter (1990) *The Politics of Social Solidarity: Class Bases of the European Welfare State, 1875–1975.* Cambridge: Cambridge University Press.

Baldwin, Peter (2005) 'Beyond Weak and Strong: Rethinking the State in Comparative Policy History', *The Journal of Policy History* 17/1: 12–33.

Bale, Tim (2003) 'Cinderella and Her Ugly Sisters: The Mainstream and the Extreme Right in Europe's Bipolarising Party Systems', *West European Politics* 26/3: 67–90.

Balibar, E. (2004 [2001]) *We, the People of Europe: Reflections on Transnational Citizenship.* Princeton: Princeton University Press.

Balibar, E. and Wallerstein, I. (1991) *Race, Nation, Class: Ambiguous Identities.* London: Verso.

Banton, Michael (1983) *Racial and Ethnic Competition.* Cambridge: Cambridge University Press.

Barone, Enrico (1908) 'Il Ministro della Produzione nello Stato Collettivista', *Giornale degli Economisti* 2 (Sept./Oct.): 267–93, trans. as 'The Ministry of Production in the Collectivist State', in F. A. Hayek (ed.) (1935), *Collectivist Economic Planning.* London: Routledge, pp. 245–90.

Barraclough, G. (1967 [1964]) *An Introduction to Contemporary History.* Harmondsworth: Penguin.

Bauman, Zygmunt (2004) *Europe: An Unfinished Adventure.* Cambridge: Polity.

Bayly, C. A. (2004) *The Birth of the Modern World 1780–1914.* Oxford: Blackwell.

Bechev, Dimitar (2005) 'EU and the Balkans: The Long and Winding Road to Membership', Opinion Piece, South East European Studies Programme, European Studies Centre, St Antony's College, Oxford.

Beck, Ulrich (1987) 'Beyond Status and Class: Will There Be an Individualized Class Society?', in Volker Meja, Dieter Misgeld and Nico Stehr (eds), *Modern German Sociology*. New York: Columbia University Press, pp. 340–55.

Beck, Ulrich (1992 [1986]) *Risk Society*. London: Sage.

Beck, Ulrich (2004) *Der kosmopolitische Blick*. Frankfurt: Suhrkamp. Trans. *The Cosmopolitan Vision*. Cambridge: Polity, 2006.

Beck, Ulrich and Grande, Edgar (2004) *Das kosmopolitische Europa*. Frankfurt: Suhrkamp. Trans. *Cosmopolitan Europe*. Cambridge: Polity, 2007.

Beck, Ulrich and Grande, Edgar (2007 [2005]) *Power in the Global Age: A New Global Political Economy*. Trans. Kathleen Cross. Cambridge: Polity.

Beck, Ulrich and Grande, Edgar (2007) 'Cosmopolitanism: Europe's Way out of Crisis', *European Journal of Social Theory* 10/1: 67–85.

Beck, Ulrich, Giddens, Anthony and Lash, Scott (1994) *Reflexive Modernization: Politics, Tradition and Aesthetics in the Modern Social Order*. Cambridge: Polity.

Berend, I. (1996) *Central and Eastern Europe, 1944–1993: Detour from the Periphery to the Periphery*. Cambridge: Cambridge University Press.

Bernal, M. (1987, 1991) *Black Athena: The Afroasiatic Roots of Classical Civilization*. 2 vols. London: Free Association.

Best, Geoffrey (ed.) (1988) *The Permanent Revolution: The French Revolution and its Legacy 1789–1989*. London: Fontana.

Bhabha, Homi (ed.) (1990) *Nation and Narration*. London: Routledge.

Bhambra, Gurminder K. (2007) *Rethinking Modernity*. Basingstoke: Palgrave.

Billig, Michael (1995) *Banal Nationalism*. London: Sage.

Blair, Tony and Schröder, Gerhard (1999) *Europe: The Third Way*, available online at: <http://www.socialdemocrats.org/blairandschroeder6-8-99.html#top>.

Blaut, J. M. (1993) *The Colonizer's View of the World: Geographical Diffusionism and Eurocentric History*. New York and London: The Guilford Press.

Blazyca, George (2002) 'EU Accession: The Polish Case', in Hilary and Mike Ingham (eds), *EU Expansion to the East: Prospects and Problems*. Cheltenham: Edward Elgar, pp. 205–21.

Blech, Klaus (1995) 'Germany Between East and West', *SAIS Review* 15: 23–38.

Bleich, Erik (2003) *Race Politics in Britain and France*. Cambridge: Cambridge University Press.

Blokker, Paul (2005) 'Populist Nationalism, Anti-Europeanism, Post-Nationalism, and the East–West Distinction', *German Law Journal* 6/2 (Feb.).

Blokker, Paul (2006) 'The Post-enlargement European Order: Europe "United in Diversity"?', *European Diversity and Autonomy Papers* – EDAP; 2006/1.

Blyth, Mark (2003) 'From Comparative Capitalism to Economic Constructivism: The Cornell Series in Political Economy', *New Political Economy* 8/2 (July): 263–74.

Bohle, Dorothee (1999) 'Der Pfad in die Abhängigkeit? Eine kritische Bewertung institutionalistischer Beiträge in der Transformationsdebatte', Discussion Paper FS 1 99–103, Wissenschaftszentrum Berlin für Sozialforschung.

Bohle, Dorothee and Greskovits, Béla (2005) 'Capital, Labor and the Prospects of the European Social Model in the East', *Central and Eastern Europe Working Paper 58*. Harvard: Center for European Studies.

Bohle, Dorothee and Greskovits, Béla (2007) 'Neoliberalism, Embedded Neoliberalism and Neocorporatism: Towards Transnational Capitalism in Central–Eastern Europe', *West European Politics* 30/3: 443–66.

Boltanski, Luc and Chiapello, Ève (1999) *Le nouvel esprit du capitalisme*. Paris: Gallimard. Trans. by Gregory Elliott as *The New Spirit of Capitalism*. London: Verso, 2005–2006.

Boltanski, Luc and Chiapello, Ève (2005) 'The Role of Criticism in the Dynamics of Capitalism. Social Criticism versus Artistic Criticism', in Max Miller (ed.), *Worlds of Capitalism: Institutions, Governance and Economic Change in the Era of Globalization*. London: Routledge, pp. 237–67.

Bonefeld, Werner (2005) 'Europe, the Market and the Transformation of Democracy', *Journal of Contemporary European Studies* 13/1, April: 93–106.

Bönker, Frank, Klaus Müller and Andreas Pickel (eds) (2002) *Postcommunist Transformation and the Social Sciences*. Lanham, MD: Rowman and Littlefield.

Bonnett, Alastair (2004) *The Idea of the West: Culture, Politics and History*. Basingstoke: Palgrave.

Bonoli, G. (1997) 'Classifying Welfare States: A Two Dimensional Approach', *Journal of Social Policy* 26/3: 351–72.

Böröcz, József and Kovás, Melinda (eds) (2001) *Europe's New Clothes: Unveiling EU Enlargement*. Telford: Central European Review (<http:www.ce–review.org/>).

Böröcz, József and Sarkar, Mahua (2005) 'What is the EU?', *International Sociology* 20: 153–73.

Bottomore, Tom and Brym, Robert (eds) (1989) *The Capitalist Class: An International Study*. New York and London: Harvester Wheatsheaf.

Bourdieu, Pierre (1983) 'The Three Forms of Capital', reprinted in A. H. Halsey, Phillip Brown and Amy Stuart Wells (eds), *Education: Culture, Economy, and Society*. Oxford: Oxford University Press, 1997, pp. 46–58. Page references are to this edition. Originally published in German, tr. Reinhard Kreckel, in Kreckel (ed.), *Soziale Ungleichheiten*. Göttingen: Schwarz.

Boyer, Robert (2005) 'Coherence, Diversity and Evolution of Capitalisms: The Institutional Complementarity Hypothesis', unpublished paper; see also Colin Crouch et al., 'Dialogue on "Institutional Complementarity and Political Economy"', *Socio-Economic Review* 3/2 (May 2005): 359–82.

Brague, Rémi (2002) *Eccentric Culture. A Theory of Western Civilization*. Trans. *Europe, La voie romaine*. South Bend, IN: St Augustine's Press.

Braudel, Fernand (1987 [1963]) *L'Europe*. New edn. Paris: Arts et metiers graphiques.

Brenner, Robert (2005) 'After Boom, Bubble and Bust: Where is the US Economy Going?', in Max Miller (ed.), *Worlds of Capitalism: Institutions, Governance and Economic Change in the Era of Globalization*. London: Routledge, pp. 200–34.

Brubaker, Rogers (1991) *Citizenship and Nationhood in France and Germany*. New York: University Press of America.

Brubaker, Rogers (1996) *Nationalism Reframed: Nationhood and the National Question in the New Europe*. Cambridge and New York: Cambridge University Press.

Brückner, Wolfgang (1987) 'Nord-Süd im kulturellen Selbstverständnis der Deutschen', in Hans-Georg Wehling (ed.), *Nord–Süd in Deutschland? Vorurteile und Tatsachen.* Stuttgart: Kohlhammer, pp. 11–28.

Bruszt, Laszlo and Stark, David (2003) 'Who Counts? Supranational Norms and Social Needs', *East European Politics and Societies* 17/1: 74–82.

Bruter, Michael (2005) *Citizens of Europe? The Emergence of a Mass European Identity.* Basingstoke: Palgrave.

Buchen, Clemens (2006) 'Estonia and Slovenia as Antipodes', in David Lane and Martin Myant (eds), *Varieties of Capitalism in Post-Communist Countries.* Basingstoke: Palgrave Macmillan, pp. 65–89.

Budge, I. and Newton, K. (eds) (1997) *The Politics of the New Europe.* London: Longman.

Burawoy, Michael (ed.) (2001) *Review Symposium, American Journal of Sociology*, special issue.

Burawoy, Michael and Krotov, Pavel (1993) 'The Soviet Transition from Socialism to Capitalism: Worker Control and Economic Bargaining in the Wood Industry', in Simon Clarke, Peter Fairbrother, Michael Burawoy and Pavel Krotov, *What About the Workers? Workers and the Transition to Capitalism in Russia.* London: Verso, pp. 56–90.

Buruma, Ian and Margolit, Avishai (2004) *Occidentalism: The West in the Eyes of its Enemies.* New York: Penguin.

Calhoun, Craig (2003) 'European Studies: Always Already There and Still in Formation', *Comparative European Politics* 1: 5–20.

Calvacoressi, Peter (1991) *Resilient Europe: A Study of the Years 1870–2000.* London and New York: Longman.

Cameron, Fraser (ed.) (2004) *The Future of Europe: Integration and Enlargement.* London: Routledge.

Cameron, K. (ed.) (1999) *National Identity.* Exeter: Intellect.

Carling, Alan (1991) *Social Division.* London: Verso.

Carpenter, Michael (1997) 'Slovakia and the Triumph of Nationalist Populism', *Communist and Post-Communist Studies* 30/2: 205–20.

Carrier, James (1995) *Occidentalism: Images of the West.* Oxford: Clarendon Press.

Castles, Francis (2004) *The Future of the Welfare State: Crisis Myths and Crisis Realities.* Oxford: Oxford University Press.

Castles, Francis (2007) *The Disappearing State? Retrenchment Realities in an age of Globalisation*. Cheltenham: Edward Elgar.

Castles, S., Booth, H. and Wallace, T. (1984) *Here for Good: Western Europe's New Ethnic Minorities*. London: Pluto Press.

Ceruti, Fario (2003) 'A Political Identity of the Europeans?', *Thesis Eleven* 72 (February): 26–45.

Ceserani, David and Fulbrook, Mary (eds) (1996) *Citizenship, Nationality and Migration in Europe*. London: Routledge.

Chavance, Bernard, (1999) 'Le capitalisme et le socialisme comme espèces systémiques: formation, co-évolution, transformation', in Chavance et al. (1999), pp. 295–315.

Chavance, Bernard, Magnin, Éric, Motamed-Nejad, Ramine, Sapir, Jacques (eds) (1999) *Capitalisme et socialisme en perspective*. Paris: La Découverte.

Cheneval, Francis (2003) 'Die Europäische Union und das Problem der demokratischen Repräsentation', *Basler Schriften zur europäischen Integration* Nr. 67, 38pp.

Chirot, D (ed.) (1989) *The Origins of Backwardness in Eastern Europe: Economics and Politics from the Middle Ages until the Twentieth Century*. Berkeley: University of California Press.

Chryssochou, D. (1998) *Democracy in the European Union*. London/ New York: Tauris.

Clark, Christopher (2006) *Iron Kingdom: The Rise and Downfall of Prussia 1600–1947*. London: Allen Lane.

Clarke, Simon (1993) 'Privatisation and the Development of Capitalism in Russia', in Simon Clarke, Peter Fairbrother, Michael Burawoy and Pavel Krotov, *What About the Workers? Workers and the Transition to Capitalism in Russia*. London: Verso, pp. 199–241.

Claval, Paul (2001) 'Multiculturalism and the Dynamics of Modern Civilizations', <http://www.unu.edu/dialogue/papers/claval–s2.pdf>.

Clift, Ben (2004) 'The French Model of Capitalism: Still Exceptional?', in Perraton and Clift, pp. 91–110.

Cohen, Daniel (1999) *Nos temps modernes*. Paris: Flammarion.

Colas, Dominique (2002) 'Société civile, État, Nation', in Dominique Colas (ed.), *L'Europe post-communiste*, part 1. Paris: PUF.

Cook, Robin (2005) 'A Manifesto Like This Would Actually Motivate Our Voters', the *Guardian*, 4 Feb.

Cowles, Maria Green, Caporoso, James and Risse, Thomas (eds) (2001) *Transforming Europe: Europeanization and Domestic Change*. Ithaca, NY: Cornell University Press.

Cowles, Maria Green and Desmond Dinan (eds) (2004) *Developments in the European Union 2*. Basingstoke: Palgrave.

Cox, Terry (2003) 'Changing Societies: Class and Inequality in Central and Eastern Europe', in Stephen White, Judy Batt and Paul G. Lewis (eds), *Developments in Central and East European Politics*. Basingstoke: Palgrave, pp. 234–52.

Crouch, Colin (1993): 'The Future of Employment in Western Europe: Reconciling Demands for Flexibility, Quality and Security'. Twelfth Hitachi Lecture, Sussex European Institute.

Crouch, Colin (1999) *Social Change in Western Europe*. Oxford: Oxford University Press.

Crouch, Colin (2001) 'Breaking Open Black Boxes: The Implications for Sociological Theory of European Integration', in Anand Menon and Vincent Wright (eds), *From the Nation State to Europe: Essays in Honour of Jack Hayward*. Oxford: Oxford University Press, pp. 195–213.

Crouch, Colin (2003) 'Institutions Within Which Real Actors Innovate', in Renate Mayntz and Wolfgang Streeck (eds), *Die Reformierbarkeit der Demokratie*. Frankfurt: Campus, pp. 71–98.

Crouch, Colin (2005) *Post-Democracy*. Cambridge: Polity.

Crouch, Colin and Streeck, Wolfgang (eds) (1997) *Political Economy of Modern Capitalism: Mapping Convergence and Diversity*. London: Sage.

Crow, Graham (1997) *Comparative Sociology and Social Theory: Beyond the Three Worlds*. Basingstoke: Palgrave Macmillan.

Czada, Roland (2006) 'Der Begriff der Verhandlungsdemokratie und die vergleichende Policy-Forschung', in Renate Mayntz and Wolfgang Streeck (eds), *Die Reformierbarkeit der Demokratie*. Frankfurt: Campus, pp. 173–204.

Dauderstädt , Michael (1999) 'Der Kirchturm und sein Horizont. Identität und Grenzen Europas', Bonn: Friedrich-Ebert-Stiftung, *Reihe Eurokolleg* 42: 1–21.

Davies, Norman (1996) *Europe: A History*. Oxford: Oxford University Press.

de Beauvoir, Simone (1949) *Le deuxième sexe*. Paris: Gallimard. Tr. as *The Second Sex*. London: Cape, 1953.

Debray, Régis (1981) *Critique de la raison politique*. Paris: Gallimard. Trans. by David Macey, *Critique of Political Reason*. London: Verso, 1983.

Deeg, Richard and Jackson, Gregory (2006) 'Towards a More Dynamic Theory of Capitalist Variety'. King's College, London: Department of Management Research Papers, number 40.

Delanty, Gerard (1995) *Inventing Europe: Idea, Identity, Reality*. Basingstoke: Macmillan.

Delanty, Gerard (1996) 'The Frontier and Identities of Exclusion in European History', *History of European Ideas* 22/2: 93–103.

Delanty, Gerard (1999) 'Die Transformation nationaler Identität und die kulturelle Ambivalenz europäischer Identität', in R. Viehoff and R. T. Segers, *Kultur, Identität, Europa*. Frankfurt: Suhrkamp, pp. 267–89.

Delanty, Gerard (2003) 'The Making of a Post-Western Europe: A Civilizational Analysis', *Thesis Eleven* 72: 8–24.

Delanty, Gerard (2004) 'Multiple Modernities and Globalization', *Protosociology* 20: 165–85.

Delanty, Gerard (2005) 'Cultural Translations and European Modernity', in Eliezer Ben-Rafael and Y. Sternberg (eds), *Comparing Modern Civilizations: Pluralism versus Homogeneity*. Leiden: Brill, pp. 443–60.

Delanty, Gerard (ed.) (2006a) *Handbook of Contemporary European Social Theory*. London: Routledge.

Delanty, Gerard (2006b) 'The Idea of a Post-Western Europe', in Delanty (ed.), *Europe and Asia Beyond East and West*. London: Routledge, pp. 1–5.

Delanty, Gerard (2007) 'The European Heritage: History, Memory and Time', in Chris Rumford (ed.), *Handbook of European Studies*. London: Sage.

Delanty, Gerard and Rumford, Chris (2005) *Rethinking Europe: Social Theory and the Implications of Europeanization*. London: Routledge.

Delhey, Jan (2001) *Osteuropa zwischen Marx und Markt: Soziale Ungleichheit und soziales Bewusstsein nach dem Kommunismus*. Hamburg: Krämer.

Djilas, Milovan (1966) *The New Class: An Analysis of the Communist System*. London: Unwin Books.

Domański, Henryk (2000) *On the Verge of Convergence: Social Stratification in Eastern Europe.* Budapest: CEU Press. (First published as *Na progu konwergencji* (Warsaw: IfiS PAN), 1996.)

Donald, James (1992) *Sentimental Education: Schooling, Popular Culture and the Regulation of Liberty.* London: Verso.

Donzelot, Jacques (1980 [1977]) *The Policing of Families.* London: Hutchinson.

Donzelot, Jacques (1984) *L'invention du social.* Paris: Fayard.

Dunkerley, David et al. (2002) *Changing Europe.* London: Routledge.

Dyker, David (ed.) (1999) *The European Economy*, 2nd edn. Harlow: Longman.

Dyker, David (2004) *Catching Up and Falling Behind: Post-Communist Transformation in Historical Perspective.* London: Imperial College Press.

Dyson, Kenneth (1980) *The State Tradition in Western Europe.* Oxford: Martin Robertson.

Ebbinghaus, B. and Manow, P. (eds) (2001) *Comparing Welfare Capitalism: Social Policy and Political Economy in Europe, Japan and the USA.* London/New York: Routledge.

Eder, Klaus (2000) 'Zur Transformation nationalstatlicher Öffentlichkeit in Europa', *Berliner Journal für Soziologie* 10/2: 167–84.

Eder, K. and Giesen, B. (eds) (2001) *European Citizenship between National Legacies and Postnational Projects.* Oxford: Oxford University Press.

Edwards, Sobrina (2005) 'Explaining Enlargement: Space, Identity and Governance', unpublished paper delivered at UACES conference, University of Zagreb.

Einhorn, Barbara (1993) *Cinderella Goes to Market: Citizenship, Gender and Women's Movements in East Central Europe.* London: Verso.

Einhorn, Barbara (2006) *Citizenship in Contemporary Europe.* Basingstoke: Palgrave.

Einhorn, Barbara, Kaldor, Mary and Kavan, Zdenek (eds) (1996) *Citizenship and Democratic Control in Contemporary Europe.* Cheltenham: Edward Elgar.

Eisenstadt, S. N. (ed.) (1987) *Patterns of Modernity.* 2 vols. New York: New York University Press.

Eley, Geoff and Suny, Ronald Gregor (eds) (1996) *Becoming National.* New York: Oxford University Press.

Elster, Jon et al. (1998) *Institutional Design in Post-communist Societies: Rebuilding the Ship at Sea*. Cambridge: Cambridge University Press.

Emigh, Rebecca Jean, Fodor, Eva and Szelényi, Iván (1999) 'The Racialization and Feminization of Poverty during the Market Transition in the Central and Southern Europe'. TRSC 1999/10. EUI Florence: Robert Schuman Centre for Advanced Studies, European University Institute.

Engler, W. (1995) *Die ungewollte Moderne. Ost-West-Passagen*. Frankfurt: Suhrkamp.

Eriksen, E. O. (2005) *Making the European Polity: Reflexive Integration in the EU*. London: Routledge.

Eriksen, E. O. and Fossum, J. E. (eds) (2000) *Democracy in the European Union: Integration through Deliberation?* London: Routledge.

Esping-Andersen, G. (1990) *The Three Worlds of Welfare Capitalism*. Princeton: Princeton University Press.

Etzioni, A. (1968) *The Active Society*. New York: Collier-Macmillan.

Eyal, Gil, Szelényi, Ivan and Townsley, Eleanor (1998) *Making Capitalism without Capitalists: Class Formation and Elite Struggles in Post-communist Central Europe*. London: Verso.

Falter, J. W., Gabriel, O. W., Rattinger, H., and Schoen, H. (eds) (2006) *Sind wir ein Volk? Ost- und Westdeutschland im Vergleich*. Munich: Beck, pp. 212–34.

Feminist Review (2004) Special Issue no. 76 'Post-communism: Women's lives in transition'.

Fine, R. and Rai, S. (eds) (1997) *Civil Society: Democratic Perspectives*. London: Cass.

Finer, Samuel (1975) 'State- and Nation-Building in Europe: The Role of the Military', in Charles Tilly (ed.), *The Formation of National States in Western Europe*. Princeton: Princeton University Press, pp. 84–163.

Fischer, E. (1943) *The Passing of the European Age*. Cambridge, MA: Harvard University Press.

Flora, Peter et al. (1983) *State, Economy and Society in Western Europe 1815–1975: A Data Handbook in Two Volumes*. Frankfurt: Campus; London: Macmillan; Chicago: St James Press.

Follesdal, Andreas and Hix, Simon (2005) 'Why There is a Democratic Deficit in the EU: A Response to Majone and

Moravcsik', *European Governance Papers (EUROGOV)* No. C–05–02, <http://www.connex–network.org/eurogov/pdf/egp–connex–C–05–02.pdf>.

Fontana, Josep (1995) *The Distorted Past: A Reinterpretation of Europe.* Oxford: Blackwell.

Fossum, John Erik and Trenz, Hans-Jörg (2006) 'When the People Come In: Constitution-making and the Belated Politicisation of the European Union'. *European Governance Papers (EUROGOV)* No. C–06–03, Basingstoke: Palgrave; <http://www.connex–network.org/eurogov/pdf/egp–connex–C–06–03.pdf>.

Frank, André Gunder (1998) *ReOrient: Global Economy in the Asian Age.* Berkeley: University of California Press.

Fried, Johanes (2003) 'Ein dunkler Leuchtturm', in Aust and Schmidt-Klingenberg, pp. 40–60.

Furet, François (1981) *Interpreting the French Revolution* (trans. Elborg Forster). Cambridge: Cambridge University Press.

Gallant, Thomas (2006) 'Europe and the Mediterranean: A Reassessment', in Gerard Delanty (ed.), *Europe and Asia Beyond East and West.* London: Routledge, pp. 120–37.

Garcia, S. (1993) *European Identity and the Search for Legitimacy.* London: Pinter.

Garton Ash, Timothy (2004) *Free World.* London: Penguin.

Geissler, Rainer (2000) *Sozialer Wandel in Deutschland.* Informationen zur politischen Bildung Nr. 269. Bonn: Bundeszentrale für politische Bildung.

Gershuny, Jonathan (1978) *After Industrial Society? The Emergent Self-Service Economy.* London: Macmillan.

Giddens, Anthony (1973) *The Class Structure of the Advanced Societies.* London: Hutchinson.

Giddens, Anthony (1991) *Modernity and Self-Identity.* Cambridge: Polity.

Giddens, Anthony (2004) *Beyond Left and Right: The Future of Radical Politics.* Cambridge: Polity.

Giddens, Anthony (2007) *Europe in the Global Age.* Cambridge: Polity.

Giddens, Anthony, Diamond, Patrick and Liddle, Roger (eds) (2006) *Global Europe, Social Europe.* Cambridge: Polity.

Gilbert, F. (1970) *The End of the European Era, 1890 to the Present.* New York: Norton.

Gillingham, John (2006) *Design for a New Europe.* Cambridge: Cambridge University Press.

Gilroy, P. (1993) *The Black Atlantic: Modernity and Double Consciousness.* London: Verso.

Girard, Charlotte (2005) 'Contracting and Founding in Times of Conflict', in Nathalie Karagiannis and Peter Wagner (eds), *Ways of Worldmaking.* Liverpool: Liverpool University Press.

Goldberg, D. (1993) *Racist Culture: Philosophy and the Politics of Meaning.* Cambridge, MA, and Oxford: Blackwell.

Goodin, R. E. and Le Grand, J. (1987) *Not Only the Poor: The Middle Classes and the Welfare State.* London: Allen and Unwin.

Gough, Roger and Reid, Anna (eds) (2004) *The Perfect Union? New Europe and the EU.* London: Policy Exchange.

Gowan, Peter and Anderson, Perry (eds) (1997) *The Question of Europe.* London: Verso.

Grabbe, Heather (2006) *The EU's Transformative Power: Europeanization through Conditionality in Central and Eastern Europe.* Basingstoke: Palgrave.

Grabher, Gernot and Stark, David (1997) *Restructuring Networks in Post-Socialism. Legacies, Linkages and Localities.* Oxford: Oxford University Press.

Gray, Anne (2004) *Unsocial Europe: Social Protection or Flexploitation?* London: Pluto.

Gray, John (1998) *False Dawn: The Delusions of Global Capitalism.* London: Granta.

Green, David Michael (2000) 'On Being European: The Character and Consequences of European Identity', in Maria Green Cowles and Michael Smith (eds), *The State of the European Union, vol 5. Risks, Reform, Resistance, and Revival.* Oxford: Oxford University Press, pp. 292–322.

Greenfeld, Liah (1992) *Nationalism: Five Roads to Modernity.* Cambridge, MA: Harvard University Press.

Greenfeld, Liah (1995) 'Nationalism in Western and Eastern Europe Compared', in Stephen E. Hanson and Willfried Spohn (eds), *Can Europe Work? Germany and the Reconstruction of Postcommunist Societies.* Seattle and London: University of Washington Press.

Greenfeld, Liah (2006) *Nationalism and the Mind: Essays on Modern Culture* Oxford: Oneworld.

Greskovitz, Béla (1998) *The Political Economy of Protest and Patience: East European and Latin American Transformations Compared.* Budapest: Central European University Press.

Grix, Jonathan (2001) 'Social Capital as a Concept in the Social Sciences: The State of the Debate', *Democratization* 8/3: 189–210.

Gros, Daniel and Suhrcke, Marc (2001) 'Ten Years After: What is Special about Transition Countries?', *Aussenwirtschaft* 56/II: 201–4.

Groys, Boris (2006) *Das Kommunistische Postskriptum*. Frankfurt: Suhrkamp.

Grundy, Sue and Jamieson, Lynn (2005) 'Are We All Europeans Now? Local, National and Supranational Identities of Young Adults', *Sociological Research Online* 10/3 <http://socresonline. org.uk/10/3/grundy.html>.

Grundy, Sue and Jamieson, Lynn (2007) 'European Identities: From Absent-Minded Citizens to Passionate Europeans', *Sociology* 41/4, August: 663–80.

Habermas, Jürgen (1976) 'Können komplexe Gesellschaften eine vernünftige Identität ausbilden?', in *Zur Rekonstruktion des historischen Materialismus*. Frankfurt: Suhrkamp.

Habermas, Jürgen (1990) *Die nachholende Revolution*. Frankfurt: Suhrkamp.

Habermas, Jürgen (1991) 'Europe's Second Chance', trans. in Habermas, *The Past as Future*. Cambridge: Polity, 1994.

Habermas, Jürgen (1996) *Die Einbeziehung des Anderen*. Frankfurt: Suhrkamp.

Habermas, Jürgen (1999) 'The European Nation-State and the Pressures of Globalization', *New Left Review* 235: 46–59.

Habermas, Jürgen (1998) *Die postnationale Konstellation*. Frankfurt: Suhrkamp. Trans. as *The Postnational Constellation*. Cambridge: Polity, 2001.

Habermas, Jürgen (2003) 'Intolerance and Discrimination', *I.CON* 1/1: 2–12.

Habermas, Jürgen (2004) *Der Gespaltener Westen*. Frankfurt: Suhrkamp.

Hall, John A. (2006) 'Plaidoyer pour l'Europe des Patries', in Ralf Rogowski and Charles Turner (eds), *The Shape of the New Europe*. Cambridge: Cambridge University Press, pp. 107–24.

Hall, Peter and Soskice, David (eds) (2001) *Varieties of Capitalism: The Institutional Foundations of Comparative Advantage*. Oxford: Oxford University Press.

Haverland, Markus (2005) 'Does the EU Cause Domestic Developments? The Problem of Case Selection in Europeanization

Research.' *European Integration online Papers* (EIoP) 9/2 <http://eiop.or.at/eiop/texte/2005–002a.htm>.

Hay, Colin, Watson, Matthew and Wincot, Daniel (1999) 'Globalisation, European Integration and the Persistence of European Social Models', Birmingham: POLSIS working paper 3/99.

Hay, Denys (1957) *Europe: The Emergence of an Idea.* Edinburgh: Edinburgh University Press.

Hearn, Jonathan (2007) 'National Identity: Banal, Personal and Embedded', *Nations and Nationalism* 13/4: 657–74.

Hechter, Michael (1975) *Internal Colonialism: The Celtic Fringe in British National Development, 1536–1966.* London: Routledge and Kegan Paul.

Heidenreich, Martin (2003) 'Regional Inequalities in the Enlarged Europe', *Journal of European Social Policy* 13/4: 313–33.

Held, David (1995) *Democracy and the Global Order: From the Modern State to Cosmopolitan Governance.* Cambridge: Polity.

Hemerijk, Anton, Keune, Maarten and Rhodes, Martin (2006) 'European Welfare States: Diversity, Challenges and Reforms', in Paul Heywood, Erik Jones, Martin Rhodes and Ulrich Sedelmeier (eds), *Developments in European Politics.* Basingstoke: Palgrave, pp. 259–79.

Herrmann, R. K., Risse, T. and Brewer, M. B. (eds) (2004) *Becoming European in the EU.* New York: Rowman and Littlefield.

Heywood, Paul and Krastev, Ivan (2006) 'Political Scandals and Corruption', in Paul M. Heywood, Erik Jones, Martin Rhodes and Ulrich Sedelmeier (eds), *Developments in European Politics.* Basingstoke: Palgrave, pp. 157–77.

Heywood, Paul, Jones, Erik, Rhodes, Martin and Sedelmeier, Ulrich (eds) (2006) *Developments in European Politics.* Basingstoke: Palgrave.

Hicks, Simon, Noury, Abdul and Roland, Gérard (2006) *Democratic Politics in the European Parliament.* Cambridge: Cambridge University Press.

Higley, John and Lengyel, György (eds) (2000) *Elites After State Socialism: Theories and Analysis.* Lanham, MD: Rowman and Littlefield.

Hildermaier, Manfred, Kocka, Jürgen and Conrad, Christoph (eds) (2000) *Europäische Zivilgesellschaft in Ost und West: Begriffe, Geschichte, Chancen.* Frankfurt: Campus.

Hill, Michael (2006) *Social Policy in the Modern World*. Oxford: Blackwell.

Hirst, Paul Q. and Thompson, Grahame (1996) *Globalization in Question*. Cambridge: Polity.

Hix, Simon, Noury, Abdul and Roland, Gerard (2006) 'Dimensions of Politics in the European Parliament', *American Journal of Political Science* 50/2: 494–511.

Hjerm, Michael (2003) 'National Sentiments in Eastern and Western Europe', *Nationalities Papers* 31/4, December: 413–29.

Hoffman, S. and Kitromilides, P. (eds) (1981) *Culture and Society in Contemporary Europe*. London: George Allen and Unwin.

Hollingsworth, J. R. and Boyer, Robert (eds) (1997) *Comparative Capitalism*. Cambridge: Cambridge University Press.

Hölscher, B. and Dittrich, R. (1999) 'Russia Goes West?', *Journal of Sociology and Social Anthropology* 2/1: 66–89.

Hopper, Paul (2004) '"Who Wants to be a European?" Community and Identity in the European Union', *Human Affairs* 14/2: 141–51.

Hradil, S. (2001) *Soziale Ungleichheit in Deutschland*, 8th edn. Opladen: Leske and Budrich.

Hradil, S. and Schiener, J. (2002) *Soziale Ungleichheit in Deutschland*. Stuttgart: UTB.

Hudson, R. and Williams, A. (eds) (1999) *Divided Europe*. London: Sage.

Hutton, Will (2002) *The World We're In*. London: Little Brown.

Hutton, Will (2007) *The Writing on the Wall: China and the West in the 21st Century*. London: Little, Brown.

Ingham, Hilary and Ingham, Mike (eds) (2002) *EU Expansion to the East: Prospects and Problems*. Cheltenham: Edward Edgar.

Jackson, Gregory and Deeg, Richard (2006) 'How Many Varieties of Capitalism? Comparing the Comparative Institutional Analyses of Capitalist Diversity', Max Planck Institute for the Study of Societies Discussion Paper 06/2. Cologne: MPIfG.

Jacobs, Dirk and Maier, Robert (1998) 'European Identity: Construct, Fact and Fiction', in M. Gastelaars and A. de Ruijter (eds), *A United Europe: The Quest for a Multifaceted Identity*. Maastricht: Shaker, pp. 13–34.

Jacoby, Wade (2001) *Imitation and Politics: Redesigning Modern Germany*. Ithaca, NY: Cornell University Press.

Jacquot, Sophie and Wolf, Cornelia (2003) 'Usage of European Integration: Europeanisation from a Sociological Perspective', *European Integration online Papers (EIoP)* 7/12: <http://eiop.or.at/eiop/texte/2003–012a.htm>.

Jardine, Lisa (1996) *Worldly Goods: A New History of the Renaissance*. London: Macmillan.

Jessop, Bob (2005) 'The European Union and Recent Transformations in Statehood', in Sonja Puntscher Riekmann (ed.), *Transformations of Statehood from a European Perspective*. Cambridge: Cambridge University Press.

Jönsson, Christer, Tägil, Sven and Törnqvist, Gunnar (2000) *Organizing European Space*. London: Sage.

Jöppke, Christian and Morawska, Ewa (eds) (2003) *Towards Assimilation and Citizenship*. Basingstoke: Palgrave.

Judt, Tony (2005) *Postwar: A History of Europe since 1945*. London: Heinemann.

Kaelble, Hartmut (ed.) (2004) *The European Way: European Societies During the Nineteenth and Twentieth Centuries*. Oxford; New York: Berghahn.

Kaelble, H. and Schmidt, G. (eds) (2004) *Das europäische Sozialmodell: Auf dem Weg zum transnationalen Sozialstaat (WZB Jahrbuch)*. Berlin: Sigma.

Kaldor, Mary and Vejvoda, Ivan (1999) *Democratisation in Central and Eastern Europe*. London: Pinter.

Kantner, Cathleen (2006) 'Collective Identity as Shared Self-Understanding: The Case of the Emerging European Identity', *European Journal of Social Theory* 9/4, November: 501–23.

Karagiannis, Nathalie (2004) *Avoiding Responsibility: The Politics and Discourse of European Development Policy*. London: Pluto; and Ann Arbor: University of Michigan Press.

Karagiannis, Nathalie (ed.) (2007) *European Solidarity*. Liverpool: Liverpool University Press.

Katenhusen, Ines and Lamping, Wolfram (eds) (2003) *Demokratien in Europa. Der Einfluss der europäischen Integration auf Institutionenwandel und neue Konturen des demokratischen Verfassungsstaates*. Opladen: Leske und Budrich.

Katzenstein, Peter (1978) *Between Power and Plenty: Foreign Policies of Advanced Industrialized States*. Madison: University of Wisconsin Press.

Keating, Michael (2006) 'Territorial Politics in Europe', in Paul M. Heywood, Erik Jones, Martin Rhodes and Ulrich Sedelmeier (eds), *Developments in European Politics*. Basingstoke: Palgrave, pp. 136–54.

Kempny, Marian and Jawlowska, Aldona (eds), *Identity in Transformation: Postmodernity, Postcommunism, and Globalization*. Westport, CT, and London: Praeger.

Kenedi, János (1981) *Do it Yourself: Hungary's Hidden Economy*. London: Pluto.

Kennedy, Michael (2002) *Cultural Formations of Postcommunism: Emancipation, Transition, Nation, and War*. Minneapolis: University of Minnesota Press.

Kiernan, V. G. (1972 [1969]) *The Lords of Human Kind: European Attitudes towards the Outside World in the Imperial Age*. Harmondsworth: Penguin.

Kiernan, V. G. (1995) *Imperialism and its Contradictions*, ed. Harvey J. Kaye. London: Routledge.

King, Lawrence P. (2001) *The Basic Features of Postcommunist Capitalism in Eastern Europe: Firms in Hungary, the Czech Republic, and Slovakia*. Westport, CT, and London: Praeger.

King, Russell and Donati, Marco (1999) 'The Divided Mediterranean: Re-defining European Relationships', in Ray Hudson and Allan Williams (eds), *Divided Europe*. London: Sage, pp. 132–62.

Klinger, Cornelia and Knapp, Gudrun-Axeli (2005) 'Achsen der Ungleichheit – Achsen der Differenz. Verhältnisbestimmungen von Klasse, Geschlecht, »Rasse«/Ethnizität'. *Transit – Europäische Revue* 29.

Knell, Mark and Srholec, Martin (2006) 'Diverging Pathways in Central and Eastern Europe', in David Lane and Martin Myant (eds), *Varieties of Capitalism in Post-communist Countries*. Basingstoke: Palgrave Macmillan, pp. 40–63.

Koch, Thomas and Thomas, Michael (1997) 'The Social and Cultural Embeddedness of Entrepreneurs in East Germany', in Gernot Grabher and David Stark (eds), *Restructuring Networks in Post-Socialism*, pp. 242–61.

Kohler-Koch, Beate (2005a) 'European Governance and System Integration', *European Governance Papers (EUROGOV)* No. C–05–01, <http://www.connex–network.org/eurogov/pdf/egp–connex–C–05–02.pdf>.

Kohler-Koch, Beate (2005b) 'Network Governance within and beyond an Enlarged European Union', in Amy Verdun and Osvaldo Creci (eds), *The European Union in the Wake of*

Eastern Enlargement: Institutional and Policy-making Challenges. Manchester: Manchester University Press, ch. 3, pp. 35–53.

Kolankiewicz, George (1996) 'Social Capital and Social Change', *British Journal of Sociology* 47/3 (September): 427–41.

Konrád, György and Szelényi, Ivan (1979) *The Intellectuals on the Road to Class Power.* Brighton: Harvester.

Kornai, János (2000) 'What the Change of System from Capitalism to Socialism Does and Does Not Mean', *Journal of Economic Perspectives* 14/1, Winter: 27–42.

Kosta, J. (1997) 'Die ökonomische Transformationsstrategie Tschechiens im Vergleich zur Slowakei, Ungarn und Polen', Discussion Paper FS II 97–602. Berlin: WZB.

Kovács, Melinda (2001) 'Putting Down and Putting Off: The EU's Discursive Strategies in the 1998 and 1999 Follow-up Reports', in József Böröcz and Melinda Kovács (eds), *Europe's New Clothes: Unveiling EU Enlargement.* Telford: Central European Review (<http:www.ce–review.org/>), pp. 196–234.

Kreckel, Reinhard (1992) *Politische Soziologie der sozialen Ungleichheit.* Frankfurt: Campus.

Krus, Merje (2004) 'Europe's Eastern Expansion and the Reinscription of Otherness in East-Central Europe', *Progess in Human Geography* 28/4: 472–89.

Krygier, Martin (1997) 'Virtuous Circles: Antipodean Reflections on Power, Institutions and Civil Society', *East European Politics and Societies* 11/1 (Winter): 36–88.

Krzyzanowski, M. (2005) '"European Identity Wanted": On Discursive and Communicative Dimensions of the European Convention', in R. Wodak and P. Chilton (eds), *A New Agenda for Critical Discourse Analysis: Theory, Methodology, and Interdisciplinarity.* Amsterdam, Philadelphia: J. Benjamins, pp. 137–63.

Kühnhardt, Ludger (2006) 'European Integration: Challenge and Response. Crises as Engines of Progress in European Integration History'. University of Bonn: Center for European Integration Studies, Discussion Paper C157.

Kumar, Krishan (1978) *Prophecy and Progress: The Sociology of Industrial and Post-Industrial Society.* London: Allen Lane.

Kumar, Krishan (2001) 'Civil Society', in Krishan Kumar, *1989: Revolutionary Ideas and Ideals.* Minneapolis: Minnesota University Press.

Kumar, Krishan (2003) *The Making of English National Identity.* Cambridge: Cambridge University Press.

Kuus, Merje (2004) 'Europe's Eastern Expansion and the Reinscription of Otherness in East-Central Europe', *Progress in Human Geography* 28/4: 472–89.

Ladányi, János and Szelényi, Iván (2006) *Patterns of Exclusion: Constructing Gypsy Ethnicity and the Making of an Underclass in Transitional Societies of Europe.* Boulder, CO: East European Monographs.

Lane, Christel (2003) 'Changes in Corporate Governance of German Corporations: Convergence to the Anglo-American Model?', *Competition and Change* 7/2–3, June–September: 79–100.

Lane, David (2006) 'Post-State Socialism: A Diversity of Capitalisms?', in David Lane and Martin Myant (eds), *Varieties of Capitalism in Post-communist Countries.* Basingstoke: Palgrave Macmillan: 13–39.

Lange, O. and Taylor, F. M. (1938) *On the Economic Theory of Socialism.* Minneapolis: University of Minnesota Press.

Lavenex, Sandra (2004) 'EU External Governance in "Wider Europe"', *Journal of European Public Policy* 11/4, August: 680–700.

Leadbeater, Charles (2000) *The Weightless Society.* New York and London: Texere.

Le Carré, John (1968) *A Small Town in Germany.* London: Heinemann.

Lee, D. and Turner, Bryan S. (eds) (1966) *Conflicts about Class: A Selection of Readings Debating Inequality in Late Industrialism.* London: Longman.

Le Grand, Julian (1982) *The Strategy of Equality: Redistribution and the Social Services.* London: Allen and Unwin.

Leibfried, Stephan and Zürn, Michael (eds) (2005) *Transformations of the State?* Cambridge: Cambridge University Press.

Leisering, Lutz and Leibfried, Stefan (2001) *Time and Poverty in Western Welfare States,* trans. John Veit-Wilson. Cambridge: Cambridge University Press.

Lenin, V. I. (1939 [1916]) *Imperialism: A Popular Outline: The Highest Stage of Capitalism.* New York: International Publishers.

Lepsius, M. Rainer (2004) 'Prozesse der europäischen Identitätsstiftung', in *Aus Politik und Zeitgeschichte* B38/2004, pp. 3–5.

Lewis, Paul and Mansfeldová, Zdenka (2006) *The European Union and Party Politics in Central and Eastern Europe*. Basingstoke: Palgrave Macmillan.

Liotta, P. H. (2005) 'Imagining Europe: Symbolic Geography and the Future', *Mediterranean Quarterly* 16, Summer: 67–85.

Lipset, Seymour Martin (1964) *The First New Nation: The United States in Historical and Comparative Perspective*. London: Heinemann.

Lukes, Steven (2005) 'Invasions of the Market', in Max Miller (ed.), *Worlds of Capitalism: Institutions, Governance and Economic Change in the Era of Globalization*. London: Routledge: 298–321.

McCann, Leo (ed.) (2004) *Russian Transformations: Challenging the Global Narrative*. London; New York: RoutledgeCurzon.

McCann, Leo (2005) *Economic Development in Tatarstan: Global Markets and a Russian Region*. London : RoutledgeCurzon.

Mair, Peter (2005) 'Popular Democracy and the European Union Polity', *European Governance Papers (EUROGOV)* No. C-05-03, <http://www.connex—network.org/eurogov/pdf/egp-connex-C-05-03.pdf>.

Mandel, David (2005) '"Managed Democracy": Capital and State in Russia', *Debatte* 13/2, August: 117–36.

Mann, Michael (1986, 1993) *The Sources of Social Power*, 2 vols. Cambridge: Cambridge University Press.

Mann, Michael (1998) 'Is there a Society Called Euro?', in Roland Axtmann (ed.), *Globalization and Europe*. London: Continuum.

Mannheim, Karl (1927) *Conservatism*. London: Routledge and Kegan Paul, 1986.

Manning, Nick (2004) 'Diversity and Change in Pre-accession Central and Eastern Europe since 1989', *Journal of European Social Policy* 14/3: 211–32.

Marshall, T. H. (1950) *Citizenship and Social Class and Other Essays*. Cambridge: Cambridge University Press.

Marx, Karl (1957 [1844]) 'Critique of Hegel's Philosophy of the State: Introduction.' *Marx-Engels Werke (MEWE)* 1. Berlin: Dietz: 383.

Mastnak, T. and Sumic-Riha, J. (eds) (1993) 'Questioning Europe', *Filozofski Vestnik* (Ljubljana), 2.

Mateju, Petr, Rehakova, Blanka and Evans, Geoffrey (eds) (2005) 'The Politics of Interests and Class Realignment in the Czech

Republic, 1992–1996', in Geoffrey Evans (ed.), *The End of Class Politics? Class Voting in Comparative Context*. Oxford: Oxford University Press.

Mau, Steffen (2004) 'Soziale Ungleichheit in der Europäischen Union', in *Aus Politik und Zeitgeschichte* B38/2004, pp. 38–46.

Mayhew, Alan (2000) 'Enlargement of the European Union: An Analysis of the Negotiations with the Central and Eastern European Countries', SEI Working Paper 39.

Mendras, Henri (1970) *La Fin des paysans: changements et innovations dans les sociétés rurales françaises*. Paris: Librairie Armand Colin.

Mendras, Henri (1997) *L'Europe des Européens*. Paris: Gallimard.

Meyer, Thomas (2001) *Identity Mania: The Politicization of Cultural Difference*. London: Zed.

Meyer, Thomas (2002) *Identitätspolitik. Vom Missbrauch kultureller Unterschiede*. Frankfurt: Suhrkamp.

Middlemas, Keith (1995) *Orchestrating Europe: The Informal Politics of the European Union, 1943–95*. London: HarperCollins.

Miller, Max (ed.) (2005) *Worlds of Capitalism: Institutions, Governance and Economic Change in the Era of Globalization*. London: Routledge.

Milward, Alan (1992) *The European Rescue of the Nation-State*. London: Routledge.

Moore, Barrington (1966) *Social Origins of Dictatorship and Democracy*. Harmondsworth: Penguin.

Moore, Barrington (1978) *Injustice*. London: Macmillan.

Morgan, Glyn (2005) *The Idea of a European Superstate: Public Justification and European Integration*. Princeton: Princeton University Press.

Motamed-Nejad, Ramine (1999a) 'Le capitalisme et le socialisme: similitudes et différences', in Bernard Chavance, Éric Magnin, Ramine Motamed-Nejad and Jacques Sapir (eds), *Capitalisme et socialisme en perspective*. Paris: La Découverte, pp. 217–47.

Motamed-Nejad, Ramine (1999b) 'Approches de la transition et nature des économies post-socialistes', *Revue d'études comparatives Est-Ouest* 30/2–3: 11–59.

Mudde, Cas (2006) 'Anti-System Politics', in Paul Heywood, Erik Jones, Martin Rhodes and Ulrich Sedelmeier (eds), *Developments in European Politics*. Basingstoke: Palgrave, pp. 178–95.

Müller, Jan-Werner (2004) 'Verfassungspatriotismus: eine europäische Verbindlichkeit?', *Transit – Europäische Revue* 28.

Münch, Richard (1993) *Das Projekt Europa. Zwischen Nationalstaat, regionaler Autonomie und Weltgesellschaft.* Frankfurt: Suhrkamp.

Münch, Richard (1999) Europäische Identitätsbildung', in R. Viehoff and R. T. Segers, *Kultur, Identität, Europa.* Frankfurt: Suhrkamp.

Myrdal, Gunnar (1944) *An American Dilemma.* New York and London: Harper & Bros.

Nagle, J. D. and Mahr, A. (1999) *Democracy and Democratization: Post-Communist Europe in Comparative Perspective.* London: Sage.

Nairn, Tom (1977) *The Break-Up of Britain: Crisis and Neo-Nationalism.* London: Verso. 2nd edn 1981; 3rd edn 2003.

Nederveen Pieterse, Jan (2002) 'Europe Traveling Light: Europeanization and Globalization', in Maran Kempny and Aldona Jawlowska (eds), *Identity in Transformation: Postmodernity, Postcommunism and Modernization.* Westport, CT: Praeger, pp. 127–44.

Needham, Joseph (1969) *The Grand Titration: Science and Society in East and West.* London: Allen and Unwin.

Neller, Katja (2006) 'Getrennt vereint? Ost-West-Identitäten, Stereotypen und Fremdheitsgefühle nach 15 Jahren deutscher Einheit', in J. W. Falter, O. W. Gabriel, H. Rattinger and H. Schoen (eds), *Sind wir ein Volk? Ost- und Westdeutschland im Vergleich.* Munich: Beck, pp. 13–36.

Neocleous, Mark (2003) *Imagining the State.* Maidenhead: Open University Press.

Nolte, Hans-Heinrich (1997) 'Europäische innere Peripherien im 20. Jahrhundert', *Historische Mitteilungen* 23 (Supplement). Stuttgart: F. Steiner.

Nolte, Hans-Heinrich (2002) 'Die Osterweiterung der EU', in K. Lamping and I. Katenhusen (eds), *Demokratien in Europa.* Opladen: Leske and Budrich.

Norman, Peter (2005) *The Accidental Constitution: The Story of the European Convention.* Brussels: EuroComment.

Oberhuber, F. (2005) 'Deliberation or "Mainstreaming"? Empiricially Reaserching the European Convention', in R. Wodak and P. Chilton (eds), *A New Agenda for Critical Discourse Analysis: Theory, Methodology, and Inter-disciplinarity.* Amsterdam, Philadelphia: J. Benjamins, pp. 165–87.

Obinger, Herbert, Leibfried, Stephan, Bogedan, Claudia, Gindulis, Edith, Moser, Julia and Starke, Peter (2005) 'Welfare State

Transformation in Small Open Economies', in Stephan Leibfried and Michael Zürn (eds), *Transformations of the State?* Cambridge: Cambridge University Press, pp. 161–85.

Offe, Claus (1985) *Disorganized Capitalism*. Cambridge: Polity.

Offe, Claus (1995) 'Designing Institutions in East European Transitions', in Robert Goodin (ed.), *The Theory of Institutional Design*. Cambridge: Cambridge University Press.

Offe, Claus (2000) 'The Democratic Welfare State: A European Regime under the Strain of European Integration', *Reihe Politikwissenschaft* 68. Vienna: Institute for Advanced Studies.

Offe, Claus (2003) 'Is There, or Can There Be, a "European Society"?', in Ines Katenhusen and Wolfram Lamping (eds), *Demokratien in Europa. Der Einfluss der europäischen Integration auf Institutionenwandel und die Zukunft des demokratischen Verfassungsstaates*. Opladen: Leske und Budrich, pp. 71–90.

Offe, Claus (2005) 'The European Model of "Social" Capitalism: Can It Survive European Integration?', in Max Miller (ed.), *Worlds of Capitalism: Institutions, Governance and Economic Change in the Era of Globalization*. London: Routledge, pp. 146–78.

Offe, Claus and Preuss, Ulrich (2006) 'The Problem of Legitimacy in the European Polity: Is Democratization the Answer?', in Colin Crouch and Wolfgang Streeck (eds), *The Diversity of Democracy: Corporatism, Social Order and Political Conflict*. Cheltenham: Edward Elgar pp. 175–204.

Ohmae, K. (1994) *The Borderless World, Power and Strategy in the Interlinked Economy*. London: HarperCollins.

Opp, Karl–Dieter (2005) 'Decline of the Nation-State? How the European Union Creates National and Sub-National Identifications', *Social Forces* 84/2: 653–80.

O'Reilly, Jacqueline (2006) 'Framing Comparisons: Gendering Perspectives on Cross-national Comparative Research on Work and Welfare', *Work, Employment and Society* 20/4: 731–50.

Ossowski, Stanislaw (1963 [1957]) *Class Structure in the Social Consciousness*, trans. S. Patterson. London: Routledge and Kegan Paul.

Outhwaite, William (1999) 'The Myth of Modernist Method', *European Journal of Social Theory* 2/1: 5–25.

Outhwaite, William (2001) 'What is European Culture?', in W. Ehlert and G. Széll (eds), *New Democracies and Old Societies in Europe*. Frankfurt: Peter Lang pp. 92–101.

Outhwaite, William (2006a) *The Future of Society*. Oxford: Blackwell.

Outhwaite, William (2006b) 'Is There a European Civil Society?', in Ralf Rogowski and Charles Turner (eds), *The Shape of the New Europe*. Cambridge: Cambridge University Press, pp. 87–103.

Outhwaite, William (2006c) 'Europe after the EU Enlargement: "Cosmopolitanism by Small Steps"', in Gerard Delanty (ed.), *Europe and Asia Beyond East and West*. London: Routledge, pp. 193–202.

Outhwaite, William (2007) 'Who Needs Solidarity?', in Nathalie Karagiannis (ed.), *European Solidarity*. Liverpool: Liverpool University Press, pp. 75–93.

Outhwaite, William and Ray, Larry (2005) *Social Theory and Postcommunism*. Oxford: Blackwell.

Pakulski, J. and Waters, M. (1995) *The Death of Class*. London: Sage.

Parkin, Frank (1971) *Class Inequality and Political Order: Social Stratification in Capitalist and Communist Societies*. London: Paladin.

Payne, Geoff (ed.) (2006) *Social Divisions*, 2nd edn. Basingstoke: Palgrave Macmillan.

Pérez-Días, Victor (1998) 'The Public Sphere and a European Civil Society', in Jeff Alexander (ed.), *Real Civil Societies*. London: Sage, pp. 211–38.

Perraton, Jonathan and Clift, Ben (2004) *Where are National Capitalisms Now?* Basingstoke: Palgrave.

Peters, Bernhard, Sifft, Stefanie, Wimmel, Andreas, Brüggemann, Michael and Kleinen-von Königslöw, Katherina (2005) 'National and Transnational Public Spheres: The Case of the EU', in Stephan Leibfried and Michael Zürn (eds), *Transformations of the State?* Cambridge: Cambridge University Press, pp. 139–60.

Pickles, John and Smith, Adrian (eds) (1998) *Theorising Transition: The Political Economy of Post-Communist Transformations*. London: Routledge.

Pierson, Christopher (1991) *Beyond the Welfare State? The New Political Economy of Welfare*. Cambridge: Polity.

Pierson, Christopher (1996) *The Modern State*. London: Routledge.

Pohoryles, R. et al. (eds) (1994) *European Transformations: Five Decisive Years at the Turn of the Century*. Aldershot: Avebury.

Pollack, Mark (2000) 'Blairism in Brussels', in Maria Green Cowles and Michael Smith (eds), *The State of the European Union, vol 5. Risks, Reform, Resistance, and Revival*. Oxford: Oxford University Press, pp. 266–91.

Pollock, G. (2001) 'Civil Society and Euro-Nationalism', *Studies in Social and Political Thought* 4: 31–56.

Pollock, G. (2002) 'Civil Society and Nation', unpublished PhD thesis, University of Sussex.

Portes, Richard, Baldwin, Richard E. and François, Joseph F. (1997) 'The Costs and Benefits of Eastern Enlargement', *Economic Policy* 12/24 (April 1997): 125–76; cited in Hilary and Mike Ingham (eds), *EU Expansion to the East: Prospects and Problems*. Cheltenham: Edward Elgar, 2002, p. 20.

Poznanski, Kasimierz (2002) 'The Crisis of Transition as a State Crisis', in Frank Bönker, Klaus Müller and Andreas Pickel (eds) (2002), *Postcommunist Transformation and the Social Sciences*. Lanham, MD: Rowman and Littlefield, pp. 55–76.

Pratt, Geoff (2003) *Class, Nation and Identity: The Anthropology of Political Movements*. London: Pluto.

Pridham, Geoffrey (2005) *Designing Democracy: EU Enlargement and Regime Change in Post Communist Europe*. Basingstoke: Palgrave.

Prior, Pauline and Sykes, Robert (2001) 'Globalization and the European Welfare States: Evaluating the Theories and Evidence', in Robert Sykes, Bruno Palier and Pauline M. Prior (eds), *Globalization and European Welfare States: Challenges and Change*. Basingstoke: Palgrave.

Prodi, Romano (2000) *Europe as I See It*. Cambridge: Polity.

Pryce-Jones, David (1995) *The War that Never Was: The Fall of the Soviet Empire 1985–1991*. London: Weidenfeld and Nicolson.

Putnam, Robert (1993) *Making Democracy Work: Civic Traditions in Modern Italy*. Princeton: Princeton University Press.

Ray, Larry (1995) 'The Rectifying Revolutions? Organizational Futures in the New Eastern Europe', *Organization* 2/3–4: 441–65.

Ray, Larry (1996) *Social Theory and the Crisis of State Socialism*. Cheltenham: Edward Elgar.

Rhodes, Martin and van Apeldoorn, Bastiaan (1997) 'The Transformation of West European Capitalism?', EUI Working paper 97/60. Florence: European University Institute.

Riboud, Michelle, Sánchez-Páramo, Carolina and Silva-Jauregui, Carlos (2002) 'Does Eurosclerosis Matter? Institutional Reform and Labor Market Performance in Central and Eastern Europe', *World Bank Technical Paper no. 519*. Washington, DC: World Bank.

Rieu, A.-M. and Duprat, G. (eds) (1993; rev. edn 1995) *European Democratic Cultures*. Milton Keynes: Open University; and London: Routledge.

Rifkin, Jeremy (2004) *The European Dream: How Europe's Vision of the Future is Quietly Eclipsing the American Dream*. New York: Penguin.

Rogowski, Ralf and Turner, Charles (eds) (2006) *The Shape of the New Europe*. Cambridge: Cambridge University Press.

Rothstein, Bo (2001) 'The Future of the Universal Welfare State: An Institutional Approach', in Stein Kuhnle (ed.), *Survival of the European Welfare State*. London: Routledge, pp. 217–33.

Ruiz Jiménez, Antonia M. et al. (2004) 'European and National Identities in EU's Old and New Member States: Ethnic, Civic, Instrumental and Symbolic Components', *European Integration Online Papers (EIoP)* 8/11: <http://eiop.or.at/eiop/texte/2004–011a.htm>.

Rumford, Chris (2002) *The European Union*. Oxford: Blackwell.

Rumford, Chris (2003) 'European Civil Society or Transnational Social Spaces', *European Journal of Social Theory* 6/1: 36–7.

Rumford, Chris (ed.) (2007) *Cosmopolitanism and Europe*. Liverpool: Liverpool University Press.

Rumford, Chris (ed.) (2008) *Sage Handbook of European Studies*. London: Sage.

Ruzza, Carlo (2005) 'EU Public Policies and the Participation of Organized Civil Society', University of Milan, Department of Social and Political Studies Working Papers 23/11/2005.

Sachs, Jeffrey (1990) 'Eastern Europe's Economies – What is to be Done?', *The Economist* (13 Jan. 1990).

Sakwa, Richard (1999) *Postcommunism*. Buckingham: Open University Press.

Sakwa, Richard (2006) 'Russia as Eurasia: An Innate Cosmopolitanism', in Gerard Delanty (ed.), *Europe and Asia Beyond East and West*. London: Routledge, pp. 215–27.

Sakwa, Richard and Stevens, Anne (eds) (2000) *Contemporary Europe*. 2nd edn 2006. Basingstoke: Palgrave Macmillan.

Sassen, Saskia (2005) 'When National Territory is Home to the Global: Old Borders to New Borderings', *New Political Economy* 10/4, December: 532–41.

Scharpf, Fritz (2004) 'Legitimationskonzepte jenseits des Nationalstaats', Cologne: MPIfG Working paper 04/6, November.

Schecter, Darrow (2000) *Sovereign States or Political Communities? Civil Society and Contemporary Politics*. Manchester: Manchester University Press.

Schimmelfennig, Frank (2007) 'European Regional Organizations, Political Conditionality, and Democratic Transformation in Eastern Europe', *East European Politics and Societies* 21/1: 126–42.

Schimmelfennig, Frank and Sedelmeier, Ulrich (eds) (2005a) *The Europeanization of Central and Eastern Europe*. Ithaca, NY, and London: Cornell University Press.

Schimmelfennig, Frank and Sedelmeier, Ulrich (eds) (2005b) *The Politics of EU Enlargement*. London: Routledge.

Schlesinger, Philip and Kevin, Deirdre (2000) 'Can the European Union Become a Sphere of Publics?', in Erik Oddvar Eriksen and John Erik Fossum (eds), *Democracy in the European Union: Integration Through Deliberation?* London: Routledge, pp. 206–29.

Schmalz-Bruns, Rainer (2005) 'On the Political Theory of the Euro-Polity', in E. O. Eriksen (ed.), *Making the European Polity: Reflexive Integration in the EU*. Cambridge: Polity, pp. 59–83.

Schmidt, Vivien (2002) *The Futures of European Capitalism*. Oxford: Oxford University Press.

Schmidt, Vivien (2006) *Democracy in Europe: The EU and National Polities*. Oxford: Oxford University Press.

Schmitter, Philippe (2000) *How to Democratize the European Union . . . and Why Bother?* Lanham, MD: Rowman and Littlefield.

Schneider, Peter (1982) *Der Mauerspringer*. Neuwied: Luchterhand.

Schöpflin, George (1993) *Politics in Eastern Europe 1945–1992*. Oxford: Blackwell.

Schöpflin, George (2003) 'Identities, Politics and Post-Communism in Central Europe', *Nations and Nationalism* 9/4: 477–90.

Schöpflin, George and Nancy Wood (eds) (1989) *In Search of Central Europe*. Cambridge: Polity.

Schumpeter, Joseph (1921) 'Sozialistische Möglichkeiten von heute', *Archiv für Sozialwissenschaft und Sozialpolitik* 48/2: 305–60.

Schumpeter, Joseph (1951) *Imperialism and Social Classes.* Oxford: Blackwell.

Schumpeter, Joseph (1987 [1944]) *Capitalism, Socialism and Democracy.* London: Allen and Unwin.

Schwengel, H. (1999) *Globalisierung mit europäischen Gesicht. Der Kampf um die politische Form der Zukunft.* Berlin: Aufbau-Verlag.

Senghaas, D. (1982) *Von Europa Lernen. Entwicklungsgeschichtliche Betrachtungen.* Frankfurt: Suhrkamp. Tr. K. H. Kimmig as *The European Experience. A Historical Critique of Development Theory.* Leamington Spa: Berg, 1985.

Senghaas, D. (1994) *Wohin Driftet die Welt? Über die Zukunft friedlicher Koexistenz.* Frankfurt: Suhrkamp.

Sennett, Richard (1998) *Corrosion of Character: The Personal Consequences of Work in the New Capitalism.* New York: W.W. Norton.

Shaw, Jo and Wiener, Antje (2000) 'The Paradox of the European "Polity"', in Maria Green Cowles and Michael Smith (eds), *The State of the European Union, vol 5. Risks, Reform, Resistance, and Revival.* Oxford: Oxford University Press, pp. 64–88.

Shaw, M. (2001) *Theory of the Global State: Globality as Unfinished Revolution.* Cambridge: Cambridge University Press.

Shelly, M. and Winck, M. (eds) (1993) *Aspects of European Cultural Diversity.* Milton Keynes: Open University; rev. edn London: Routledge, 1995.

Shonfield, Andrew (1965) *Modern Capitalism: The Changing Balance of Public and Private Power.* Oxford: Oxford University Press.

Shore, Cris (2000) *Building Europe: The Cultural Politics of European Integration.* London; Routledge.

Siedentop, Larry (2000) *Democracy in Europe.* London: Allen Lane.

Sil, Rudra and Cheng Cheng (2004) 'State Legitimacy and the (In)signficance of Democracy in Post-Communist Russia', *Europe-Asia Studies* 56/3, May: 347–68.

Silver, H. and Wilkinson, F. (1995) 'Policies to Combat Social Exclusion: A French–British Comparison', in G. Rodgers, C.

Gore and J. Figueiredo (eds), *Social Exclusion: Rhetoric, Reality, Responses*. Geneva: International Labour Organization, pp. 183–end.

Silverman, M. (1992) *Deconstructing the Nation: Immigration, Racism and Citizenship in Modern France*. London and New York: Routledge.

Smith, Adrian, Rainnie, Al, Dunford, Mick, Hardy, Jane, Hudson, Ray and Sadler, David (2000) '"Where the Jobs will be in the United States of Europe": Networks of Value, Commodities and Regions in Europe after 1989'. *One Europe or Several?* Working Paper No. 4. ESRC: <www.one-europe.ac.uk>.

Smith, Anthony (1992) 'National Identity and the Idea of European Unity', *International Affairs (Royal Institute of International Affairs 1944–)* 68/1 (Jan.): 55–76.

Sombart, Werner (1976 [1906]) *Why is There No Socialism in the United States?* Basingstoke: Macmillan.

Sørensen, Georg (2004) *The Transformation of the State: Beyond the Myth of Retreat*. Basingstoke: Palgrave Macmillan.

Soysal, Y. (1995) *Limits of Citizenship. Migrants and Postnational Membership in Europe*. Chicago and London: Chicago University Press.

Spence, David and Stevens, Anne (2006) 'Staff and Personnel Policy in the Commission', in David Spence with Geoffrey Edwards (eds), *The European Commission*, 3rd edn. London: John Harper, pp. 173–208.

Spittler, Gerd (1981) *Verwaltung in einem afrikanischen Bauernstaat: das koloniale Französisch-Westafrika 1919–1939*. Wiesbaden: F. Steiner.

Spittler, Gerd (1983) 'Administration in a Peasant State', *Sociologia Ruralis* 23/2: 130–44.

Spohn, Willfried (2001) 'The Role of Collective Identities in the Eastern Extension of European Integration – A Western/Eastern European Comparison', Robert Schuman Centre for Advanced Studies, European University Institute, Project Report. <www.iue.it/RSCAS/Research/EURONAT/Spohncollid.doc>.

Spohn, Willfried (2003) 'Civil Society Discourse on Europe and the Nation in Germany: Qualitative Interviewing', Robert Schuman Centre for Advanced Studies, European University Institute, Project Report, June.

Srubar, Ilja (1996) 'Neoliberalism, Transformation and Civil Society', *Thesis Eleven* 47, November: 33–47.

Srubar, Ilja (2003) '"Kampf der Kulturen" und die EU-Osterweiterung', in Stephan Beetz, Ulf Jakob and Anton Sterbling (eds), *Soziologie über die Grenzen. Europäische Perspektiven.* Hamburg: Krämer, pp. 327–41.

Staniszkis, J. (1999) *Post-Communism: The Emerging Enigma.* Warsaw: ISP/PAN.

Stark, David and Bruszt, László (1998) *Postsocialist Pathways: Transforming Politics and Property in East Central Europe.* Cambridge: Cambridge University Press.

Stark, David and Bruszt, László (2001) 'One Way or Multiple Paths: For a Comparative Sociology of East European Capitalism', *American Journal of Sociology* 106/4, January: 1129–37.

Stasiuk, Andrzej (2000) 'Mein Europa', *Transit* 20, <http://www.ivm.at/t–20txt2.htm>.

Steingart, Gabor (2006) *Weltkrieg um Wohlstand. Wie Macht und Reichtum neu verteilt werden.* Munich: Piper.

Stockmann, U. (2005) 'Beobachtungen zu unterschiedlichen Politikkulturen im Europäischen Parlament', in R. Fikentscher (ed.), *Kultur in Europa. Einheit und Vielfalt.* Halle: Mitteldeutscher Verlag.

Stråth, Bo (2002) 'A European Identity: To the Historical Limits of a Concept', *European Journal of Social Theory* 5/4: 387–401.

Stråth, Bo (2005) 'Methodological and Substantive Remarks on Myth, Memory and History in the Construction of a European Community, *German Law Journal*, Special Issue, 6/2: 255–71.

Streeck, Wolfgang (1997) 'Beneficial Constraints: On the Economic Limits of Rational Voluntarism', in J. Rogers Hollingsworth and Robert Boyer (eds), *Contemporary Capitalism: The Embeddedness of Institutions.* New York: Cambridge University Press, pp. 197–219.

Streeck, Wolfgang (1999) 'Competitive Solidarity: Rethinking the "European Social Model"', *Max Planck Institute for the Study of Societies Working Paper* 99/8. Cologne: MPIfG.

Streeck, Wolfgang and Thelen, Kathleen (eds) (2005) *Beyond Continuity: Institutional Change in Advanced Political Economies.* Oxford: Oxford University Press.

Szelényi, I. and Konrad, G. (1990) 'Intellectuals and Domination in Post-Communist Societies', in Pierre Bourdieu and James Coleman (eds), *Social Theory in a Changing Society.* Boulder, CO: Westview Press (1991), pp. 337–61.

Széll, György and Ehlert, Wiking (eds) (2001) *New Democracies and Old Societies in Europe*. Frankfurt: Peter Lang.

Teschke, Benno (2003) *The Myth of 1648: Class, Geopolitics, and the Making of Modern International Relations*. London: Verso.

Therborn, Göran (1986) 'Neo-Marxist, Pluralist, Corporatist Statist Theories and the Welfare State', in Ali Kazancigil, *The State in Global Perspective*. Aldershot: Gower, pp. 204–31.

Therborn, Göran (1995) *European Modernity and Beyond: The Trajectory of European Societies 1945–2000*. London: Sage.

Therborn, Göran (1997) 'Europe in the Twenty-First Century: The World's Scandinavia?', in P. Gowan and P. Anderson (eds), *The Question of Europe*. London: Verso, pp. 357–84.

Therborn, Göran (2002) 'Asia and Europe in the World: Locations in the Global Dynamics', *Inter-Asia Cultural Studies* 3/2: 287–305.

Therborn, Göran (2004) *Between Sex and Power: Family in the World, 1900–2000*. London: Routledge.

Therborn, Göran (2006) 'Post-Western Europe and the Plural Asias', in G. Delanty (ed.), *Europe and Asia Beyond East and West*. London: Routledge, pp. 24–44.

Thumfart, Alexander (2002) *Die Politische Integration Ostdeutschlands*. Frankfurt: Suhrkamp.

Tilly, Charles (ed.) (1975) *The Formation of National States in Western Europe*. Princeton: Princeton University Press.

Tilly, Charles (1992) *Coercion, Capital, and European States, A.D. 990–1990*. Oxford: Basil Blackwell.

Tocqueville, Alexis de (1971) *Recollections*, edited by J. P. Mayer and A. P. Kerr. London: Macdonald.

Todd, Emmanuel (1987) *The Causes of Progress: Culture, Authority and Change*. Oxford: Blackwell.

Triandafyllidou, Anna (2005) 'Media, Elite and Popular Views on European Integration', RSCAS-EUI: EURONAT Project Report, January.

Vachudová, Milada and Snyder, Tim (1997) 'Are Transitions Transitory? Two Types of Political Change in Eastern Europe since 1989', *East European Politics and Societies* 11/1: 1–35.

van der Pijl, Kees (1984) *The Making of an Atlantic Ruling Class*. London: Verso.

van der Pijl, Kees (2006a) 'A Lockean Europe?', *New Left Review* 37, Jan–Feb: 9–37.

van der Pijl, Kees (2006b) *Global Rivalries: From the Cold War to Iraq*. London: Pluto.

Van Ees, Hans and Garretsen, Harry (1994) 'The Theoretical Foundation of the Reforms in Eastern Europe: Big Bang versus Gradualism and the Limitations of Neo-Classical Theory', *Economic Systems* 18/1, March: 1–13.

Verdun, Amy and Croci, Osvaldo (2005) *The European Union in the Wake of Eastern Enlargement: Institutional and Policy-making Challenges*. Manchester: Manchester University Press.

Vogel, Dita (2006) 'What does Europe Mean to Third Country Students in the European Union?', University of Oldenburg: POLITIS working paper 4.

von Beyme, Klaus (2005) 'Asymmetric Federalism between Globalization and Regionalization', *Journal of European Public Policy* 12/3 (June): 432–47.

Von Tunzelmann, Nick (1999) 'Growth and the Supply Side in Europe since the Second World War', in David Dyker, *The European Economy*. Harlow Longman, pp. 11–42.

Voslensky, M. (1984) *Nomenklatura: Anatomy of the Soviet Ruling Class*. London: Bodley Head.

Wagner, Peter (2003) 'Die westliche Demokratie und die Möglichkeit des Totalitarismus', in Antonia Grunenberg (ed.), *Fünfzig Jahre The Origins of Totalitarianism von Hannah Arendt*. Frankfurt: Peter Lang, pp. 131–45.

Wagner, Peter (2005) 'The Political Form of Europe, Europe as a Political Form', *Thesis Eleven* 80, February: 47–73.

Wallace, Claire, Datler, Georg and Spannring, Reingard (2005) *Young People and European Citizenship*. Vienna: Institut für Höhere Studien.

Wang Hui (2005a) 'Imagining Asia: A Genealogical Analysis', <http://www.cscsban.org/html/Wang>.

Wang Hui (2005b) 'Reclaiming Asia from the West: Rethinking Global History', <http://www.japanfocus.org/article.asp?id=226>.

Warren, Tracey (2004) 'Operationalising "Breadwinning Work": Gender and Work in 21st Century Europe'. IRISS Working Paper 2004–08, pp. 1–41.

Waters, M. (1997) 'Inequality after Class', in David Owen (ed.), *Sociology after Postmodernism*. London: Sage, pp. 23–39.

Waters, Sarah (2006) 'A l'attac: Globalisation and Ideological Renewal on the French Left', *Modern and Contemporary France* 14/2: 141–56.

Weber, Eugen (1977) *Peasants into Frenchmen: The Modernization of Rural France, 1870–1914.* London: Chatto and Windus.

Wehling, Hans-Georg (ed.) (1987) *Nord–Süd in Deutschland? Vorurteile und Tatsachen.* Stuttgart: Kohlhammer.

Weiler, Joseph (2001) 'Federalism without Constitutionalism Europe's *Sonderweg*', in K. Nicolaïdes and R. Howse (eds), *The Federal Vision: Legitimacy and Levels of Governance in the US and the EU.* Oxford: Oxford University Press pp. 54–70.

Weiler, Joseph (2002) 'A Constitution for Europe? Some Hard Choices', *Journal of Common Market Studies* 40/4: 563–80.

White, Paul (1999) 'Ethnicity, Racialization and Citizenship as Divisive Elements in Europe', in Ray Hudson and Allan Williams (eds), *Divided Europe.* London: Sage, pp. 210–30.

White, Stephen, Batt, Judy and Lewis, Paul G. (eds) (2003) *Developments in Central and East European Politics.* Basingstoke: Palgrave.

Whitley, Richard (2003) 'How National are Business Systems?', Manchester Business School: Working Paper No. 450.

Wiener, Antje (1997) 'Making Sense of the New Geography of Citizenship: Fragmented Citizenship in the European Union', *Theory and Society* 26: 529–60.

Wild, Gérard (2002) 'Économie de la transition: le dossier', in Dominique Colas (ed.), *L'Europe post–communiste.* Paris: PUF, pp. 257–389.

Williams, Alan M. and Balaz, Vladimir (1999) 'Transformation and Division in Central Europe', in R. Hudson and A. Williams (eds), *Divided Europe*, ch.7.

World Bank (2002) *Transition – The First Ten Years: Analysis and Lessons for Eastern Europe and the Former Soviet Union.* Washington, DC: World Bank.

Wydra, Harald (2007) *Communism and the Emergence of Democracy.* Cambridge: Cambridge University Press.

Yamamura, Kozo and Streeck, Wolfgang (eds) (2003) *The End of Diversity? Prospects for German and Japanese Capitalism.* Ithaca, NY: Cornell University Press.

Zielonka, Jan (2006) *Europe as Empire: The Nature of the Enlarged European Union.* Oxford: Oxford Unversity Press.

INDEX

1989 2, 18, 21, 29, 31, 33, 41, 48, 58, 81, 82, 102, 154, 155
see also revolutions of
accession 24, 30, 34, 43, 60, 68, 94, 115, 144
accession countries, states 32, 46, 64, 66–7, 147
accumulation 66
acquis communautaire 131
Adorno, T. 143
Africa 2, 7, 10, 11, 38, 76, 131, 135, 142, 146
Ágh, A. 84
agriculture 102, 104, 115, 138, 153 n.3
Albania 24, 25, 117, 121
Albert, M. 47–8, 54
Algeria 117
Amable, B. 50–3, 57, 80, 146
America 2, 7, 8, 11, 17, 19–24, 47, 44, 71, 73, 76, 113, 140
see also USA
America, Latin/South 10, 134, 138

Americanization 13
Anderson, B. 76
Anderson, J. 87
apparatchik 155 n.11
Appiah, K. A. 142
Arato, A. 30
Archer, M. 12
Armenia 24, 38, 135
Arnason, J. 18, 145
Aron, R. 18, 148
Asia 2, 7, 11, 17, 20–1, 23–5, 32, 34, 50–2, 133–6, 138, 143
see also Eurasia
association, associational 88–9, 112, 134, 137
asylum 119
Atlantic/Atlanticist 24, 26, 35, 42, 61, 70, 96
Attali, J. 33, 134
Auer, S. 26–7
Australia 58
Australasia 2, 17, 24, 54, 138
Austria 41, 47, 50, 79, 81, 93, 145, 147, 156

Austro-Hungarian Empire 73
Azerbaijan 24, 38, 135

Bachrach, P. 93
Bagnasco, A. 147
Bahro, R. 34, 101
Bailey, D. 152
Bakunin, M. 8
Baldwin, P. 33, 77, 155
Balibar, E. 31, 127, 143, 155
Balkans, Balkan states 24, 36,
    38, 47, 67–8, 135
Baltic, Baltic republics/
    states 32, 42, 58, 66, 84,
    120
Baratz, M. 93
Barone, E. 45
Basque Country 73, 120–1,
    127
Bauman, Z. 1
Beck, U. 1, 33, 95, 111–12,
    142, 152
Belarus 24, 28, 36, 38, 47,
    66–7, 135
Belgium 37–8, 42, 50, 75, 85,
    93, 117, 120, 134
Berlin 23–5, 37, 148
Berlusconi, S. 83–4
Bhabha, H. 14
Bhambra, G. 2
Black Sea 5
Blair, A. 20, 53, 151, 80, 84,
    97, 101, 151
Bohle, D. 56, 64, 147
Bonn 37, 145
Böröcz, J. 34, 144
Bosnia 25
Bourdieu, P. 103, 105–7, 111
bourgeoisie 62, 101, 103–4,
    107, 153
Boyer, R. 49, 145

Brandt, W. 86
Braudel, F. 8, 143
Brezhnev doctrine 74
Britain 1, 5, 36–7, 59, 75, 77–
    8, 88, 93, 101, 115, 117,
    129, 134, 142, 149, 156
  break–up of 120
  role in EU 151–2
  see also UK
British Isles 23, 36, 42, 85
Brittany 73, 120
Brown, G. 53
Brussels 19, 37, 39, 90, 121,
    128, 136, 141, 151
Bruszt, L. 59–60, 63–4, 104
Bruter, M. 128
Bulgaria 36, 42–3, 46, 63,
    66–7, 148
  crime and corruption in 153
  and EU 32, 34, 43, 67,
    150–1
Burawoy, M. 106, 147
bureaucracy 62, 73–4, 77, 79,
    91
Bush, G. W. 90, 97

Calais 73
Calhoun, C. 2
Calvacoressi, P. 142
Cameron, F. 31
capital 31, 56, 62, 96, 104,
    106, 110
  capital-intensive 145
  city 23, 37, 128, 145
  cultural, political, social 55,
    61–2, 105–6, 154
capitalism 2–3, 9–10, 13, 17,
    29–31, 44, 46–50, 54,
    56–7, 63–8, 71–2, 103–6,
    108, 111, 138, 145
  advanced/late/mature 62

and convergence 53, 68
political 60–2, 106
postcommunist 30, 61, 63,
 103
without classes 111
see also 'comparative
 capitalism', 'varieties of
 capitalism'
Caspian Sea 5
Castles, F. 55, 146
Castoriadis, C. 76
Catalonia 17, 120–1
Catholic 36–7, 42, 116
Central Europe 26, 28–9, 32–
 5, 41–2, 60, 62, 65, 67–8,
 81, 84, 88, 107, 113, 130,
 156
Charlemagne, Carolingian 5,
 26, 135, 137, 144
China, Chinese 7, 10, 17, 19,
 69–71, 90, 134, 145
Christendom 7, 19, 25
Christian democracy 112
Christianity 5, 24, 36, 81,
 132, 142, 148
citizen 93–5, 97–8, 119, 125,
 127, 130, 136
citizenship 78, 130, 155
civic culture 26
Civic Forum 29
civil society 29, 81, 124, 137,
 152
civil war 28, 58, 150
'clash of civilizations' 142
class 3, 22, 38, 60, 62, 65,
 96–113, 116, 130–1, 149,
 153–5
class conflict, struggle 101,
 131
clientelism 37
Clift, B. 146

Coal and Steel
 Community 85–6
coalition 52–3, 80, 148, 151
Cold War 27, 33, 47, 81, 102,
 124
Coleman, J. 105
colonialism 9, 10, 16, 25,
 143–4
colonies 7, 9, 73, 117
Commission, European 57,
 87, 90–1, 151, 157
Common Agricultural
 Policy 57, 85, 90
common currency 85, 94,
 141
see also euro
Commonwealth of
 Independent States
 (CIS) 24
communism 28, 33, 61, 64,
 82, 84, 150
Communist Party, Parties 78,
 82–3, 111, 148
see also Party
community, political 136–7
'comparative capitalism' 54,
 57, 60, 68
conservatives 8, 54, 113, 150
constitution 31, 78, 83, 85,
 87, 92, 96–7
constitutional
 Convention 31
consumption 39, 113
convergence 30, 53, 68, 142,
 148
Cook, R. 155
corporatism 48–50, 64, 80,
 141
corruption 37–9, 153
cosmopolitan(ism) 14–15,
 33–5, 95, 135–7, 141

cosmopolitan democracy
    126–7
Council of Europe 140
crime 28
crisis 64, 70, 82, 102, 151–2
Croatia 46, 66–7
Crouch, C. 1, 20, 50, 53,
    102, 111, 119, 138, 144,
    152
Crusades 5, 8
cultural capital *see* capital
culture 11–15, 17–18, 23, 38,
    75, 108, 112, 142–3
    see also civic culture
Cyprus 38
Czech Republic,
    Czechoslovakia 27–9, 32,
    36, 42, 45–6, 56, 58–9,
    63–4, 66, 75, 82, 147,
    149, 153–4, 156

Dahrendorf, R. 107
Debray, R. 97
decommodification 54–5
Deeg, R. 54, 146
Delanty, G. 1, 5, 25, 87–8,
    97, 137, 143
Delhey, J. 43, 110, 113
deliberative democracy 31,
    95
democracy 9, 10, 29, 43, 59,
    73–4, 79, 80, 92, 95–8,
    125–7, 142, 150–2, 154
    see also Christian democracy,
    deliberative democracy
demography 90, 133, 142
democratization/
    democratizing 15, 31, 94,
    96–7, 144
Denmark 42, 50, 68, 85, 145,
    147

development 27, 29, 39, 44–5,
    53, 61, 67, 69–70, 77,
    97, 104–5, 130, 138, 141,
    149
    studies 108
dictatorship 3, 71, 74, 117,
    148, 150, 155
differentiation 26, 108, 110,
    113, 154
division of labour 109
Djilas, M. 101
Domański, H. 67
domestic service 115
    labour 116
Donati, M. 117
Donzelot, J. 10
Dore, R. 61
Dyker, D. 58, 60, 68
Dyson, K. 74, 76, 78–9

East Germany 27–8, 45, 138,
    148, 153
    see also GDR
economic 2, 6, 7, 9, 10, 19,
    21, 28
    policies 28, 43, 110,
    131
    reconstruction,
    transformation 28, 83
economy 8, 22, 43–8, 52,
    54, 58, 61, 65–6, 69–71,
    96, 99, 101, 104, 147,
    152
    informal/second
    economy 82
    see also market economy
Einhorn, B. 131
elections 93, 152
elective affinity
    (*Wahlverwandtschaft*) 21,
    52

elite 15, 21, 30, 33, 38, 58, 62, 106, 108, 113, 153–5
  nomenklatura elite 101, 110
Elster, J. 63, 150
emancipation (of women) 115, 131
embeddedness 3, 50, 60, 62, 96
empire 3, 5–6, 8–10, 13, 25–6, 34–5, 72–3, 76, 81, 136, 143–4, 146
  EU as 94–5
Engels, F. 29, 45, 78, 131
England 36–9, 46, 72–4, 77, 104, 119, 121, 127, 149
Enlightenment 6, 7, 81, 134
environment/
  environmental 71, 88
equality 37, 70, 115, 144
Esping-Andersen, G. 54
Estonia 36, 38, 65, 147
ethnic cleansing 73
ethnicity, ethnic groups 18, 26, 100, 116–17, 132, 135, 153
Etzioni, A. 12
EU 1, 3, 5, 11, 13, 19, 24–5, 27–34, 38–9, 41, 43, 46–7, 53, 57, 64, 66–8, 71, 85, 95, 127, 134, 136, 138, 156
  Enlargement 25, 29, 31–2, 67, 85, 88, 90, 94, 108, 111, 135, 144, 154
  see also accession, membership
Eurasia 3, 5, 135–6
EURATOM 85, 87
euro 85, 119, 144, 151
  see also common currency

Eurocentrism 7, 15–16, 25, 143
Eurocommunism 14
European Bank for Reconstruction and Development (EBRD) 33, 128
European Economic Area 33, 74
European integration 11, 12, 15, 19, 26, 31, 49, 66, 74, 79, 86, 88, 90–2, 94, 96, 98–9, 126, 128, 130, 134–5, 140–1, 152, 156
  critique of concept 88
'European miracle' 16, 23
European Parliament 84, 95–6, 111
European social charter 57
European social model 10, 55–7, 90, 141
European studies 2, 137
European Union see EU
Europeanization 57, 68, 108, 126, 137, 148
Euroscepticism 25, 89, 91, 121, 140
Eurozone 47, 64, 68–9, 145
extracomunitari 94

family 36, 42, 48, 55–6, 105, 115, 125
Fanon, F. 100
fascism/fascist 3, 9, 73, 93, 97–8, 117, 150
federal(ism) 37, 64, 75, 80, 85, 87, 89–96, 126, 145, 150–1
  in Europe 85, 87, 89–97, 126

federal(ism) (cont.)
  in Germany 69, 80, 116,
    145, 150–1
  in US 75
feminism 100–1, 115–16,
    131–2
First World War 9, 13, 72–3,
    131
Fordism 147
Former Soviet Union
    (FSU) 38, 48, 62, 67, 84,
    146, 153
  see also Commonwealth of
    Independent States (CIS)
Foucault, M. 152
France 5, 8, 23, 36–9, 42, 46,
    48, 65, 70, 72, 77, 93,
    96, 102, 116–17, 119–20,
    124, 134, 142, 144, 146,
    149–51
Frankfurt 37, 39
freedom 8, 27, 64, 83, 85, 95,
    125
French (language) 15, 20
French Revolution 8, 73, 78
  see also revolution
Fukuyama, F. 142

Galicia (Spain) 120–1
Gellner, E. 91
gender 3, 22, 54, 99–100,
    103, 115–16, 130–2, 138,
    146
Georgia 24, 38, 66, 135
GDR 37, 75, 113, 153
  see also East Germany
genocide 32
Germany 9, 10, 15, 26, 28,
    30, 35–7, 39, 41–2, 45,
    47, 50, 52, 54, 58, 63–4,
    66, 69–70, 73, 77–80, 82,

    86, 93, 108, 113, 116–17,
    119–20, 124, 128, 133–5,
    138, 144–5, 149, 155–7
  Nazi 70
  (re)unification of 39, 41,
    152
  see also East Germany, West
    Germany, GDR
Gershuny, J. 101
Giddens, A. 10, 18, 19, 57,
    101, 147, 152
Gillingham, J. 90–1, 134
Gini coefficient 43, 113,
    144
global, globalization 2, 3, 13,
    14, 17, 22, 44, 48, 64–6,
    89, 97, 108, 126–7, 129,
    134, 137
God 42
Goethe, J. W. 21
Goldman Sachs 69
governance 50, 64, 77, 88–9,
    94, 126, 146
Grabher, G. 60, 63
Gramsci, A. 81
Grande, E. 1, 33, 95, 142
Greece 3, 32, 38, 52, 115,
    129, 133, 135
Greenfeld, L. 26, 121
Gresham's Law 47, 71
Groys, B. 30
Grundy, S. 128–9, 156

Habermas, J. 18, 29, 34, 74,
    124, 127
Hall, J. A. 91
Hall, P. 48, 67
Hallstein, W. 91
Hanseatic League 5
Hayek, F. von 59
health 55, 77, 88, 126

history 1, 5, 14, 16, 41, 44,
  69, 70, 81, 90, 101, 144,
  148, 150
  colonial 30, 34
  end of 142
Holy Roman Empire 72
human capital 105
human rights 78
  see also rights
Hungary 6, 32, 45–6, 58,
  63–6, 73, 81–3, 108, 120,
  150, 153–4, 156
Huntington, S. 21, 142
Hutton, W. 70

Iceland 85
identity 9, 38, 74, 95, 110,
  120–1, 124–5, 127–131,
  134, 151–2, 156
  see also national identity
ideology 10, 35, 65, 70, 78,
  131, 150
imaginary 8, 96, 98
imagined community 5, 76
IMF 64
imitation 155
income 43, 54, 65–6, 77, 113,
  144
  see also inequality
India 11–13, 19, 20, 69–71,
  90, 134
individualism 2, 8, 13, 42
industrial society/societies 17–
  18, 66, 108
industrialism 16–17, 101
industrialization 8, 45, 101,
  135, 149
inequality/inequalities 42–3,
  46, 65, 68, 100, 105,
  110, 112–13, 131, 138,
  144

information technology 103
infrastructure 41, 77, 96
institutions 47, 54, 59, 63–4,
  78–9, 126, 151
  democratic,
    representative 79, 83,
    124
  European Union 19, 39, 53,
    93, 96, 128, 135, 144
  financial 50, 103, 124
  in postcommunism 59, 63
  social policy 125
intellectuals 32, 62, 101
intelligentsia 62, 107, 155
internal colonialism 10, 25,
  143
internationalism/
  internationalization
  14–15, 73
investment 39, 52, 67, 105,
  107, 153
Iran 135
Iraq 135
Ireland, Irish Republic 32, 38,
  42, 48, 54–6, 73–4, 115,
  120–1, 127, 145, 155
Islam 5, 7, 24, 132
Islamism 119
Italy 19, 23, 35–9, 41, 46, 48,
  50, 52, 55, 73, 75, 78,
  80, 83, 86, 93–4, 105,
  116–17, 120

Jackson, G. 54, 146
Jacoby, W. 155
Jamieson, L. 128–9, 156
Japan 17, 21, 47–9, 70–1,
  131, 133, 135, 145
Jews 32, 73
judiciary 39, 93
justice 124–5, 131

Kaczynski(s) 83
Kaelble, H. 126
Kaldor, M. 144
Kant, I. 86
Karaganov, S. 136
Karagiannis, N. 141, 155
Kazakhstan 66
Kazan 39
Khrushchev, N. 148
King, L. 154
King, R. 117, 140
Kipling, R. 16
Kissinger, H. 14, 140
Klaus, V. 147
Kohl, H. 28, 41
Korea 48–9
Kovács, M. 33
Kreckel, R. 111
Kumar, K. 101

labour market 54, 115
Länderfinanzausgleich 69
Lane, D. 51, 54, 65–7, 147
language 11, 14–15, 19–20,
    37, 94, 106, 117, 119,
    129–30, 148, 156
Lash, S. 152
Latin 15
Latvia 36, 42, 67, 153
law 7, 26, 78, 80, 83, 92, 103,
    149, 151
Le Grand, J. 55
Lega Nord 37, 120
legitimacy, legitimation 83,
    94, 96, 124–6, 152, 154
Lenin, V. I. 9
Lepsius, M. R. 91
Lewandowski, J. 59
liberalism 3, 59
    see also neo-liberalism
liberties 7

life expectancy 28
lifestyle 110, 112–13, 131
Liotta, P. H. 24
Lipset, S. M. 8
Lithuania 42, 67
London 12, 23, 37, 76, 128,
    147, 151
Ludz. P. C. 62
Luxemburg 36, 39, 128

McCann, L. 39
Major, J. 20, 53
Mali 77
Malta 33
managerialism 59, 61–2,
    103
managers 43, 54, 103–4, 108,
    113
Mandel, D. 38
Mann, M. 7, 19
market 45–6, 57, 61, 64–67,
    107, 109, 112, 115, 137,
    146
  economy 47, 49, 50–4,
    57–8, 61, 67, 147, 152
  social market economy 54,
    152
  socialism 46
Marks and Spencer 47
Marshall Plan 27, 138
Marx, K. 6, 45, 60–1, 78, 89,
    97, 103, 105, 112, 131,
    152
Marxism 64, 99, 101, 103,
    106, 111, 147
Marxism-Leninism 10, 13,
    73
Mateju, P. 111
media 83, 84, 156
Mediterranean 23, 38, 51–2,
    117, 140, 146

membership (of EC/EU) 24,
    33–4, 38, 46, 49, 63, 68,
    124, 128, 135, 150, 152
memory 35
Mendras, H. 102
middle class 55
migration 9, 21, 23, 32, 93,
    100–1, 117, 119, 136,
    140, 146, 155
military 7, 9, 70–1, 155
Milward, A. 140
minority/minorities 71, 73,
    116, 119
modernity 1–2, 14, 16–18,
    22, 25–6, 41, 99, 112,
    136–7
modernization 16, 19, 37,
    81–2
Mohács 6
Moldova 38, 66, 135
Moore, B. 104, 149, 154
morality 125
Morgan, G. 89–90
Morocco 38
Mudde, C. 98
multiculturalism 21, 119
multinational 95
    see also transnational
multiple modernities 8
Myrdal, G. 100

nation/national 1, 2, 6, 8, 9,
    13–14, 26, 45, 49, 64–5,
    74–6, 85–99, 102, 112,
    116, 119–21, 124, 126–9,
    134, 142–3
    identity 74, 128–9, 151,
        156
    insurance 55
    liberation movements
        149

state 8–9, 13, 74, 76, 86–7,
    89, 91, 95, 97, 120–1,
    124, 126–8, 131, 136,
    152
nationalism 9, 11, 26–7, 30,
    35, 73–6, 81, 85, 89, 91,
    102, 121, 124, 127, 148,
    155
nationality 112
nationalization 14
NATO 23, 124, 140
Nazism 13, 70, 73, 100
Neocleous, M. 149
neo-liberalism 59, 64, 71, 147,
    151
neo-Marxism 49, 53, 64
Netherlands 15, 23, 34, 36,
    50, 73, 75, 96, 115–17,
    120, 146, 149
networks 5, 62–3, 105, 112,
    140, 147
network state 88
New Zealand 55, 147
NGOs 63
Nolte, H.-H. 32
nomenklatura 62–3, 101, 104,
    110
nomenklatura privatization 62,
    104
Nordic countries 36, 42, 115,
    146, 151
Northern Ireland 42, 120–1,
    127
Norwegian Study of Power
    and Democracy
    151

Offe, C. 94, 97, 125–6
O'Reilly, J. 54–5, 146
Orthodoxy 36
Ossowski, S. 100–1, 112

Ottoman Empire 25, 73
Owen, R. 45

Pakulski, J. 110
Palestine 25
Parkin, F. 101
participation 85, 103,
    115–16
Party 74, 78–9, 82–4, 104,
    111–12, 148–50, 155
    see also Communist Party
    and parties
Pavlovski, G. 38
peasants 60, 102, 110, 114,
    154
peoples' democracies 45, 74,
    110
Perraton, J. 146
petty bourgeoisie 102
Peter the Great 23
plan, planning 44–5, 47, 53–4,
    107
Poland 23, 29, 32–3, 37, 42,
    45, 58–9, 62, 66, 75, 81,
    84, 104, 113, 116, 145,
    153–4
police 35, 39
political capital 61
political capitalism 60–2,
    106–7
politics 2, 10, 43, 79, 81,
    84, 92–4, 96–9, 108,
    110–11, 113, 124, 129,
    135–51
    third way 10, 43, 46, 53,
    110
polyarchy 5
population 46, 71
    ageing of 90
    see also demography

Portugal 3, 9, 39, 42, 46, 52,
    69, 102, 116–17, 146,
    149
postcolonial theory 1, 7, 34,
    100
postmodernism 12, 16
postnational 126
post-western Europe 25, 135
poverty 66
power 3, 6–10, 34, 63, 70–1,
    75–99, 107, 121, 134,
    149, 151
Poznanski, K. 82
Prague Spring 35
Preuss, U. 94, 97
privatism 21
privatization 31, 58–60, 65,
    82, 147, 153
    see also nomenklatura
    privatization
Prodi, R. 1
production 2, 8, 12, 17, 44–5,
    47, 49, 69–70, 86, 103,
    106–7, 133
proletariat 113, 148
property 59–60, 63, 104,
    110
Protestantism 19, 36, 113
Prussia 77
public sphere 17, 95
Putin, V. 48
Putnam, R. 105–6, 154

race 99–100, 117, 132
racism 33, 35, 116
Radikalenerlass 78
recombinant property 63
Red Army 27
reflexivity 18, 37, 95, 127
Reformation 6, 7, 36, 81

region 1–3, 7, 13–16, 19–23,
    25, 30, 32–3, 38–9, 41–2,
    47–50, 64, 66, 68–9, 75,
    80–1, 85, 87–8, 92–4,
    98–9, 106–7, 115,
    119–21, 127–9, 134,
    137–8, 140–1, 144, 156
regional policy 57, 69, 140,
    152
regulation 34, 49, 54, 82, 116,
    145–6
religion 7, 24, 36, 132,
    148
Renaissance 6–7, 14, 23, 81,
    134
Renan, E. 86, 92
revolution 1, 6–8, 10, 17–18,
    73–4, 78, 81, 101–2
    revolutions of 1989 21, 29,
    69–70, 154
Rhodes, M. 146
Rifkin, J. 71
rights 8, 10, 34, 54, 78, 83,
    94, 97, 126, 130
    see also human rights,
    property
role 112
Roma 28, 35, 120
Roman law 7
Romania 32, 34, 43, 46,
    66–7, 120–1, 144, 150–1,
    154
Rome/Roman Empire 5, 7, 23,
    37, 72, 94, 121
Rorty, R. 142
Rostock 35
Ruiz Jiménez, A. 129
ruling class 62
Rumford, C. 1, 2, 24, 87–8,
    97, 137

Russia 72–3, 81–2, 90, 104,
    106–8, 113, 120, 134–6,
    143, 149, 153, 157

Sacks. J. 59
Said, E. 143
Saint-Simon, H. de 86
Sakwa, R. 35, 60, 134
Sarkar, M. 34, 144
Schengen 85, 93
Schmidt, V. 48, 50, 80, 88,
    92–4, 96, 126, 145–6,
    148, 151–2
Schmitter, P. 94, 97
Schneider, P. 143
Schöpflin, G. 41, 81–2,
    150
Schröder, G. 53
Schumpeter, J. 45, 130
Scotland 36, 72–3, 80, 120–1,
    151
second economy 82
    see also informal economy
Second World War 10, 13,
    24, 45, 56, 102, 121, 135,
    140, 152
self-determination 73
Senghaas, D. 16
Sennett, R. 145
Serbia 36, 83
Sinus 113–14
Slovakia 43, 56, 67, 75, 83,
    120, 153–4, 156
Slovenia 38, 41, 46, 58, 65–6,
    117, 151
Smith, A. 26, 148
social capital 55, 62, 105,
    154
social democracy 10, 52, 54,
    59, 71, 85, 110, 155

social policy 56–7, 90, 102, 124, 126, 152
social science 12, 193
social security 57
social structure 85, 104–5, 107, 111
social theory 1, 12
society 1–3, 11, 28, 75, 79, 81, 91, 97, 99, 101, 108, 112, 137, 150, 155
  see also civil society, industrial society
sociology 1, 8, 12, 16–17, 59–60, 91, 112, 121, 137
solidarity 49, 86, 97, 124–6, 155
Solidarity (*Solidarność*) 29
Sombart, W. 10, 138
Soskice, D. 48, 67
South America *see* America
sovereignty 10, 74, 79, 88, 92, 151
Soviet Union (including former Soviet Union) 38, 48, 62, 67, 74, 84, 133, 136, 148, 153, 157
  see also USSR
Spain 3, 9, 37, 48, 52, 75, 93, 117, 120–1, 129, 133, 146, 149–50, 156
Spence, D. 151
Spiegel 69
Spittler, G. 77
Staatenverbund 152
Stalin, J. V., Stalinist 10, 21, 45, 81
Staniszkis, J. 60–1
Stark, D. 60, 63–4
state(s) 2, 3, 5–11, 13–16, 18–22, 24–5, 27–8, 30, 34–5, 37–9, 47–50, 54, 60–7, 69–70, 74–97, 99–100, 102–4, 116–17, 120–1, 124–9, 131, 133–8, 141–57
EU as state 134
EU member-states 24–5, 27, 32, 38, 41, 64, 88, 92–3, 124, 145
postcommunist state 30–1, 103
state capitalism 48, 61, 66
state crisis 82
state power 107
state socialism 3, 27, 41, 44–6, 60–1, 65, 101–3
  see also communism
Steingart, G. 69–70, 134, 148
Stråth, B. 86, 130
stratification, social 67–8, 107, 110
Streeck 63–4, 126, 145–6
suicide 28
surveillance 75, 77
Sussex 38
Sweden 42, 50, 54, 59, 68, 85, 120, 144–5
Switzerland 34, 36, 47, 78, 85, 93, 115, 117, 119, 145–7
Szelényi, I. 111

Taiwan 48
tax/taxation 55, 65, 69, 70, 77
technology 2, 7, 15, 21, 23, 37, 115, 138
terrorism 29, 73, 90, 132
Thatcher, M., Thatcherism 20, 53, 59, 80, 151
Therborn, G. 1, 19, 28, 41–2, 115, 133, 138, 143–4, 157

Third Way 10, 43, 46, 53, 91, 110–11
Tilly, C. 77, 148–9
TINA ('There is No Alternative') 30
Tocqueville, A. de 8, 29, 71
Todd, E. 36–7
totalitarianism 3, 30, 75
Townsley, E. 62, 106, 111
tradition 19, 21, 34–5, 39, 41, 47–8, 103, 112, 114–15, 126, 129, 136, 138, 143
transition 2, 27–31, 34, 57–9, 64–6, 82, 88, 101, 104, 107, 111, 147–50, 153
transnational/transnationalism 38, 98, 111, 126
transparency 38, 152–3
Treuhandanstalt 108
Trotskyist 62, 101
trust 125, 154
Tudors 73–4
Turkmenistan 66
TV 14, 17, 70

UK 69, 75, 79–80, 84–5, 93, 100, 102, 115–16, 119–21, 128, 131, 140, 144–5, 151, 156
Ukraine 135
'uncivil economies' 63
unemployment 52, 66, 119
US/USA 8, 9, 17, 20, 26, 30, 42, 46, 48, 54, 58, 69–71, 75, 87, 90, 100, 105, 131, 133–4, 138, 141–2, 148, 157
see also America
USSR 18–19, 34, 45, 65, 70, 72–3, 75, 105, 115, 133
see also Russia, Soviet Union

Uzbekistan 66

values 42, 112, 127, 150, 155
van Apeldoorn, B. 146
van der Pijl, K. 70, 96
'varieties of capitalism' 49, 65, 67–8
Vejvoda, I. 144
Verhandlungsdemokratie 80
Vietnam 153
violence 28
Visegrád Group 32, 154
von Beyme, K. 96
von Tunzelmann, N. 148

Wales 73, 80, 120–1, 151
Wallerstein, I. 8, 127
war, warfare 2, 6, 9, 28, 45, 73, 76, 141, 148
see also Cold War, First World War, Second World War
Warsaw 37
Warsaw Pact 10, 23, 28
Waters, M. 108–11
Weber, M. 21, 36, 60, 91, 102–3, 107, 112, 155
'weightless economy' 101
Weiler, J. 91–2, 97, 126
welfare 52, 54
see also social security, social welfare
welfare state 41, 52, 54, 102, 110, 115
West Germany 78–9, 90–100, 102, 114, 117, 135
Westphalia 142
White, P. 119
Wiener, A. 130
'wild' West 26
Wodak, R. 32

Wollstonecraft, M. 131
women 9, 103, 115–16, 119,
    131
work 37, 103, 115–16
workers 43, 46–7, 54, 88,
    100, 102, 113–14, 126,
    131, 148
'workers' states' 101
working class 107, 110, 113,
    149

world history 16
World Values Survey 42

Yugoslavia, Yugoslav
    Federation 24, 28, 45, 58,
    75, 117, 121, 124, 149,
    153

Ziełonka, J. 83, 94, 150

EUROPEAN SOCIETY